*Direct Practice Research
in Human Service Agenci*

Direct Practice Research
in Human Service Agencies

Betty Blythe
Tony Tripodi
Scott Briar

Columbia University Press
New York

Columbia University Press
New York   Chichester, West Sussex
Copyright © 1994 Columbia University Press
All rights reserved

Library of Congress Cataloging-in-Publication Data

Blythe, Betty J.
        Direct practice research in human service agencies   /   Betty Blythe,
    Tony Tripodi, Scott Briar.
            p.   cm.
        Includes bibliographical references and index.
        ISBN 0–231–07366–6 (cloth   :   acid-free paper)   : $49.50.   —   ISBN
    0–231–07367–4 (paper)   : $22.50
        1. Human service—Research—United States.   2. Social service—
    Research—United States.   I. Tripodi, Tony.   II. Briar, Scott,
    1926-   .   III. Title.
    HV11.B594   1995   94-24325
    361.3′2—dc20

Casebound editions of Columbia University Press books are printed on permanent and
durable acid-free paper.

Printed in the United States of America

c 10 9 8 7 6 5 4 3 2 1
p 10 9 8 7 6 5 4 3 2 1

To
Mary Ann Blythe,
Tommy Torchia,
and
Jennifer Briar

Contents

1. *Introduction*

The authors of this book contend that social workers engaged in direct practice can carry out research tasks that will facilitate their practice. We focus on social workers who work with individuals, couples, families, or groups, and who carry out their practice activities in social agencies, hospitals, community centers, clinics, and other human service organizations. We consider direct practice research to be a vital component of practice: it is not auxiliary or incidental. Hence we conceptualize direct practice as incorporating research tasks and concepts that are instrumental to practice.

This book presents a selection of research strategies and procedures that can be incorporated into the practice activities of direct service practitioners, including supervisors and students. We also discuss research tasks that are compatible with the routine work of direct service practitioners, who work within the constraints of human service agencies, where money, resources, and time are precious commodities.

This book is not intended for social workers who spend the bulk of their time conducting basic clinical research, full-scale program evaluations, or research concerned with the fundamental processes of clinical activities. It is not written for social workers who practice as administrators, social planners, policy developers, or community organizers, nor is it written for social researchers who use social agencies as laboratories for testing hypotheses related to theories of social psychology.

This book is for direct service practitioners who are ethically bound to develop and utilize knowledge in their professional practice (National Association of Social Workers 1987) but have little experience in research and even less time to engage in large-scale investigations. Accordingly, the following criteria guided the selection of research concepts, principles, and tasks for presentation in subsequent chapters:

1. The research tasks and functions should be easily integrated into the job duties of direct service practitioners who are employed by social agencies and other organizations that use social workers.
2. They should be applicable to a wide range of activities and problems social workers confront in direct practice.
3. They should be time-limited and focused within the confines of agency practice.
4. They should require only a basic understanding of research concepts and principles.
5. They should provide information that is useful for making practice decisions or for effectively completing practice tasks.

Thus the book discusses research concepts, principles, and tasks that pertain to the human service agency as a context for conducting direct practice research, assessing client needs, implementing social work interventions, monitoring client progress, evaluating effectiveness, and incorporating research results into practice.

What is Direct Practice Research?

Direct practice research involves the use of social research methods in direct practice. While social research can be conceived as the "systematic application of logical strategies and observational techniques for purposes of developing, modifying and expanding knowledge about social phenomena" (Tripodi 1974:18), direct practice research has the following characteristics:

1. It is conducted by practitioners in social agencies and human service organizations;
2. It is integrated into the worker's other practice activities;
3. It contributes to empirically based practice;
4. It can employ a wide variety of research techniques; and
5. Its basic goal is to provide information that is directly helpful to practitioners.

Direct practice research is conducted by practitioners as part of their practice. It can be incorporated into assessment, planning, implementation of interventions, and termination and follow-up activities (Blythe and Tripodi 1989). The practitioner or supervisor generates questions for research; the research questions are not imposed on practice by non-practitioners.

Single-subject design methodology is the research tool most frequently employed by practitioners. While single-subject designs can provide information on the effectiveness of practitioners' interventions, other research techniques are may be more appropriate for other research questions that practitioners might formulate. For example, certain principles of constructing questionnaires and drawing samples can aid in determining client needs or in selecting members for groupwork interventions.

Similarly, empirically based practice is more than conducting an evaluation of the effects of one intervention. According to Siegel (1984:329), a social worker engaged in empirically based practice

1. makes maximum use of research findings,
2. collects data systematically to monitor the intervention,
3. demonstrates empirically whether or not interventions are effective,
4. specifies problems, interventions, and outcomes in terms that are concrete, observable, and measurable,
5. uses research ways of thinking and research methods in defining clients' problems, formulating questions for practice, collecting assessment data, evaluating the effectiveness of interventions and using evidence,
6. views research and practice as part of the same problem-solving process, and
7. views research as a tool to be used in practice.

Finally, direct practice research, like applied social research, seeks to provide information that is directly relevant to practice tasks and decisions. For example, a social worker who works in intensive family preservation services can apply research techniques to determine whether progress has been made in restoring family functioning subsequent to a crisis (Blythe 1990). A supervisor in a sexual abuse treatment program may be interested in identifying factors associated with clients who respond better to individual therapy than to group counseling. A medical social worker can systematically gather data on the degree to which clients are complying with their medical regimens. A social worker dealing with juvenile delinquents and their families requires information about family interactions, social supports, and basic human needs in order to make informed social assessments; such assessments can be facilitated by the use of research techniques.

These examples indicate the many types of information necessary for the conduct of effective and efficient practice. In addition to generating data specific to the needs of practitioners, direct practice research can contribute to the development of empirically based models of direct practice. By accumulating information on the effectiveness of interventions, hypothetical or empirical models of practice might be generated that prescribe interventions for specific situations (Blythe and Briar 1985).

Who Conducts Direct Practice Research?

Because we consider direct practice research to be a component of interpersonal practice that deals with individuals, families, and groups, it is obvious that direct service practitioners will become involved in the conduct of such research. Using research tools and concepts in direct practice is the *sine qua non* of direct practice research. Although social workers who use research methods as part of their practice in administration, community organization, or policy development provide information that is potentially relevant to direct practice, we do not regard their activities as direct practice research.

Social researchers who are not currently employed as direct service practitioners can provide knowledge that sheds light on direct practice research. Social researchers from psychology, sociology, or psychiatry may conduct research that is indirectly or directly related to direct practice in social work. For example, psychologists and psychiatrists have validated cognitive and behavioral interventions that some social workers now use in direct practice. Information from the study of organizations and agencies produced by organizational and community psychologists, sociologists, and anthropologists also may offer insight on the work of social work practitioners.

Social workers who conduct research in agencies and organizations are involved in direct practice research if they produce knowledge that clarifies the tasks and functions of social workers in direct practice. For example, Rose (1981) explored the relationships between group attributes (such as group participation and group cohesion) and behavioral changes in clients who received assertiveness training. Rose's findings might compel direct practitioners to use group cohesion exercises.

In our view, however, direct service practitioners and their supervisors offer the greatest potential for knowledge production that contributes to practice. The bulk of practicing social workers function in direct practice positions. Even if they only spend a modest amount of their time on practice-relevant research, the profession of social work will be well-served. The profession's increased knowledge about practice is in the best interests of our clients.

Why Should Social Workers do Direct Practice Research?

We believe that social workers must engage in direct practice research for the following reasons:

1. Direct practice research provides a way for social workers to be accountable. As social workers, we owe it to our clients to use all available tools so that we are providing the best possible services to them. Moreover, the National Association of Social Workers and the Council of Social Work Education mandate that social workers must be accountable to clients, employers, and the profession. Note the following excerpts from the NASW Code of Ethics, the NASW Standards for the Practice of Clinical Social Work, and the Council on Social Work Education's Curriculum Policy for the Master's Degree and Baccalaureate Degree Programs in Social Work Education:

The social worker should provide clients with accurate and complete information regarding the extent and nature of the services available to them.   *(National Association of Social Workers 1980)*

The social worker should apprise clients of their risks, rights, opportunities, and obligations associated with social service to them.   *(National Association of Social Workers 1980)*

The social worker should terminate service to clients, and professional relationships with them, when such service and relationships are no longer required or no longer serve the clients' needs or interests.   *(National Association of Social Workers 1980)*

Clinical social workers shall have and continue to develop specialized knowledge and understanding of individuals, families, and groups and of therapeutic and preventive interventions.
    (NASW Standards for the Practice of Clinical Social Work 1984)

The curriculum content relating to practice must include the knowledge base, i.e., theory, research, and practice wisdom. It must also include the practice skills, i.e., exploration and data-gathering, differential assessment and differential planning, intervention, and evaluation relevant to social work practice. The plan for teaching practice should explicitly demonstrate how content on practice relates to that knowledge base and skills that are included in the curriculum content of research.

(Council on Social Work Education 1991:112)

The professional foundation content in research should thus provide skills that will take students beyond the role of consumers of research and prepare them to evaluate their own practice systematically. *(Council on Social Work Education 1991:113)*

2. Direct practice research can facilitate the development of empirically based models, which are needed in social work (Blythe and Briar 1985).
3. Direct practice research provides a context in which practitioners can evaluate the effectiveness of their interventions with clients (Bloom and Fischer 1982).
4. Direct practice research focuses on the development of knowledge that can be useful for social workers who work in agencies or organizations. (Reid 1987).
5. Direct practice research can point to gaps in knowledge that might stimulate large-scale research projects.
6. Direct practice research can help social workers provide concrete feedback to clients.

In addition to these general reasons for engaging in direct practice research, there are reasons for using each research concept and tool discussed in this book. Each instance of direct practice research has some very specific benefits for practitioners and clients.

Where is Practice Research Conducted?

Direct practice takes place in a variety of human service agencies. Practitioners work with people from all walks of life who are confronted with social and psychological problems (Meyer 1987). Social workers who provide direct practice services are employed wherever people seek help. Hospitals, mental health clinics, welfare departments, family service agencies, and correctional institutions are just a few common examples. As new social movements result in changing programs and services, direct practice can occur in different settings or locations. Recently developed contexts for direct practice include agencies that deal with problems of the homeless (Koroloff and Anderson 1989), programs that provide in-home services to prevent child placement when parents are abusing substances (Blythe, Jiordano, and Kelly 1991) and services that help individuals mediate decisions such as child custody or care for elderly family members (Parsons and Cox 1989).

Practice research can occur wherever direct practice is conducted, because it is a component of direct social work practice. It takes place in human service agencies, broadly conceived as including the gamut of organizations and programs where direct services are provided (Reid 1987). The sites of practice research can be categorized by their organizational contexts. Holland and Petchers (1987) offer a schema for classifying agencies into one of four categories: people-changing agencies, where the goals are to change specific attributes and behaviors of clients (such as residential treatment centers and day treatment programs), agencies that support normal functioning (such as retirement counseling centers), agencies that respond to dysfunctional behaviors (such as psychiatric hospitals, mental health clinics, and child welfare agencies) and agencies that focus on socialization and normal development (such as schools). We recognize that social workers also work in settings where the larger organization is not a human service agency, such as in an industry's employee assistance program.

The minimum requisites for practice research in a human service agency are:

1. The agency should have the basic goal of providing services by means of direct service practitioners.
2. The agency should employ one or more social workers.
3. The social workers and their immediate superiors should be knowledgeable about or be willing to apply research concepts, principles, and tasks in their practice.
4. The *supports* for practice research should outweigh the *constraints* against its conduct.

We consider social work students as potential direct practice researchers. To the extent that students in the field provide direct services in human service agencies, they can be considered to be direct service practitioners. Correspondingly, students function as direct practice researchers to the degree to which they comply with the spirit of standards promulgated by the Council on Social Work Education.

Hence, fieldwork placements for social work students can be considered as settings for practice research. In fact, student practice research has been conducted in field placements, as in the evaluation of a cognitive-behavioral treatment package for reducing aggressive behaviors in an eleven-year-old boy (Collins, Kayser, and Tourse 1994; Taber 1981).

Sources of Support for Practice Research

Factors that facilitate the conduct of practice research involve the social worker, the profession of social work, the human service agency, and the community environment (Weinbach 1989). These factors are both interrelated and interactive, and they can stimulate and enhance the effectiveness and efficiency of the occurrence and utility of practice research.

Practitioner Factors

At least four factors influence the extent to which social workers themselves become practice-researchers: (1) conceptions of direct practice; (2) knowledge of practice research methods; (3) motivation to pursue practice research; and (4) adherence to professional values.

Each practicing social worker is influenced by one or more theoretical orientations toward the conduct of practice. Conceptions of practice can include notions about how information is gathered, how workers determine if clients are making progress, and about the application of research methods. If research is conceptualized as a component of practice, social workers will conduct practice research. If a theory of practice is compatible with the tasks of practice research, then it is likely that social workers practicing within these theories will apply research methods. As an example, a practitioner who espouses a problem-solving approach, in which diagnosis, assessment, and evaluation are integral to practice, is more likely to conduct practice research than is a practitioner whose theoretical framework is concerned only with the interaction between worker and client. The practitioner operating in the interactional framework, however, could also benefit from applying practice research methods.

Practitioners may strongly believe that research should be an integral part of their practice, but do not know how to conduct practice research. Obviously, these practitioners are less likely to conduct research than are practitioners who know applicable research methods. We contend that this knowledge will become commonplace in the coming years. It is now available, and it should be (and is being) taught in schools of social work and in postgraduate training programs.

Worker motivation also influences whether practice research occurs. If social workers are motivated to acquire knowledge about research methods for practice, they will do so. As the priority for research knowledge in social work practice increases, the social worker will learn how to conduct such research—by reading, consulting with colleagues and others, by taking courses, and by doing it. Some of the worker's motivation will come from understanding how research can facilitate and even improve practice. On the other hand, motivation can be diminished if workers believe research is too difficult to understand or undertake.

An extremely important factor that affects whether workers conduct practice research is their view of their ethical responsibilities to clients, colleagues, and the community. Without question, research methods constitute an approach to improving practice that is consistent with social work values, but adhering to these values has some important consequences for the nature of one's practice. For example, workers who believe that only effective interventions should be employed in practice will need to obtain information about the relative effectiveness of interventions and base their treatments on this information.

Professional Factors

Each profession has its own requisites and its code of ethics. Social workers obtain their standards for practice and education from the National Association of Social Workers, the Council on Social Work Education, and various states' licensure requirements for professional practice. Three interrelated factors impinge on social workers' conduct of practice research: (1) the profession's position on its knowledge base; (2) the profession's ethical proclamations; and (3) the professions' view of responsibility toward clients, colleagues, and agencies.

The profession of social work *does* call for the development of knowledge related to practice. Social workers are expected to provide the best services available and if none are effective with a client, to not use them(National Association of Social Workers 1987). Schools of social work are responsible for training practitioners, and increasingly students are being trained to validate practice by means of research methods taught in social work courses.

Agency Factors

The agency is the basic context in which practice research is conducted. Several interrelated factors within the agency influence the degree to which social workers can do research. These include basic organizational goals, agency priorities, demands on accountability, computerized information systems, resources, and rewards.

Organizational goals differ between agencies, and each organization's goals call for unique information. These goals influence the type of information that interests members of the organization. A people-changing organization is more likely to possess (or be more willing to collect) information on client change than is an organization that is not concerned with changing the attitudes and/or behavior of its clients. A substance abuse treatment center may collect information on changes in client drug use; a child and youth protective services shelter may not have any information on client change resulting from detention. An organization concerned with normal socialization for teenagers such as the YMCA is more apt to gather information about client activities than information about client change. When an agency requires the collection of certain types of information, it can be easier to conduct practice research with similar types of information. This is especially true if the information demands of practice research are identical to routine information-gathering tasks in the agency. For example, a substance abuse treatment center would be a good place to examine behavioral changes of clients.

Agency priorities are important for determining the allocation of resources for the tasks and functions of agency management and operation. If an administrator conceptualizes practice research as a component of practice that requires five percent of the practitioner-researcher's week, then "research time" will be regarded as "practice time." Management and staff members may support practice research; their interest becomes evident when research is discussed in supervisory and staff conferences, highlighted in agency newsletters, presented at agency board meetings, or reported to funders. When research efforts are recognized, the agency environment supports practice research.

Agency pressures for obtaining information about the effectiveness and relevance of practice activities can be termed *accountability de-*

mands. The administrator may require practice research or other types of research to satisfy requirements of funding agencies, boards of directors, and the local community. Administrators may require information about clients as a result of their conceptions of accountability or for public relations and fundraising activities. As an example, a child-service agency with sites in Pennsylvania, West Virginia, and Maryland meets the administration's notion of accountability by publishing an annual follow-up report of clients served in the past year.(Fabry and Kaminski 1991).

In recent years, human services agencies have begun to collect increasingly large amounts and types of information (Nurius, Hooyman, and Nicoll 1991). Computerized client information systems have greatly facilitated data collection. Ideally, computer data are readily available to practitioners and agency workers, given adequate protection to ensure client confidentiality (Grasso and Epstein 1989) . Most agencies have information about clients in hard copy files, but practitioners' efforts to conduct practice research are greatly facilitated when the information is already compiled and readily accessible via computer. Moreover, data stored on computers are likely to be more accurate and reliable because it calls for a systematic framework for recording the information.

Agency resources include the availability of time allocated for activities related to practice research, as well as support such as clerical assistance, computers, supplies, and telephones. The more an agency administration makes these resources available to practitioner-researchers, the more supportive the administration is of practice research. An administration may not allocate resources to practice research per se, but if agency administration devotes sufficient resources to practice activities and accepts the notion that practice research is a component of practice, then resources for practice research can be conceived of as that portion of practice that is devoted to practice research. Some agencies are complex and may even have their own research departments that can be resources for consultation and information. Recall, however, that our definition of practice research does not encompass research conducted by professional researchers.

Finally, rewards to workers for doing practice research can be beneficial. For example, the practice-researcher might be given financial support to attend conferences on practice research, receive extra secretarial support or an extra salary increment as a result of publishing practice research in a professional journal. For some, recognition alone may be sufficient reinforcement.

Community Environmental Factors

Community environmental factors can facilitate practice research by sanctioning research activities or by making provisions that facilitate gathering information about clients. As used here, *community* encompasses other human service agencies as well as other institutions in the community.

Every community supports research efforts in its own way. Community support may take the form of grants from sponsoring organizations and foundations. The grants may include incentives to gather data assessing needs or evaluating the activities of direct practice. Government agencies that contract for services may decide to require that all of its contractors routinely collect practice data. Other organizations that might sanction practice research include agency advisory boards, client advocacy groups, or local or state associations of agencies serving a particular population. Finally, laws, statutes, and local ordinances affect the work of social workers. Mandatory reporting laws regarding child abuse, for example, may aid rather than hinder the development of practice research into the needs of abused children.

In addition to sanctioned research, there may be instances in which data are shared between agencies. There may be interagency agreements on sharing information. Such reciprocal agreements can result in sharing client data. For example, a state association of private providers of services for the elderly may require its member agencies to collect data on their clients. A member agency might share these data with other organizations not belonging to this association.

Barriers to Practice Research

Factors that prevent or hinder research are barriers to practice research. Because research barriers are diametrically opposed to research supports, the preceding discussion of sources of support can serve as a stimulus for locating research barriers (that is, there is an inverse relationship between supports and barriers). In contrast to the previously cited support factors, the following are regarded as barriers:

1. Research not integrated as a component of direct practice
2. Practitioners with no knowledge of research methods
3. Practitioners not motivated to do research
4. Practitioners who do not ascribe to professional values toward knowledge development and dissemination

The same analysis can be extended to other areas where supportive factors have been identified. The three major sources of barriers to practice research are practitioners, agencies, and community environments.

Practitioner Barriers

Our collective experiences in practice, practice research, and teaching leads us to believe that the major practitioner barriers to research result from unfounded fears and misconceptions about practice research, which can be corrected through education and training in research concepts.

Some persons are in awe of research. They believe it is primarily mathematical and statistical, and that it is not research unless it involves complicated computer programs, mathematical formulas, and the like. They view themselves as technically incompetent and leave research to the academics and technocrats. This conception of research is distorted. Research in practice is driven by the questions of practice, not by mechanistic tools that may or may not be relevant. Although some knowledge of statistics is necessary, expertise in advanced mathematical and statistical methods is not required to conduct practice research. The few statistical procedures that *are* employed require nothing more than a comprehensive liberal arts education in high school and college.

A similar and sometimes overlapping group are practitioners who view research as uninteresting and unrelated to practice. This belief is fostered by numerous dry research reports, which indeed offer little insight into practice dilemmas or decisions. But this is not an accurate conception of *practice* research, which should directly address the questions most interesting to practitioners.

Although they seldom admit it, some social workers fear self-exposure and being identified as failing to help clients. This can lead to an avoidance of obtaining information about effectiveness. Yet we know that we do not have all the answers about how to best help our clients, and our knowledge is in a relatively early stage of development. Therefore, it is incumbent on us to learn from our practice what we do, how well we do it, and what results derive from our work. In this way, we can continually raise questions, refine our practice, and specify areas for training and development.

Some social workers believe that important aspects of practice can only be described qualitatively. On the contrary, many practice decisions involve nominal (classificatory) and ordinal (rank ordering) scales of measurement—existence of child abuse; placement for adoption; return to the community from an institution; degree of perceived depression; and abstinence from drug use, to name a few examples (Blythe and Tripodi 1989). In chapter 2, we present a conception of measurement that facilitates measuring many, if not all, practice decisions. Regardless of one's theoretical orientation, measurement concepts can be applied to specify assessment and evaluation variables in practice.

Agency Barriers

We have observed that human service agencies raise many barriers to conducting practice research. These barriers include: (1) the nature of practice in agencies; (2) conflicts between treatment and research goals; (3) possible incompetence of agency management and supervision; (4) inadequate files and information systems; (5) insufficient availability of resources and/or low priority given to practice research; and (6) punitive agency environments.

For better or worse, practice in the "real world" is not always a stable, orderly process. There are many crises and unexpected events in direct practice that can pose difficulties when practitioners attempt to carry out treatment objectives or research activities. For instance, a family may unexpectedly find itself in an emergency, requiring the immediate and full attention of the practitioner. In this case, it may be difficult or even inappropriate to gather routine research information that is not immediately relevant to the emergency. On the other hand, some facets of practice in agencies may actually point to the importance of carrying out practice research. All too often, clients discontinue services by missing appointments or by dropping out of agency programs or services. While they may not be able to participate in follow-up surveys, over time, these clients may stimulate opportunities for practice research on factors related to drop-out or continuance of service.

Certain types of research may be especially difficult to pursue when, as in some experimental manipulations, the goals of service conflict with those of research (Thomas 1978). In practice research, the research goals must always be consistent with practice goals. When a research procedure, such as withdrawing an effective intervention, is not compatible with the goals of practice, the procedure is *not employed*. In the subsequent discussions of research designs, we will show how research designs can be used to take advantage of natural occurrences in practice. Examples are the withdrawal of interventions during vacations, weekends, holidays, and illnesses. But research designs will always follow, not conflict with, the treatment or service goals for clients.

As demonstrated by Weissman (1974), administrators and supervisors sometimes can be incompetent, which in turn, may pose a barrier to practice research and other practice innovations. If supervisors are incompetent or simply ignorant of practice research, they may avoid dealing with the topic and, consequently, not function as adequate role models. They may not provide necessary supports for social workers attempting practice research (Briar and Blythe 1985). As a result, educators in social work are stressing the importance of integrating classroom content on research into practice field placements. As a corollary, it is apparent that supervisors must also know what their students know if they are to provide effective leadership in developing practice research.

Inadequate agency records may pose a barrier to practice research. They may contain inaccurate and unreliable information, or the information may not be accessible. Information systems may be organized so that files cannot easily be combined for analysis. Such problems are common when the information systems have been developed for administrative purposes, with little thought given to other applications. For example, a child welfare organization may organize its information by child, to facilitate "head counts." By doing so, it may be impossible to aggregate information by family, although siblings often are served by the same practitioners. An examination of agency files is one activity in which a practitioner-researcher can be engaged. In chapter 2, criteria for determining the usability of available records and files are presented. If, in the worse case, nothing is adequate or available, it is necessary for practitioner-researchers to compile their own information.

Perhaps the most difficult situation occurs when there is no administrative and staff support for practice research. Resources may be scarce, and there may be a low priority for obtaining information pertinent to client progress. No rewards may be available, and there may be no encouragement for practice research. Fortunately, this phenomenon occurs less frequently than in the previous decade. Nonetheless, it is still possible to conduct practice research under these circumstances, focusing activities on one's current case load. A number of illustrations are provided in subsequent chapters as examples of gathering and analyzing client information to monitor and evaluate client progress and/or client needs.

In some cases, the agency may discourage research, experimentation, and creativity. In such instances, administrators often are interested in high numbers of cases served and client contact hours, but not in outcomes. The environment may even be so harsh that worker-generated data indicating lack of client progress would be used as an indication of worker failure, rather than of ethical practice. Such an environment can bolster practitioners' fears of self-exposure and pose a huge barrier to the conduct of practice research and to good practice.

Community Environmental Barriers

The local community may pose barriers to practice research, but these generally are not insurmountable. The community may restrict the sharing of information. As long as the client's rights are protected, however, interagency agreements can be negotiated for sharing information relevant to the conduct of practice.

Community pressures may make it difficult to collect accurate information, particularly when one practices with clients who bear the social stigmas of contemporary society, such as drug addicts, the mentally ill, juvenile delinquents, spouse abusers, and sexual offenders. These pressures, however, can be counteracted by community boards' and associations' demands to know what their human services are doing, whether they're providing relevant services, and whether these services are meeting client needs effectively.

Ethical Issues in Direct Practice Research

Direct practice researchers owe their primary responsibility to their clients. They must be cognizant of ethical issues that confront them as practitioners and as researchers. Social workers generally encounter ethical dilemmas in direct practice with individuals, families and groups, during the development of policies and programs for distributing resources, and in their professional and collegial conduct toward clients (Reamer 1983). In direct practice, social workers deal with ethical dilemmas that involve

> Truth-telling in relationships with clients; conflicts between a law, rule, or policy and treatment goals; conflicts between social workers' obligations to their employers and to their clients; confidential-

ity and privileged communication; terminating services against a client's wishes; and providing services against a client's wishes. (Reamer 1983:31).

To deal with these dilemmas, professional associations such as the National Association of Social Workers promulgate standards that serve as guidelines for the conduct of practice and research. Various writers have provided interpretations (Gillespie 1987; Reamer 1983; Reynolds 1982). Cited most often by researchers in social work are those standards in the NASW Code of Ethics (1987:953) that refer to the social worker's responsibility for scholarship and research:

1. The social worker engaged in research should consider carefully its possible consequences for human beings.
2. The social worker engaged in research should ascertain that the consent of participants in the research is voluntary and informed, without any implied deprivation or penalty for refusal to participate, and with due regard for participants' privacy and dignity.
3. The social worker engaged in research should protect participants from unwarranted physical or mental discomfort, distress, harm, danger, or deprivation.
4. The social worker who engages in the evaluation of services or cases should discuss them only for the professional purposes and only with persons directly and professionally concerned with them.
5. Information obtained about participants in research should be treated as confidential.
6. The social worker should take credit only for work actually done in connection with scholarly and research endeavors and credit contributions made by others.

To reconcile conflicting values about the conduct of research in practice, social workers must weigh the practical merits of the research against potential harm to the client (Gillespie 1987). Sponsored research, which involves institutional review boards, often requires the researcher follow specified standards. In human service agencies, social workers in practice or in research follow the written policies and procedures developed for the ethical boundaries of work with clients. Most often, these policies involve interpretations of confidentiality, consent, the privacy of clients, and the release and exchange of information about clients, their families, and other significant relationships.

Perhaps the most thorough analysis of ethical dilemmas and strategies for comparing the risks and benefits of research has been provided by Reynolds (1982). Reynolds examined a series of questions concerned with the rights of all parties participating in research; the costs and benefits of the research; the risks and benefits for research participants; expected distributions of costs and benefits; respect for the rights and welfare of participants; the personal treatment of those involved in research; and the professional acceptability of professional judgments about the ethics of research. This framework would be helpful to individual practitioner-researchers who have ethical questions about planned research activities as well as to agencies wanting to develop ethical guidelines for practice and other research activities.

Because research is incorporated in practice, the goals of practice research are consistent with (and served by) those of direct practice. The ethical concerns confronting the practitioner-researcher are the same as those that confront any direct service practitioner. The ethical issues involved in research are applicable to direct practice research. Influenced by the analysis of Monette, Sullivan, and DeJong (1990), we believe that (1) agency context, (2) confidentiality, (3) informed consent, (4) privacy, (5) accurate information and the lack of deception, and (6) no intended physical or psychological harm evoke interrelated, crucial questions for practitioner-researchers.

Agency Context

Practitioner-researchers must understand the policies and procedures of the agency in which they work, as well as in other relevant agencies, and the supporting statutes and ordinances that pertain to the welfare and rights of their clients. If, for example, the agency has a policy against exchanging client information with other agencies without the client's informed consent, then the practitioner-researcher needs to consider making appropriate arrangements. If there are compelling reasons for sharing the information without informed consent, then the practitioner-researcher must discuss this with the agency body that deals with the ethical dilemma. This agency body may be an ad hoc committee of administrators and staff, a committee of the board of directors, or some other group. Suppose that the agency has information pertinent to an adult son's abuse of his elderly mother. The son, as a client of the agency, may wish to have no information divulged. The mother, in turn, may be a client of a hospital social worker. Because reporting is required by local ordinances and state law, and because the hospital social worker needs the information to adequately assess the nature of the client's problems, the practitioner-researcher must resolve this dilemma in cooperation with agency staff and administration.

Confidentiality

Who should gain access to information about the client? What defines clients' rights of confidentiality? Confidentiality requirements apply to any information about the client that is obtained in the conduct of direct practice and direct practice research. The information may come from a broad range of sources, including referrals, agency records, and research protocols. Further, confidentiality requirements apply to active as well as inactive clients. The limits of confidentiality need to be clearly specified for clients. They need to be informed about who will see information (both within and outside the agency), what information can be shared with others, and under what circumstances might the information be shared.

Informed Consent

Informed consent means that clients are to be informed about (and consent to undergoing) the practice and/or research protocols to be followed, their potential for harm, as well as their known effectiveness or lack of effectiveness. Informed consent may affect client participation in practice and practice research after they are fully aware of the nature of the endeavor. For example, most people would not wish to submit to a medical treatment if there was little or no evidence of its effectiveness. Similarly, social work clients should be informed about the known effectiveness of the therapy or the treatment techniques their workers will be using.

Reynolds (1982) discusses four legal standards involved in assessing informed consent: (1) client's capacity to make a rational, mature judgment; (2) freedom from coercion; (3) information about expected practice and research procedures; and (4) comprehension of possible results. Reynolds goes on to discuss instances where problems might occur. For example, it is not possible to definitively inform the client about what will occur, because a social worker is not a fortune teller. In situations where the client is designated as incompetent by the courts, the agency, or other sources, informed consent must be obtained by some representative of the client such as a guardian, parent, the court, or institution *in loco parentis*. This issue needs to be considered with many client groups served by human service agencies, including elderly clients, mentally ill persons, foster children, and juvenile delinquents. In essence, informed consent is relevant in many social work settings where clients do not necessarily seek services on their own volition.

Privacy

Clients are entitled to privacy in their dealings with human service agencies. They, of course, are known by the direct service workers with whom they are engaged in treatment. Privacy also involves the protection of their identities during the exchange of information with other agencies and institutions, or with other branches of the agency where they receive services. Privacy concerns also are relevant in agency research and practice reports, which may be disseminated in-house or beyond the agency. If there are plans to identify clients, informed consent issues should be considered. In most reports that go beyond the specific worker-client interactions, client's names are not necessary; and a degree of anonymity can be retained. A worker may survey a group of clients who dropped out of treatment prematurely without asking for their names. As another example, a practitioner-researcher may discuss the results of an intervention by aggregating or combining the results found with several clients, without identifying specific clients.

Accurate Information and Lack of Deception

Clients need information to decide if they wish to participate in social work treatment. In order for the worker to fulfill the conditions of informed consent, they need to inform their clients both before and during treatment. If practice goals are not being achieved, the client should be told. This constitutes an operational definition of accountability to clients. Clients should be given honest, accurate information about their progress, and not be misinformed, misled, or deceived. Such deception is highly unlikely when practitioners are involved in direct practice research, because the social worker seeks the involvement of the client in identifying and developing measures of effectiveness and progress, and possibly in data collection (Blythe and Tripodi 1989). If experimental or untested treatment methods are used, clients should be informed of potentially harmful side-effects.

If clients are not competent to understand the information, then it must be accurately described to a designated representative. Then, the representative can make informed decisions about the intervention, about switching to other modes of intervention, or terminating the case.

Physical and Psychological Harm

The practitioner-researcher should examine practice and research protocols to determine the extent to which they might lead to physical or psychological harm. In addition, the consequences of actions by the social worker that might harm the client should be considered. For example, the social worker may think about sharing negative thoughts a man has conveyed about his partner to the partner. If a child reveals that he or she has been emotionally abused in the past, the worker may not want to offer this information to the alleged perpetrator because it could lead to further emotional abuse. The consequences of practice and research procedures must, as much as possible, be considered *prior* to their implementation. For issues that involve potential harm, the practitioner-researcher may need to consult a supervisor, colleague, or other professional. Decisions regarding ethical issues often are difficult, and require good judgment, experience, and careful analysis.

Format of the Book

Throughout the book, agency supports, constraints, and ethical issues will be discussed in reference to using research methods in practice tasks such as assessment, implementing interventions, monitoring progress, and evaluating effectiveness.

The second chapter includes content on measurement, and is concerned with delineating variables for practice research in human service agencies. This chapter is the basis for the remaining chapters, and contains concepts and principles that deal with specifying client, worker, and intervention variables, and with locating agency information sources for constructing those variables.

Chapter 3 focuses on assessing client needs, and covers methods for assessing individual and aggregated client needs. Issues of constructing questionnaires, selecting and contacting clients, and analyzing data are considered.

In chapter 4, we discuss research strategies for determining if interventions are conforming to plans and are developing in a manner that enhances client participation. Procedures are presented for assessing client perceptions of intervention and compliance with intervention plans.

Chapter 5 examines how to describe the progress of clients and make appropriate practice modifications as a result of this information. Methods for gathering and analyzing data at one or more measurement points over time, to facilitate practitioners' analyses and decisions, are presented.

The process of evaluating effectiveness with single cases and across cases is described in chapter 6. Selected research designs that are readily applied in agency practice are presented, and ways of controlling threats to internal validity within these designs are discussed.

Chapter 7 concludes the book by outlining the process of preparing oral and written reports of direct practice research for a variety of audiences. Reasons for recording and reporting research findings are discussed, and procedures are identified for assisting practitioners in these efforts.

2. *The Measurement Process*

Measurement is vital to direct practice research. It involves identifying and specifying variables about clients, workers, and interventions. Concepts essential to studying direct social work practice are transformed into variables that allow for the consistent and replicable grouping of two or more categories of measurement. Concepts such as marital satisfaction, child abuse, drug dependency, countertransference, task completion, positive reinforcement, and stressors can be converted into variables. The conversion process involves: (1) identifying the concept to be transformed into a practice variable; (2) specifying the variable by operationally defining the procedures necessary to categorize its properties into measurement scales; (3) developing a new instrument or identifying an available instrument to gather data necessary for measurement; and, (4) determining the variable's reliability and validity (Blythe and Tripodi 1989).

Let us consider a practice-researcher who was working with a couple who were dissatisfied with their marriage and wished to achieve greater satisfaction from it. To assess client changes in marital satisfaction, the concept of marital satisfaction needed to be transformed into a variable, which is a measurable dimension of a concept that has two or more values (Tripodi 1983). The worker could have developed a marital satisfaction variable unique to the couple receiving marital counseling. The worker could have used a standardized instrument that was constructed by a process of measurement, such as Hudson's (1982) Index of Marital Satisfaction (IMS). Following the steps of the measurement process, the IMS is a questionnaire designed to measure problems in a marital relationship. It is comprised of twenty-five items (such as "I feel that my partner treats me badly";

"I feel that my partner doesn't understand me"; and "I feel that I cannot rely on my partner"). The respondent (client) answers each item by indicating whether it is true (1) "rarely or none of the time"; (2) "a little of the time"; (3) "some of the time"; (4) "a good part of the time"; or (5) "most or all of the time." These scale values are assigned the numbers 1 to 5. Following simple scoring procedures (fully explained in Hudson 1982), a variable of marital satisfaction is obtained. The score ranges from 0 to 100. The lower score, the higher the degree of marital satisfaction. In this way, the IMS categorizes levels of marital satisfaction. From reviewing Hudson (1982), we find that the scale has adequate reliability and validity. The questionnaire was tested on 1,803 respondents. Hudson found that a given person's response to an item was highly correlated to his or her responses to other items (known as internal consistency), which suggests that the IMS will provide consistent (or the same) results each time the person completes the IMS, assuming that there are no changes in his or her marital satisfaction. Moreover, the "clinical cutting score" for the IMS suggests that individuals who are categorized as more highly dissatisfied with their marriages, based on their answers to the IMS, are more likely to be identified as having marital problems and to seek professional help, when compared with individuals who are satisfied with their marriages. Hudson has examined the validity of the IMS, using several different methods, and found it to be sufficient. Thus, it is reasonable to assume that the IMS is measuring the concept of marital satisfaction.

As often occurs in practice, the practitioner examined different facets of the couple's marital satisfaction. Through interviews, the worker learned that a major source of dissatisfaction in their marriage stemmed from perceptions that household chores were inequitably distributed. Both partners believed they were doing more than 50 percent of the household tasks. Accordingly, a treatment goal to increase sharing of household chores was developed. The goal of sharing household tasks was operationally defined as the degree to which each spouse indicates that she or he shared in a specified list of chores, determined by both spouses, on a scale that ranges from 0 percent to 100 percent. The variable of perceived sharing of chores was measured weekly for each member of the couple, so that desired changes in relation to clinical goals could be monitored. This procedure was used in conjunction with Hudson's IMS, although it could have been used separately.

The process of measurement will be described in more detail

throughout this chapter. First, we present ideas about practice concepts that can be transformed into variables of clients, workers, and interventions. Second, we discuss concepts necessary for specifying levels of measurement, and for estimating the reliability and validity of variables. Finally, we point to agency records as a common source of variables in human service agencies, and present criteria for determining the potential applications of agency records. Altogether, the chapter provides the information essential for practice-researchers to carry out the types of research described in subsequent chapters.

Identifying Practice Concepts

Concepts are necessary to communicate phenomena observed in direct practice. A concept is a verbal or symbolic representation. A key step in the measurement process is identifying those concepts to be measured. Although we will not discuss every conceivable concept and variable that pertains to practice, we can furnish guidelines that will assist in locating salient variables. Variables can be developed which pertain to clients, workers, interactions, environments, and interventions. For the purpose of illustrating the kinds of concepts and variables practice-researchers might identify, we shall consider the categories of clients, workers, and interventions. A typology for classifying practice concepts will be presented, as applied to client and worker variables, and then intervention variables will be discussed.

Client/Worker Variables

Variables describing clients and workers can be organized according to the typology presented in table 2.1 (Adapted from Blythe and Tripodi 1989:32).

Type 1 variables refer to characteristics obtained from worker and client histories and from observation. Client characteristics, for exam-

TABLE 2.1
Typology of Worker/Client Variables

Type 1	Personal and Demographic Characteristics
Type 2	Moods, Feelings, Attitudes, Beliefs, and Values
Type 3	Knowledge, Ability, and Achievement
Type 4	Observable Behavior

ple, include education, income, employment, age, gender, health status, place of residence, psychiatric diagnosis, nationality, race, marital status, number of children, previous mental health placements, and number of delinquent or criminal adjudications. Relevant worker characteristics, in addition to demographic variables such as age, gender, nationality, race, and social class, include variables related to the practice of social work, such as education in social work, degrees and/or certificates in social work practice, membership in relevant professional associations, years of experience with specific types of clients, and years of experience in the use of particular interventions.

Variables in Type 2 refer to current moods, feelings, attitudes, beliefs, and values. These usually are transformed into variables by eliciting responses via measurement scales or questionnaires. The concepts of anxiety, depression, expectations about treatment outcome, belief in the value of social work interventions, and attitudes toward controversial issues such as abortion, capital punishment, incarceration, or drug and alcohol use can be converted into variables for measurement. Although these variables usually are examined because they relate to a client goal (such as decreasing anxiety), Type 2 variables also can be obtained for workers. For example, the social worker's mood may affect clients' progress. Type 2 variables also may include worker-client congruence of moods, attitudes, beliefs, or values. High levels of congruence or incongruence might affect progress in treatment.

Type 3 variables include knowledge, ability, and achievement, as reflected on diagnostic paper-and-pencil tests, such as those testing the reading comprehension of a learning disabled child. Type 3 variables can also be created from knowledge and abilities as they relate to the achievement of treatment goals. For example, variables might include a client's knowledge of what steps to take if he relapses to drug use, the ability of a client with mild retardation to write a résumé and/or to interview for jobs, and the ability of a client with schizophrenia to maintain an independent life after institutionalization.

Type 3 variables, when examined in the worker, may include knowledge about client problems, and the ability to effectively deliver appropriate social work interventions. For example, a social worker who works with chronic schizophrenics needs to understand the psychopharmacology of the patient's drugs. A practitioner acting as a case manager needs to be familiar with community resources. Variables describing social workers' knowledge may be especially relevant for supervisors. For example, it might be helpful for a supervisor of a new community-based program to test the extent of the workers' knowledge about community resources.

Type 4 variables can be observed when a worker and a client are actively working to achieve specified goals. For clients, these often are variables that refer to observable client problems or strengths. In marital counseling, the practice-researcher might develop procedures for observing or for having the clients and significant others observe phenomena as number of arguments, or time shared in pleasurable activities. Parent-child interactions are important to social work practice with families, and variables can be developed to measure them. Social interactions or other social behaviors might be observed in autistic children. Systems for counting the intake of alcohol, drugs, or cigarettes can be devised. Positive behaviors denoting clients' self-concepts, physical fitness, and vocational and social aspirations also may be observed.

Type 4 variables pertaining to workers are most likely to describe worker-client interactions. For example, a practice-researcher may want to maintain neutral affect when a client is expressing a transference wish. If the worker emits positive expressions but is unaware of it, the intervention is not being implemented as intended. To study this, expressions of worker affect could be discerned and categorized as positive, neutral, or negative by analyzing the contents of tape-recorded interviews. Workers depend upon the creation of rapport and good relationships with their clients. These also are Type 4 variables. Client satisfaction, based on client observations, can provide workers with clues to difficulties in the relationship. For example, clients may report on their observations of the worker's planned follow-up activities, promptness in keeping appointments, listening to client's description of their problems, eye contact, or proportion of time client and worker talk during their interactions.

The four types of variables can be used for all stages of practice, from assessing the client's problems to implementing, monitoring, and evaluating interventions (Blythe and Tripodi 1989). Their relative importance depends on the problems that are being addressed, the worker-client relationship, and the interventions employed by the social worker.

Intervention Variables

Interventions are the techniques, strategies, and procedures employed by practitioners to achieve specified practice objectives or goals. An intervention may be comprised of one or more techniques. For example, to reduce delinquent behavior by an adolescent and increase positive interactions among family members, a social worker might employ techniques from cognitive-behavior therapy, family therapy, and groupwork. The techniques, used together or in sequence, constitute the social worker's intervention. This notion is similar to that of Thomas (1984) who regards intervention as a program comprised of intervention components. Thomas states that a program can vary as a result of "such factors as their scope, number of interventions, order of intervention, strength of intervention, degree of individualization, longevity, and structure" (Thomas 1984:56).

We believe that concepts about interventions can be converted into variables that specify the nature of those interventions. In other words, interventions can be categorized and identified with their goals and techniques; in turn, notions of goals and techniques can be transformed into variables that describe social work interventions.

Intervention Goals

Intervention goals refer to the intended results of social work interventions. Goals can focus on prevention, maintenance, or client change. A prevention goal might be to help a parent avoid verbally abusing her child. A maintenance goal for a group of individuals released from a psychiatric hospital could be to facilitate independent life in a group home. A goal of client change for an older client with health problems might be increased compliance with the medical regimen.

If desired, goals can be further delineated, particularly for change objectives, by indicating: (1) the amount of change expected in terms of problem magnitude or frequency; (2) a schedule for change; and/or (3) forecast of the duration of the change (Blythe and Tripodi 1989). It may be expected that an elderly male client will comply with the medical regimen (e.g., ingesting two pills per day and recording his blood pressure) 100 percent of the time, one month after intervention commences, and for a duration of three months.

Given the complexity of social work practice, interventions often have several goals. Variables can be devised to identify certain things about interventions by indicating the number of goals as well as their contents. Social workers who deliver intensive family preservation services to families in crisis, for instance, typically address several family needs. Some of these goals may be focused on the family as a whole (such as cleaning the house, organizing a chore chart, or reducing arguments), while others may be set for particular individuals (such as school attendance for a teenager, or drug counseling for a parent). In this example, identifying these goals by type and number describes the purpose or scope of the intervention (Thomas 1984).

Intervention Techniques

Intervention techniques are the components of intervention. A practitioner uses one or more techniques when working with clients. Note that the concepts of intervention techniques and interventions are often used interchangeably in the literature, as they will be here, while authors such as Thomas (1984) refer to intervention components within interventions.

The contents of techniques include the procedures that a social worker follows in working with a client. The process of proceduralization refers to delineating the procedures for implementing a specific intervention technique (Thomas 1984). In a groupwork session, intervention procedures may include the seating arrangement, discussion topics, and strategies for encouraging group members to engage in self-disclosure. Procedures also can relate to clients' activities outside of the session: for example, a client might be asked to keep a journal. In essence, proceduralization focuses on those specific arrangements, interactions, and communications that a social worker employs to implement the technique. To the degree that procedures can be specified for particular techniques, it is possible to distinguish between techniques, as well as indicate whether or not a technique is being implemented.

Frequently, more than one technique is required for an intervention, and this combination of techniques (or intervention components, or interventions) can be regarded as an intervention package (Barlow and Hersen 1984). In either case, the contents of an intervention (or intervention package) must be distinct from other interventions.

Hence they can be converted into an intervention variable. The process of these transformations will be discussed in the section *Specifying Variables*.

In addition to the content and number of techniques, their amount, frequency, and duration also can lead to the creation of intervention variables. *Amount* refers to the amount of time the technique is used during a particular worker-client interaction. As an example, in a thirty-minute counseling session with a third-grade student, a school social worker may employ play therapy for fifteen minutes. Strength and dosage of the intervention technique may or may not be thought of as equivalent to amount. For instance, a drug may vary in its dosage or strength, whereas worker-client interaction can vary in amount of time, but it often is difficult to specify the intensity of the interaction on an a priori basis. *Frequency* refers to how often a technique is employed. Groupwork sessions, for example, may be held five days per week in a hospice. The *duration* of the technique refers to the period of time it is employed. Group sessions may be held for a specified period of time, say, three months.

To further depict how an intervention technique can be specified by referring to its contents, objectives, and techniques, let us offer a simple illustration. Suppose a social worker in a community center wants to help a client take her daily medication. The intervention technique consists of a telephone call, in which the social worker reminds the client to take the medicine. The call takes one minute (amount), is made three times per week (frequency) for one month (duration). Other techniques, related to other goals, are employed by the social worker during monthly face-to-face contacts with the client, such as role playing and rehearsal to help her better deal with other members of her family with whom she has interpersonal conflicts.

Multiple techniques may be employed simultaneously, intermittently, or sequentially. The worker, for example, may use different techniques to focus on different goals, or may specify a hierarchy of goals, and deal with more immediate concerns before focusing on long-range issues (Blythe and Tripodi 1989). In delineating sequential goals, the practitioner specifies a technique for a particular treatment goal and, when that goal is accomplished, employs another technique for another goal. Specifying this sequential planning is another way to further delineate interventions, making it possible to define variables.

While the process of specifying intervention techniques and goals may seem overly technical, there are several important reasons for doing so. Specifying intervention techniques and goals facilitates the replication of effective interventions and allows two or more techniques to be compared in terms of their relative effectiveness. Most important, it is critical to good social work practice. Regardless of theoretical orientation, a social worker must have a plan that identifies the goals and interventions, and when and how the interventions will be carried out. Deviations from this plan may occur (and they probably will occur), but these deviations should be made in a careful and thoughtful manner, after a critical examination of all relevant information. Specifying the intervention techniques and goals allows the plan to be identified, implemented, communicated to others, and modified in a deliberate (rather than haphazard) manner.

Specifying Variables

Variable specification is the process of transforming a concept into a variable by making an operational definition. Like recipes for cooking, operational definitions indicate the procedures necessary to convert a concept into categories, which will be at one of four levels of measurement: nominal, ordinal, interval, and ratio. Summarized in table 2.2,

TABLE 2.2
Levels of Measurement

Nominal	Mutually exclusive and exhaustive categories; classification	Male; female Registered social worker; not a registered social worker Employing positive reinforcement; not employing positive reinforcement. Homeless; not homeless
Ordinal	Classification and order between categories	Lower class; middle class; upper class. Negative interaction; neutral interaction; positive interaction
Interval	Classification, order, and equal distances between adjacent categories	Number of contacts worker makes with family in designated period of time Number of days abstaining from drugs since first worker-client contact
Ratio	Classification, order, equal distances, and an absolute zero	Number of adjudications Number of out-of-home placements

Adapted from Blythe and Tripodi (1989:30).

these levels of measurement form a continuum of increasing information about categories employed when operationally defining a variable. The following sections define each of these levels and indicate the type of information that can be derived at each level.

Nominal Measurement Scales

A nominal scale is the simplest level of measurement. It is a scale composed of two or more mutually exclusive and exhaustive categories. Categories are mutually exclusive when objects can be assigned to only one of the categories in the scale. *Male* and *female* can be considered mutually exclusive categories: a person can be classified as either a male or a female, but not as both. Categories are exhaustive if all the possibilities for a particular scale are delimited. A scale for gender with categories of male and female is exhaustive because all people can be assigned to one or the other of these categories.

When a concept is converted to a nominal scale, it is transformed into a variable with nominal measurement. This involves defining the categories and specifying their possible number and range, so that they can be distinguished from each other. In addition, the operational definition also indicates how the data will be gathered and categorized. An operational definition of gender includes specifying that the possible categories are "male" and "female" and indicating the type of data to be gathered and categorized. Thus, gender could be reported on a questionnaire by the client, in answer to this question: "What is your gender: male/female (check one)." Obviously, operational definitions and procedures for collecting and categorizing data are much more important (and more complicated) when working with more complex variables such as ego strength.

Variables about clients that have been placed in nominal scales can refer to all four types of variables described in table 2.1. For example, possessing a high school diploma (or not possessing a diploma) constitutes a client characteristic (type 1 variable). A client's belief about abortion (pro-choice or anti-abortion) represents a nominal scale (type 2 variable). Passing or failing a driver's license examination illustrates a type 3 achievement-based variable. Finally, an observable type 4 variable might be whether or not a client meets her child's school bus at the end of each school day.

Nominal scales measuring worker attributes could include ethnic category, licensure status, and knowledge of agency regulations.

Nominal scales cover the gamut of decisions resulting from social work assessments and interventions. For example, decisions to place an adoptive child, to return a mentally ill person to a psychiatric institution, and to revoke parole are variables for nominal measurement. Monitoring whether or not an intervention is implemented depends on forming operational definitions that specify the procedures needed to determine if the intervention is taking place during a social work contact, and represents nominal measurement.

Ordinal Measurement Scales

An ordinal scale has the properties of a nominal scale, that is mutually exclusive and exhaustive categories, plus that of order between adjacent categories. To illustrate, a client may indicate her degree of satisfaction with social work intervention by responding to a question that constitutes an ordinal scale:

> To what extent are you satisfied with the interview you had with your social worker today? (check one)
> _____ very satisfied   _____ satisfied
> _____ dissatisfied   _____ not at all satisfied

The category "very satisfied" indicates greater satisfaction than the category "satisfied," which in turn signifies more satisfaction than the category "dissatisfied." This variable of ordinal measurement is the result of a transformation of the concept of satisfaction.

Ordinal scales can be used for variables that describe workers, clients, interactions, and interventions. This level of measurement is particularly useful for obtaining information about private feelings, moods, and attitudes that cannot be observed. Many pencil-and-paper instruments have been developed to assess clients' moods and attitudes (see Fischer and Corcoran 1994 for a compilation of instruments). In addition, ordinal scales can be created to track moods such as depression or anxiety. Information about worker-client relationships can be determined by variables obtained from questioning clients and/or workers. For example, a client could describe his trust for the worker on a scale ranging from "I don't trust the social worker at all" to "I trust the social worker somewhat" to "I trust the social worker a great deal." Ordinal scales also allow the practice-researcher to assess concepts based in intervention techniques. For instance, ordinal rating scales could examine the degree to which the relationship between worker and client is used as a context for discussing client behaviors, or the degree to which probing techniques are employed to gather information about the client's problems.

Interval Measurement Scales

Interval scales have the properties of ordinal scales, plus the property of equal distances between categories. However, they do not have real, absolute zero points as do ratio scales. A calendar, which begins at an arbitrary point of time, say today, provides a good example of an interval scale. Today is an arbitrarily chosen beginning point, but is not thought of as "no time" or "zero time." Yet one can count what happens in successive days. The client treated for substance abuse may abstain from drugs tomorrow, thus completing one day of abstinence. He may abstain the day after tomorrow also; hence, he abstains for two days. The distance between today and tomorrow is one day, and the distance between tomorrow and the day after tomorrow is also one day; these represent equal distances between adjacent categories.

Variables employing interval measurement are used to represent observable behaviors over a duration of time, as in the above example. They can be used for clients, workers, or interventions. For example, one might count the number of days in which interventions are focused on an individual client or on her family.

Ratio Measurement Scales

Ratio scales are interval scales with zero points. They are used for counting objects and behaviors. They can be used with variables such as income, age, and number of years of education. Sometimes it is difficult to distinguish between ratio and interval scales, due to the nature of absolute zero. A test of achievement such as a test of knowledge, assuming items are of equal difficulty, can be thought of as a ratio scale, if it is conceptually meaningful to speak of "zero" knowledge. This conceptual problem leads us to use ratio and interval scales interchangeably when discussing variables based on tests of knowledge and achievement.

Ratio scales can also be used to report the frequency and amount of intervention activities. For example, the social worker may analyze a component of worker-client interaction by measuring the amount of time the worker talked in an interview in comparison to the amount of the time the client talked. The number of intervention techniques used in a session also might be recorded, as well as the number of positive and negative worker-client interactions.

Client behaviors also can be recorded on ratio scales. As an example, one can track the eating habits by counting calories, consumption of alcohol by volume, or drug intake by dosage and frequency of use. Variables that are at the level of ratio scales might also be used to refer to height, weight, and blood pressure, important measures for health and prevention programs.

Reliability of Variables

Reliability of a variable refers to the degree to which consistent results are obtained upon repeated application of the procedures employed for gathering and categorizing variables. Consistency or dependability, that is, reliability, is an important characteristic that, along with validity, allows one to confidently employ variables in practice research. If an instrument does not yield consistent or dependable information, there is no point in using it. The three basic kinds of reliability that can be examined for worker, client, and intervention variables are inter-observer agreement, test-retest reliability or stability, and internal consistency. We will define each of these kinds of reliability and describe the procedures for calculating them.

Interobserver Agreement

Interobserver agreement is also known as interrater reliability, inter-observer reliability, or interjudge reliability. As the name suggests, it is the degree to which two or more observers (raters, judges) agree on their observations, ratings, and/or classifications of data after independently observing the same phenomena. The observations can be live observations, or they can be based on recorded phenomena such as videotapes, audio tapes, or written case records. Interobserver agreement (reliability) can be easily assessed by determining an index of percentage agreement, defined as the percentage of total possible agreements between observers which are actual agreements. In other words, percentage agreement equals the number of agreements divided by the possible number of agreements multiplied by 100:

$$\text{percentage agreement} = \frac{\text{agreements}}{\text{possible number of agreements}} \times 100$$

To illustrate, let's suppose that two social workers, Mr. Allen and Ms. Rosenbaum, listen to ten tape-recorded interviews of a third worker's interviews with ten clients. After listening to each tape, Mr. Allen and Ms. Rosenbaum independently indicate whether the worker-client interaction is positive (as evidenced by statements made by the worker or the client indicating trust, concern, or positive regard for one another), neutral (neither positive nor negative), or negative (worker and client remarks are wary, non-trusting, or hostile). The observations may be observed in table 2.3. Note that Mr. Allen and Ms. Rosenbaum agree on their ratings for clients 1, 2, 3, 5, 6, 7, 8, and 9, but disagree on clients 4 and 10. Hence, interobserver agreement is

$$\frac{8 \text{ agreements}}{10 \text{ possible agreements}} \times 100 = 80\%$$

Typically, 70 to 80 percent agreement is regarded as an acceptable degree of interobserver reliability (Blythe and Tripodi 1989).

Interobserver reliability generally is employed for type 1 and type 4 worker and client variables, as well as for intervention variables based on live observations or content analyses. The data categorized as variables are measured by nominal or ordinal scales.

TABLE 2.3

*Observations of Interactions Between Worker and Client for
Ten Clients by Two Independent Raters*

Client	Mr. Allen	Ms. Rosenbaum
1	+	+
2	+	+
3	+	+
4	+	0
5	0	0
6	−	−
7	0	0
8	0	0
9	−	−
10	+	0

Key
+ = *positive interaction*
− = *negative interaction*
0 = *neutral interaction*

There are numerous practical applications of interobserver reliability. This type of reliability could determine the consistency among workers' use of classification systems, such as the Global Assessment Scale, or in making major decisions regarding the disposition of clients, such as a recommendation that a child be placed in a wilderness camp, a residential treatment center, or in a day treatment program. Interobserver reliability also could be applied in observing such phenomena as the amount of worker and client time devoted to talking and/or the content of their interactions. For example, interviewing techniques could be categorized as giving advice, probing, or clarifying and the interobserver reliability of two raters using this nominal scale to categorize a worker's interactions with clients could be assessed.

Test-Retest Reliability (Stability)

Test-retest reliability refers to consistent results obtained over time when applying the same measurement procedures. It is especially important to know the test-retest reliability of a variable that will assess client change. For example, let us suppose we developed a Marital Satisfaction Index (MSI) to administer to clients before and after marital counseling, to determine whether there is a change in scores that might be attributed to the marital counseling. If the variable of marital satisfaction is unreliable, however, the different scores that clients get when completing the MSI over time might be due to the unreliability of the MSI and not to any actual changes in their marital satisfaction. To assess test-retest reliability, the instruments would be administered to a representative group of respondents at two different points in time. The correlation (an indicator of agreement) between the two sets of responses would be examined. A Pearson correlation coefficient is appropriate when the variable is at the level of interval or ratio measurement (Hinkle, Wiersma, and Jurs 1988). Assume that the MSI is at an interval level and that the lower the score, the higher the marital dissatisfaction. And, further suppose that ten clients waiting for treatment have completed the questionnaire twice within a three-week period of time. Table 2.4 contains the clients' data for calculating a Pearson r (correlation coefficient).

To compute the Pearson r, referring to table 2.4, take the following steps:

1. Identify scores for each client and display them in columns 1, 2, and 3, as in table 2.4. For example, client A scored 20 on both test 1 and test 2; client B scored 21 and 23, and so forth. Scores in column 2 are regarded as scores for the variable at time 1, arbitrarily designated as "X"; scores in column 3 are scores for the variable at time 2, designated as "Y."

2. Obtain scores in column 4 by multiplying X by Y for each client. For example, for client A, XY = 20 × 20 = 400; for client B, XY = 21 × 23 = 483, and so forth.

3. Obtain X^2 scores in column 5 by multiplying each X score by itself (squaring it). Hence, for client A, X^2 = 20 × 20 = 400; for client B, X^2 = 21 × 21 = 441, and so forth.

4. Similarly, obtain Y^2 scores in column 6 by multiplying each Y score by itself. For client A, Y^2 = 20 × 20 = 400; for client B, Y^2 = 23 × 23 = 529, and so forth.

5. Add up all the scores in each column to obtain totals for X(where ΣX = sum of X), Y(ΣY = sum of Y), XY(ΣXY = sum of XY), X^2(ΣX^2 = sum of X^2) and Y^2 (ΣY^2 = sum of Y^2).

6. Substitute the column totals in the following formula for a correlation coefficient, where n = number of clients and r_{xy} = the Pearson correlation coefficient between X and Y scores (Hinkle, Wiersma, and Jurs 1988:111):

$$r_{xy} = \frac{n \, \Sigma xy - \Sigma x \, \Sigma y}{\sqrt{[n \, \Sigma x^2 - (\Sigma x)^2][n \, \Sigma y^2 - (\Sigma y)^2]}}$$

$$r_{xy} = \frac{(10)(9265) - (297)(296)}{\sqrt{[(10)(9297) - (297)^2][(10)(9244) - (296)^2]}}$$

$$r_{xy} = \frac{92,650 - 87,912}{\sqrt{(92,970 - 88,209)(92,440 - 87,616)}}$$

$$r_{xy} = \frac{4,738}{\sqrt{(4,761)(4,824)}}$$

$$r_{xy} = \frac{4,738}{\sqrt{22,967,064}} = \frac{4,738}{4,792} = 0.99$$

The correlation is 0.99. Note that correlations can range from 0 to 1.00, with 0 representing no correlation and 1.00 representing a perfect correlation. An acceptable correlation for test-retest reliability is 0.8 or higher.

TABLE 2.4

Responses of Ten Clients to the Marital Satisfaction Index Questionnaire on Two Administrations Over Three Weeks

(1) Client	(2) Test 1 (X)	(3) Test 2 (Y)	(4) XY	(5) X^2	(6) Y^2
A	20	20	400	400	400
B	21	23	483	441	529
C	22	21	462	484	441
D	25	24	600	625	576
E	29	28	812	841	784
F	33	32	1056	1089	1024
G	34	35	1190	1156	1225
H	36	36	1296	1296	1296
I	38	37	1406	1444	1369
J	39	40	1560	1521	1600
TOTALS	$\Sigma X = 297$	$\Sigma Y = 296$	$\Sigma XY = 9265$	$\Sigma X^2 = 9297$	$\Sigma Y2 = 9244$

Test-retest reliabilities typically are employed for data obtained from instruments serving as indices for Type 2 and Type 3 worker or client variables. They can also be determined, however, for data obtained from observations that are in the form of ordinal or nominal data. For ordinal data, Spearman's rho (ρ) is the correlation coefficient that often is used as an index of reliability. As an example of an application of Spearman's rho to ordinal data, suppose a social worker and her supervisor agree on the rank ordering of ten boys who live in a cottage at a residential drug treatment center in terms of their level of aggressiveness toward treatment staff and other residents, from 1 as least aggressive to 10 as most aggressive. Also, suppose that the rankings are made on the basis of their observations of the boys during the afternoon on two successive days to determine the consistency in their ratings over time. They also agree on their rankings at time 2 since they make the rankings in consultation with each other (as opposed to independent ratings necessary for interrater agreement). Data based on the rankings of the boys for computing Spearman's rho are contained in table 2.5:

The following steps are taken to compute rho:

1. Display the rankings of clients A through J in column 2, in order from 1 to 10 (or from 10 to 1). The clients are also ranked at time 2, as shown in column 3. Referring to table 2.5, client A was ranked 1 at both times 1 and 2; client B, 2 at time 1 and 3 at time 2, and so on.

2. For each client, subtract the rank in column 2 from the rank in column 3. For example for client A, 1-1 = 0; for client B, 2−3 = −1; and for client C, 3−4 = −1. These rank differences are referred to as d scores, and are displayed in column 4.

3. Column 5 contains the d^2 score for each client, that is, each d score is squared (multiplied by itself) and entered in column 5. Thus, for client C, $d^2 = (−1)(−1) = +1$; and for client D, $d^2 = (2)(2) = 4$.

4. The d^2 scores are summed to produce Σd^2, which is 12 in this example.

5. Using the following formula, substitute the number 12 for Σd^2, where n = the number of clients:

$$\rho = 1 - \frac{6\Sigma d^2}{n(n^2-1)} = 1 - \frac{(6)(12)}{(10)(100-1)} = 1 - \frac{72}{990} = 1 - 0.073 = .927$$

This correlation, .927, or .93 when rounded, is a relatively high correlation, and signifies a high degree of stability in the ratings of aggressiveness over two points in time.

There are several kinds of statistics that can be employed to assess correlations between nominal scales (See Hinkle, Wiersma, and Jurs 1988). One that is often used is phi (ϕ). To illustrate its calculation, suppose that a social work supervisor wants to examine the variable of assignment to foster care. The recommendation to place a child in foster care is made on the basis of compiling all the information contained in a case record. The following steps are taken:

TABLE 2.5
Rankings of Aggressiveness for Ten Boys Over Two Successive Time Periods

(1) Client	(2) Rankings at Time 1	(3) Rankings at Time 2	(4) Difference in ranks (d)	(5) d^2
A	1	1	0	0
B	2	3	−1	1
C	3	4	−1	1
D	4	2	2	4
E	5	5	0	0
F	6	6	0	0
G	7	7	0	0
H	8	10	−2	4
I	9	8	1	1
J	10	9	1	1
				$(\Sigma d^2) = 12$

1. Case records are reviewed at time 1. Of 100 children, it is recommended that 50 should be assigned to foster care.
2. The same 100 cases are reviewed at time 2, say one month later. To determine the test-retest reliability, the same information must be reviewed again at time 2. New information cannot be considered for the reliability test, although it most certainly would be used to alter these decisions in practice, if it was available. Data from time 1 and time 2 are displayed in table 2.6: those recommended for placement at times 1 and 2 (n = 45); those recommended for placement at time 1, but not at time 2 (n = 5); those recommended not to be placed at both times 1 and 2 (n = 45), and those not to be placed at time 1, but placed at time 2 (n = 5).

Notice that the cells in table 2.6 are labelled A, B, C, and D. Also, note the calculation of the sums of the columns (time 1 *placement* is A + C and *no placement* is B + D) and of the rows (time 2 *placement* is A + B and *no placement* is C + D).

Phi is calculated by substituting the obtained values of A, B, C, D, A + B, C + D, A + C, and B + D in the following formula:

$$phi\ (\phi) = \frac{AD - BC}{\sqrt{(A+B)(C+D)(A+C)(B+D)}}$$

$$\phi = \frac{(45)(45) - (5)(5)}{\sqrt{(50)(50)(50)(50)}}$$

$$\phi = \frac{2025 - 25}{(50)(50)} = \frac{2000}{2500} = 0.8$$

It is important to note that percentage agreement is not the same as the correlation. A good example of this is provided in table 2.6,

TABLE 2.6

Recommendations for Placement in Foster Care for 100 Clients over Two Successive Time Periods

Recommendations at Time 2	Recommendations at Time 1		
	Placement	No Placement	Totals
Placement	45 (A)	5 (B)	50 (A + B)
No Placement	5 (C)	45 (D)	50 (C + D)
TOTALS	50 (A + C)	50 (B + D)	

where $\phi = 0.8$ and percentage agreement is 90 percent. Percentage agreement is calculated by adding the number of agreements for placement (A) to the number of agreements for non-placement (D) to obtain the total number of agreements which, in turn, is divided by the total possible number of agreements, 100:

$$\% \ Agreement = \frac{A+D}{A+B+C+D} \times 100$$

$$= \frac{45+45}{45+5+5+45} \times 100 = \frac{90}{100} \times 100 = 90\%$$

Internal Consistency

A third type of reliability is used for data gathered in paper-and-pencil tests such as questionnaires, tests of ability, and attitude and mood scales. These are Type 2 and 3 data usually obtained for clients, but also could describe workers and their interventions. Moreover, these data are in the form of a number of items that represent one variable. For example, responses to twenty-five items represent the variable of depression in Hudson's Generalized Contentment Scale. Or, responses to a twenty-item questionnaire about a shelter for abused women might be obtained from a number of clients to indicate their satisfaction with the program.

Internal consistency is the extent to which responses to one-half of an instrument correlate with responses to the other half. The higher the correlation, the higher the degree of internal consistency. With a perfect correlation ($r = 1.0$), internal consistency indicates that respondents respond to all of the items as if they are all represented by the same variable. We will discuss three kinds of internal consistency: split-half reliability, multiple forms, and coefficient alpha.

Split-half reliability is obtained by numbering the items in an instrument and then dividing the instrument into 2 smaller segments, one segment composed of the odd-numbered items and the other composed of the even-numbered items. Responses to both halves are correlated; the higher the correlation, the higher the split-half reliability.

Parallel forms reliability is similar to split-half reliability, but is examined by a different set of procedures. In parallel forms reliability, two separate instruments represent the variable in question and they may be administered to respondents at the same time or at different points in time. This strategy places parallel forms reliability in contrast to split-half reliability, where one instrument is administered to respondents at one point in time. The correlation of responses to the two separate instruments provides an index of multiple forms reliability. The higher the reliability, the higher the internal consistency between instruments. And, the greater the degree of internal consistency, the more likely is it that the two instruments are, indeed, two forms of the same variable.

Coefficient alpha is another, related type of reliability. It reflects the internal consistency of an instrument, and is obtained by correlating responses from one-half of the items randomly selected from the total number of items in an instrument to the remaining items. Random selection refers to a process whereby each of the items in an instrument has an equally likely chance of being selected. This can be accomplished by using published tables of random numbers available in statistics texts, or by flipping an unbiased coin for each numbered item on the instrument, so that heads indicates that the item is selected for one half, and tails indicates that the item is selected for the other half.

For all of these reliabilities, correlations of .8 or higher are regarded as adequate. It is important to note that an instrument such as a questionnaire may purposely contain many items that reflect more than one variable. In a fifty-item questionnaire about parenting, for example, twenty items may refer to satisfaction with one's role as a parent, ten to knowledge about parenting techniques, ten to actual parenting practices, and the remainder to ten different demographic variables. It would be appropriate to determine the internal consistency of the twenty items reflecting satisfaction, the ten items about knowledge of parenting techniques, or the ten items for parenting practices.

Relationship of Reliabilities

Interobserver reliability is not necessarily equivalent to test-retest reliability. Agreement among judges at one period of time may be high, and it may be high at another period in time, but it may or may not be high *over time* which is called intra-observer (or intra-rater or intra-judge) reliability. Suppose that two judges ranked the level of social supports enjoyed by ten clients at two different points in time. In table 2.7, it can be observed that correlations between judges at time 1 (columns 2 and 3) and at time 2 (columns 4 and 5) are perfect, that is, rho $\rho = 1.0$. However, the intra-judge reliability for judge A

TABLE 2.7

Rankings of Ten Clients on Level of Social Supports by Two Judges Over Two
Points in Time

(1) Clients	(2) Rankings by Judge A at Time 1	(3) Rankings by Judge B at Time 1	(4) Rankings by Judge A at Time 2	(5) Rankings by Judge B at Time 2
A	1	1	3	3
B	2	2	5	5
C	3	3	4	4
D	4	4	2	2
E	5	5	1	1
F	6	6	6	6
G	7	7	9	9
H	8	8	10	10
I	9	9	7	7
J	10	10	8	8

(column 2 vs. column 4) and for judge B (column 3 vs. column 5) can both be calculated as rho $\rho = .70$.

In the same manner, internal consistency is not necessarily equivalent to test-retest reliability. It is possible for the same degree of correlation to be produced, but usually it will not be equivalent. Multiple forms reliability combines both internal consistency and test-retest reliability when each form of the same instrument is administered over separate points in time.

It is important for the practice-researcher to consider determining the appropriate kind of reliability, depending on how an instrument or instruments will be used. In other words, it is not sufficient to simply find that an instrument has a reported reliability of .8, but the type of reliability must be appropriate for the purpose for which the instrument is being administered. If, for instance, the practice-researcher is looking for an instrument to record change over time, the appropriate reliability test would be test-retest reliability. On the other hand, a high degree of interobserver reliability would be desirable if the practice-researcher is using an instrument as a classification system.

Validity of Variables

Once it has been determined that a variable has been obtained by reliable measurement, the practice-researcher needs to be concerned about another aspect of measurement. Reliability is necessary, but not sufficient for accurate measurement. A variable will only be an accurate measurement of the concept it is intended to portray, if it actually measures what it is intended to measure. Validity of variables refers to their faithful representation of the concepts being measured. There are two basic types of validity important for practice-researchers: content validity and empirical validity.

Content Validity

Content validity refers to the degree to which the manifest contents of the data, when categorized into scales of measurement, are representative of the concept being measured. Content validity is determined by a qualitative assessment of data by persons expert in the concept. In short, it is a judgment. For example, one might review the items on Hudson's Index of Marital Satisfaction to determine whether the items appear to represent areas of marriage for which there is possible satisfaction and dissatisfaction. The items on the scale dealing with relationships, interests, sex, trust, and finances appear to be relevant. Because there are no items related to children, childcare arrangements, and other such topics, however, it might be that the contents are more valid for married couples without children. As another example, if a checklist is developed to measure those procedures that are followed to implement an intervention, the contents of the checklist should be conceptually related to the intervention. A checklist related to implementing a problem-solving intervention should have items related to helping the client identify the problem, generate alternative solutions, evaluate the consequences of these alternatives, and the like. Again, a qualitative review of the checklist by someone knowledgeable about problem-solving interventions would constitute an assessment of content validity.

Content validity can be assessed for worker, client, and intervention variables. For Type 1 worker or client variables on demographic characteristics, the contents are usually quite clear. For instance, clients' reports on an agency intake form of whether they are male or female clearly represent the concept of gender.

Type 2 variables, about moods, feelings, attitudes, beliefs, and values require more complex determinations of content validity. To illustrate, depression requires a delineation of relevant symptomatology, and this determination requires the expertise of those who have worked with depressed clients and who understand the types of items that could be construed as relevant. For example, Zung's (1965) self-rating depression scale has items about feelings ("down-hearted, blue, and sad"), physiology (losing weight, constipation, and rapid heart beat), and cognition (clarity of mind). The item "I find it easy to make decisions" may or may not be judged as directly relevant to depression, because this item may be indicative of other alternative concepts such as experience, maturity, or anxiety.

The content validity of Type 3 variables about knowledge considers the extent to which the items represent the possible range and difficulty of items that could have been included in the data-gathering instrument. For example, items on a test for social workers' knowledge about psychiatric illnesses should cover a range of diagnostic and treatment questions. However, it might not be considered necessary for practitioners to know the intricacies and interactions of various drugs.

Type 4 worker-client variables and intervention variables are primarily based on observations. To be indicative of content validity, the things being observed should be both relevant and representative of observations that denote the concept being measured. For example, a test of adolescents' social skills should use language and situations that are typical for adolescents.

Empirical Validity

The empirical validity of a variable is the extent to which there is one or more expected and corroborated relationships between the variable being studied and some external criteria. There are several types of empirical validity, which are assessed by quantitative methods such as correlation coefficients. These are concurrent, predictive, and construct validity.

Concurrent validity is proportional to the strength of relationship between the variable being validated and another variable for which data were gathered at the same point in time. For example, one variable of drug use may be obtained by self-report. If there is concurrent validity, this variable should be highly correlated with another variable of drug use, such as chemical assay of a client's urine specimen. The self-reported drug use might also be correlated with other sources and ways to assess drug use, such as observations by significant others. The higher the correlations between external criteria and the variable being measured, the greater the degree of concurrent validity.

Predictive validity is a type of empirical validity that refers to the corroboration of an expected prediction between the variable being measured and an external criterion for which data are gathered at a future point in time. For example, the empirical validity of a measure of delinquency based on self-report might be enhanced if there were a high degree of correlation between self-reported delinquency and the number of adjudicated offenses over a specified period of time.

Construct validity is a third type of empirical validity and involves predicting theory-based, expected relationships between the concept being measured and one or more external criteria. It typically is employed for abstract concepts that are part of some theoretical scheme. For example, the concept of anxiety may be part of a theoretical scheme in which anxiety is thought to be related to learning, problem-solving, and other cognitive tasks. The investigator then derives from the theoretical analysis expected and non-expected relationships between anxiety and other variables. Hence it might be predicted that anxiety is inversely related to learning, problem-solving ability, and reaction time, such that the higher the anxiety, the slower the speed of learning, the lower the degree of accuracy in problem-solving, and the slower the reaction time. Moreover, it might be predicted that there is no relationship between anxiety and variables such as religious status, education, and athletic ability. The greater the number of these theory-based predictions that are validated, the greater is the amount of construct validity. Thus, construct validity consists of a set of predicted relationships between the variable in question and a set of external criteria.

There are no conventional guidelines for judging the adequacy of empirical validity, because there can be as many validity coefficients as there are external criteria. Generally speaking, the greater the degree of correlation, the greater the empirical validity. If there are multiple criteria, the greater the proportion of verified relationships out of the possible number of potential relationships the more empirically valid is the variable being measured.

Empirical validations need not be as complicated as construct validations. They vary according to the types of variables used. Type 1 variables based on personal and demographic variables are often at a relatively low level of abstraction. For example, self-reported age can be validated as a form of concurrent validity by reference to a documented birth certificate or passport. Type 2 variables on moods, feelings, attitudes, beliefs, and values tend to require more complex validity assessments, especially as the concepts become relatively more abstract. Type 2 variables are validated by all three types of validity. The validation of type 3 variables about knowledge, ability, and achievement focuses on predictive validity. In other words, they examine the extent to which performance on tests is related to education, training, or other types of performance. For instance, one might predict a greater degree of academic success for those who have higher scores on tests of mathematical and reading ability. Type 4 variables, representing observable behavior, often are validated by focusing on concurrent validity although all types of empirical validity can be employed.

Intervention variables, such as contents, duration, and number of techniques can be validated by all three types of empirical validity. In many cases, a simple determination of content validity may be sufficient. For example, if an intervention is defined as having components x, y, and z, and if the existence of x, y, and z can be easily observed (perhaps through the use of checklists and tape recordings), the variable of presence or absence of x, y, and z can be said to be relevant, meaningful, and representative.

Often an intervention variable can be indirectly validated by making predictions about the manifest contents of the client's communications. For example, there may be an educational component to an intervention that requires the client to learn stress management strategies. A simple test can be administered before and after the social work intervention to determine if the client increased knowledge of these strategies which, in turn, represent the focus of the intervention.

Relationships of Validity and Reliability

There is no necessary relationship between content validity and empirical validity. If the contents of an instrument are completely representative of the concept being measured, however, it is plausible to expect that its correlation with another instrument designed to measure the same concept would be high. In other words, high content validity should be predictive of concurrent validity.

A high degree of concurrent validity between two different measuring devices should lead to the same degrees of predictive validity for both sets of measures. On the other hand, a low degree of concurrent validity is not necessarily correlated with predictive validity. Since construct validity consists of many predictions, it is likely that its degree of relationship with other types of empirical validity will be low.

The preceding hypotheses are speculative: there is no absolute conclusion about different types of validity. It is always important for the practice-researcher to evaluate qualitatively the content validity of a variable with respect to the relevance and representativeness of the data employed for measurement. Furthermore, whatever validating empirical evidence is available should be examined, treating the different types of validity as separate predictions. The more predictions that are corroborated within a particular type of empirical validity, the greater the degree of confidence that the practice-researcher will have in the validity of that variable.

The relationship of reliability and validity varies with respect to the types of reliability and validity being discussed (Blythe and Tripodi 1989). Because interobserver reliability and content validity both rely on expert judgment and opinion about the verbal contents of instruments, there appears to be a close relationship between them. In the same vein, internal consistency of a variable bears a close relationship to judgments about the verbal contents of an instrument (content validity), so long as there seems to be a high degree of content validity. Yet because it is a subjective judgment about two phenomena that may be defined in a similar mode, it is possible that the relationship is tautological.

The relationship of test-retest reliability to the various types of empirical validity is not clear. Internal consistency and multiple forms reliability are related to the type of concurrent validity that correlates instruments that are supposed to measure the same phenomenon. In fact, if conceived in the same way, they may be related simply by definition!

In conclusion, the relationships between types of reliability and types of validity are complex and not altogether clear. Therefore, caution must be exercised when regarding reliability and validity as related concepts. The types of reliability and validity that are appropriate for the purposes of the practice research must be determined, and the existence of a particular type of reliability or validity should not be assumed unless there is evidence, qualitative or quantitative, for it.

Using Agency Records as Sources of Variables

There are many sources of variables. Practice-researchers may design their own instruments or use existing instruments such as tests, questionnaires, observational forms, rating scales, and interview schedules. Other valuable sources include published research reports and monographs, census studies, surveys, and statistical reports from human service agencies. Throughout the book, we will discuss these sources of variables in the context of chapters devoted to needs assessment, monitoring, and evaluation tasks of the practice-researcher. As a conclusion to this chapter, we discuss agency records as sources of variables, including criteria for determining their potential utility in practice research.

Agency records may include data that are collected, codified, and computerized in an agency's information system, or they may contain data that are gathered but not codified for data analysis. Agency records may contain quantitative and qualitative data. Quantitative data might include information pertaining to characteristics of clients on face sheets such as age, gender, and other demographic, social, or historical information; data on moods, attitudes, achievements, and the like; data that refer to agency interventions such as number and types of contacts between workers and clients, agency referrals, diagnoses for medical or psychiatric illnesses; and data that are relevant to specific agency objectives, such as attendance, tardiness, and grades in school settings, number of offenses, previous number and types of psychiatric placements, school achievement, role infractions in a residential treatment center, number of clients moved to less restrictive settings, and so forth. Qualitative data might be in the form of case records, narrative responses to previously administered questionnaires, tests, or interviews, or agency documents dealing with agency policies, personnel practices, or minutes of meetings, to give a few examples.

Ethical Considerations

Agency records can be used for practice research only if ethical requirements are satisfied. The primary ethical concerns are confidentiality and informed consent. For practice research with one client, the ethical issue revolves around the dissemination of the results of the practice research to other professionals. The practice-researcher must follow informed consent procedures. The client should be informed in advance that the practice-researcher will be collecting data, and how those data will be used, stored, and disseminated. Permission should be obtained from the client before one proceeds with data collection. In both formal and informal dissemination of practice research findings, the client's identity should not be revealed. Note, however, that these procedures do not vary much from those that must be followed any time information is gathered from a client, stored in a case record, and possibly shared with other professionals.

When data are to be aggregated across clients, the clients' identities still must not be revealed. Generally, informed consent procedures should also be followed with these clients. If information from closed cases is to be used, the practice-researcher should determine what provisions and policies about confidentiality and uses of client information were in effect when the data were gathered. If the data are about children, for example, permission might need to be obtained from appropriate guardians. Permission may be required from the ex-clients themselves. Unfortunately, some agencies do not have well-established guidelines for practice-researchers. If there are no guidelines and no agency institutional review board, the practice-researcher should discuss what procedures to follow with the agency administration.

Agency Supports and Constraints

Agency administration can be very supportive of practice research by providing a range of resources. Support might include access to files, clerical assistance, computer time and usage, and necessary supplies and provisions for transforming non-categorized data into variables. Agency costs are minimal if an efficient, up-to-date computerized information system is in place. Unfortunately, in small agencies that may not even have an adequate filing system, the initial cost of establishing an information system, even if it is not computerized, may be more than the agency can afford. In such instances, an alternative may be to develop proposals to local foundations for support in establishing such a system, particularly if it is regarded as vital for conducting effective practice and research.

Primary agency constraints may be encountered in agency administration, the information system, accessibility of records, and availability of resources. Agency administrators may simply be unsupportive because they regard practice research as a low priority. Administrators may be so incompetent that they don't know how to develop, use, and process agency records, let alone devise procedures to make records available for practice research. The files and the means for updating them may be inadequate, information may not be systematically filed, definitions for data may be ambiguous and inconsistently applied among agency personnel, or data may not even be recorded and filed. Accessibility to the records may involve permission from clients, legal guardians, or other social workers. Permission may not be granted to use existing records or the costs for obtaining permission to use the data may be beyond the available budget and time of the practice-researcher. This problem can be eased if resources are made available. If not, the lack of resources can affect the extent to which it is possible to use agency data.

Social workers interested in conducting practice research should carefully assess the resources and constraints presented by their current situation. Obviously, working in an environment that supports practice research, with some like-minded colleagues, is the ideal situation. Unfortunately, this type of situation is rare, although not nonexistent. If the practitioner finds somewhat fewer resources and supports, this is not a sign to give up. Rather, care must be taken in selecting topics to study, and in designing the size and scope of the project. There are many interesting topics in one's own caseload. Perhaps the advice can best be summed up as follows: it is always better to complete a small, well-designed and well-executed study than to be in the throes of a larger study that is beyond the scope of available resources and/or skills.

Criteria for Using Agency Records

While agency records appear to be a valuable source of data, it is wise to check them before undertaking a study. Accordingly, we present six criteria that can be employed for deciding whether agency records should be used as sources of variables. These are content relevance, consistent availability, accessibility, measurement potential, reliability, and validity (Tripodi 1983).

The first criterion, content relevance, is a subjective determination of whether or not the contents of the record are relevant to the variables of interest. There may be information already transformed into a variable, or information that is not categorized. In either case, the information is only relevant if it provides data necessary for measuring a variable. For instance, assume that a practice-researcher is interested in studying the involvement of group members in group problem-solving tasks. In examining agency records, the practice-researcher finds very few notes taken by the group leader, no taped recordings, and no attention paid to group involvement. The only available information is contained in brief notes in which the worker indicated the group's discussion topic and that clients seemed to have difficulty maintaining focus on the topic. Clearly, the contents are irrelevant for forming a variable of group involvement in problem-solving.

On the other hand, if the contents are relevant for direct use as a variable or for transformation into one, the next criterion to consider is whether the information is consistently available. In considering consistent availability, one might focus on availability across several clients at one point in time, across several clients over time, or on one client over time. To compare across several clients or for one client at several points in time, the same criteria must be employed in the records. The definitions of key concepts must be consistent, and the records must be complete and accurate. For example, information would not be consistently available for measuring the concept of client reluctance to participate in treatment if it is included for some clients and not for others, or if the definitions of client reluctance are ambiguous. The practice-researcher needs to determine how the data were recorded and what criteria were used over time. In addition, several different case records must be examined to assess qualitatively whether there appear to have been different criteria employed for recording and whether there are inconsistencies and gaps in the data. If there are, the data are not consistently available and would not be directly useful in studying client change.

The contents of agency records may be relevant and consistently available, but not accessible. Even with permission to access records and administrative cooperation, it is important that the practice-researcher carefully estimate the costs involved in the planned use of records. These costs include the practice-researcher's time, the time of other workers and support staff, and the cost of supplies. Case records, in essence, are not accessible if the costs associated with gathering information from them are excessive. Of course, there are many instances where the costs may simply require an investment of a few hours of time. For example, information on race, gender, age, type of problem(s), number of contacts, and type of treatment may be recorded systematically for all clients on intake and discharge summaries. Suppose that a supervisor wishes to examine the extent to which there are differentials with respect to those variables in the caseloads of her supervisees. Suppose further that she has three supervisees and wants to limit the study to thirty cases each. It would be relatively easy for the supervisor or a secretary to aggregate the information on a form for each worker. Agency board members also have been used to collect data from case records when the information was found to be relevant and consistently available, but not easily accessible because of the time involved in gathering and categorizing the information (Blythe and Goodman 1987). This strategy also offered a way to involve board members in agency activities and to educate them about the difficult cases confronted by agency staff.

Measurement potential is an important criterion when considering the extent to which qualitative data can be transformed into variables. As we have discussed in this chapter, transformation into variables is synonymous with measurement, and is defined as using an operational definition to convert data into a nominal, ordinal, interval, or ratio scale. Qualitative data must be examined to consider whether the potential exists for converting them into variables. Of course, quantitative data that are already in the form of variables may be included in the records.

The final criteria concern the reliability and validity of the variables. Quantitative data in case records may have been used in previous agency research, and there may be evidence of its reliability and validity in the professional literature or in other studies, although this would be rare for most agencies. In making judgments about the potential reliability and validity of data for which there are no reliability and validity studies, the practice-researcher should consider the following procedures:

1. Seek available agency manuals, policies, and procedures that are employed for recording information included in case records.
2. Specify the variable(s) of interest, and observe whether operational definitions are available and systematically employed. If the researcher provides the operational definition, then he or she should determine whether there is sufficient information to categorize it into a measurement scale.
3. Determine whether or not there appear to be any biases and inconsistencies in recording information. If systematic, consistent procedures are employed in recording, then reliability is enhanced.
4. Make a judgment of the content validity of the proposed variable by noting not only whether the information appears to be relevant and meaningful to the variable, but also whether the contents are sufficiently representative. For example, the social worker's case recording may contain some items about a client's motivation to change, but there may not be a sufficient amount of information about the client's willingness to change, the client's perception of the social desirability for change, the client's awareness that the behavior in question is harmful and should

be changed, the importance of change for the client, or the client's expectancy of change.

5. If there are no empirical data on reliability, apply procedures presented in this chapter for determining, on a small sample of representative clients or workers, the appropriate kind of reliability. Coupled with a judgment of adequate content validity, this information is sufficient for selecting variables in much of practice research. If tests are employed, however, additional empirical information about internal consistency and validity should be obtained. If not, they may lead to inaccurate conclusions about client status and change.

3. *Assessing Client Needs*

To effectively work with clients in human service agencies, it is necessary to identify and delineate client needs. Having identified client needs, the social worker can provide the requisite services or refer the client to other programs. In this chapter, we focus on assessing needs for persons who, whether they are voluntary or involuntary clients, have contacted the human services agency. The client population under discussion includes those individuals judged as eligible for agency services, those who are waiting to receive services, those who currently receive services, or those who have received services in the past. Although services provided by human service agencies tend to be circumscribed within a particular domain, it is possible to provide new services or to refer clients to other agencies to meet client needs. For example, clients in a substance abuse treatment program who need financial assistance may be referred to a public welfare agency. On the other hand, as more families of substance abusers become known to the substance abuse treatment center, a family counseling service may be created within the agency.

What Is Need?

The notion of need is easily misunderstood. In social work, some define need as the need for a particular service, resource, or intervention. Others define it as a required change in the state of a client. In fact, clients do not require services or interventions per se. Rather, they require them only if the services or interventions will satisfy their condition of need. Suppose that newly arrived refugees require training to change their skill levels so that they will be more likely to obtain employment. Training, as an intervention, is an independent variable, which is supposed to change the client's skill level, the dependent variable. The need for training is satisfied when there is a desirable change in skill level. This is compatible with the following definition of need: A need is actually a value judgment that a particular individual or group has a problem that can be solved. There are four aspects to this definition:

1. Because recognizing need involves values, people with different values will recognize different needs. Furthermore, the person recognizing the need and the person experiencing the need may disagree about the need.
2. A need is possessed by a particular client unit, which may be an individual, family, or group, in a certain set of circumstances.
3. A problem is an inadequate outcome, an outcome that violates expectations. There are many sources of expectations, reflecting different values. For example, adolescents' leisure activities can indicate a problem if they do not meet the expectations of their parents, or their teachers, or the students themselves.
4. Recognizing a need involves a judgment that a solution exists for a problem. A problem may have many potential solutions, solutions that vary in terms of the probability of alleviating the problem, and of the cost and the feasibility of implementation. (Adapted from McKillip 1987)

In the above definition, the problem is the dependent variable, which will be influenced by the solution, the independent variable. The designation of a problem is predicated on the values of an individual client, of a worker, and/or of society.

Needs, as problems awaiting solutions, can be regarded as dependent variables that describe clients. As we indicated in chapter 2, there are four types of variables that describe clients: (1) personal and demographic characteristics; (2) moods, feelings, attitudes, beliefs, and values; (3) knowledge, ability, and achievement; and (4) observable variables.

The task of assessing client needs, therefore, involves locating variables that are relevant to measuring client problems. This can be considered in reference to three types of client populations (McKillip 1987, 11). First, there are clients on waiting lists who may be at risk of further deterioration. Second, there are clients who currently are being served, but may continue to be in need if a discrepancy between the desired and the actual level of change persists. Third, there are clients who have discontinued services, because they completed their planned course of services or because they simply dropped out and were not reengaged with the agency workers. The last group may be at risk of further undesirable changes, while the first may not maintain the level of change achieved in treatment.

The practice-researcher identifies needs for client units (cases which may consist of one or more persons and significant others) and for aggregates of client units (the worker's caseload, or the caseloads of the workers assigned to a supervisor). The researcher then can apply research concepts and principles for gathering and analyzing data to assess needs relevant to individuals and aggregated cases can be applied to enhance the quality of the information collected.

Here are some examples of individual and aggregated client needs. There may be the need to move an older person with Alzheimer's from his home to a nursing home to decrease the probability that he will harm himself. Hence, the Type 1 variable describing the client need is a new residence. A client who has received psychotherapy to reduce her feelings of loss and depression over the death of her husband may relapse after discontinuing treatment. Here, the Type 2 variable is the feeling of loss and depression. As an example of a Type 3 variable, a parent may still need knowledge to understand her child's learning disability since there is a discrepancy between what she understands and what she would like to understand. Finally, a student in elementary school may need to receive an intervention, such as play therapy, from the school social worker to reduce the number of times he disrupts other students in his class. This would be an instance of a Type 4 variable.

Aggregated variables describing client needs, based on data gathered from a large number of clients, could lead to expanding or contracting existing services, changing the type of agency referrals, or developing new interventions and services within the human services agency. Evidence of the need to increase financial resources may be manifest in a worker's caseload, necessitating a system of referrals for possible employment opportunities and job training programs (Type 1 variable). Feelings of anger and fear among rape victims may lead to a therapeutic group for these clients (Type 2 variable). Lack of knowledge about safe sex among the clients in a recreational center for teenagers may be an indication of their high risk for contracting sexually transmitted diseases, signaling the need for educational materials and programs (Type 3 variable). Finally, a high incidence of aggressive behaviors of older children toward younger children in a residential treatment center may establish the need for alternate living arrangements for the different age groups (Type 4 variable).

Why Should Need Be Assessed?

The assessment of need is prerequisite for direct social work practice, when practice is conceptualized as a problem-solving model (Blythe and Tripodi 1989) and for program planning (Posavac and Carey 1985). The direct practice worker requires information about such things as the needs of individual clients, their motivation to deal with their problems, their strengths and resources, and the severity of their problems. This information is necessary to plan an intervention that will be relevant and effective in solving problems. Needs also can be assessed for a large number of potential, active, or terminated clients. As a result of a needs assessment of agency caseloads, workers or supervisors can recommend expanding or contracting existing programs, as well as developing new programs and interventions. For example, the analysis of responses to a questionnaire administered to current clients may reveal a desire and a willingness on the part of clients to participate in community-based programs to increase their skills in coping with their environment.

While social workers and other social agency staff frequently call for developing or expanding social programs, these requests are strengthened by accompanying data underscoring the need for such efforts. Not only will the request or suggestion carry more weight, but it also will better describe the needs of the targeted client population.

Obviously, the variables in a needs assessment will depend upon the theory and related assumptions that the practice-researcher invokes about practice phenomena. For example, Vigilante and Mailick (1988) emphasize the dynamic relationship between intrapsychic needs and social needs, and the institutional resources that are available to meet those needs. To assess these interrelationships, it is first necessary to gather and analyze information about the type and extent of intrapsychic and social needs in the population of interest. Other theoretical assumptions will point to including other variables in a needs assessment.

A fundamental reason for needs assessment is accountability. By studying the extent of need over time, social workers and their supervisors can determine the effectiveness of practice interventions. They can inform clients about the extent of their progress. Moreover, changes in need can be associated with interventions, to make decisions about the utility of those interventions. The use of baselining, that is, obtaining repeated observations on selected dependent variables, is a form of need assessment in that it can be employed to determine the severity and persistence of needs (Blythe and Tripodi 1989). The ideas of baselining problem behaviors prior to introducing an intervention and then continuing to gather information about problem behaviors is an application of single-subject design methods (which will be discussed in subsequent chapters).

By analyzing the degree to which identified client needs are reduced (or met), as well as the maintenance of those solutions, social workers have the grounds for recommending the use, expansion, or discontinuation of interventions. Ethically, social workers are accountable and responsible for developing and maintaining problem resolution (National Association of Social Workers 1987). In fact, Charlotte Towle's classic *Common Human Needs* (1945), which continues to be relatively popular today, could be interpreted as a call for social workers to be morally responsible to society by identifying and helping to resolve basic human needs.

The Process of Needs Assessment

In general, the process of needs assessment involves six interrelated activities. These activities include: (1) locating the target person(s); (2) defining and operationalizing need; (3) specifying the procedures for gathering data; (4) estimating the reliability and validity of those procedures; (5) implementing the procedures and gathering information; and (6) analyzing data and relating the conclusions to decisions about interventions.

The target for needs assessment can be a client unit (individual, family, or group), or an aggregated set of client units, ranging from an active caseload to all clients ever served by a particular agency. Note that community needs assessment includes potential clients from the community, as well as those who have received services from the agency. Our notions of needs assessment, however, are somewhat less likely to include potential clients from the community, because we are focusing on what we believe a practice-researcher can most readily study within the confines of a human services agency.

An aggregate of clients can be specified in at least three ways. First, they can be delineated according to the different workers or treatment units from which they received treatment. Second, clients can be specified by various characteristics such as gender, race, and income. For example, one may wish to assess the needs of a group of African-American females, ages seventeen to twenty-five, who are heads of households. Third, clients might be specified by the geographic area in which they live. This would be exemplified by an assessment of the community needs of residents of a housing project.

Needs should be defined as variables so that their levels (from high need to low need) can be studied for changes, which subsequently can be associated with decisions about the social worker's interventions. Needs are defined as variables by employing the concepts of measurement presented in chapter 2. In other words, needs should be operationally defined. This includes delineating the procedures for gathering data. For example, data may be obtained by administering available standardized instruments to study Type 1 to Type 4 variables. These may include questionnaires, research interview schedules, or psychological tests, as examples. Data may be obtained by forms, schedules, and questionnaires that are created by the practice-researcher.

Whatever instruments and procedures are employed, there should be estimates of reliability and validity. If the data are not reliable and valid, the needs assessment will be meaningless. Research procedures should only be implemented when the practice-researcher is confident in the reliability and validity of the procedures.

Finally, the information is analyzed and decisions are made about interventions. For example, if the level of need on a dependent variable remains high after a specified period of time, the social worker may decide to increase the intensity of the intervention, withdraw the intervention and substitute another one, or refer the case to another worker in the same agency or to another worker in another agency.

Assessing Clients' Needs

Assessing the needs of clients involves using available instruments and/or developing instruments for assessment. In the latter instance, the instruments are primarily forms and questionnaires. Research principles for using these procedures for needs assessment are described in the following sections of this chapter.

Using Available Instruments

Many instruments are available for gathering data and transforming them into measures that can be employed in direct practice. Instruments are data collection tools such as questionnaires, interview schedules, and tests. These instruments may be found in research and evaluation departments of human service agencies, in journals dealing with practice and research (*Evaluation and Program Planning, Journal of Social Service Research,* and *Social Work Research* are examples) and in reference books such as Fischer and Corcoran's *Measures for Clinical Practice: A Sourcebook* (1994) and McCubbin and Thompson's *Family Assessment Inventories for Research and Practice* (1987). Basically these assessment tools facilitate collecting client data comprised of Type 1, 2, 3, or 4 variables.

When assessing client units, the practice-researcher identifies the target person(s) such as the client who may be an adult or a child, or the client and his family. Then need is operationalized in specific terms, and various resources are reviewed for an available instrument that might be compatible with the specification of need. Of course, the worker may be interested in several needs, in which case there would be a search for more than one instrument. If there are available instruments, the costs of and time involved in conducting practice research are reduced. Suppose, for example, that the practice-researcher is beginning to work with a family in a family services agency. The worker may be interested in assessing the extent of family conflict and whether in discussion with the family there is a need to reduce that conflict. The "Self-Report Family Instrument (SFI)" described in Fischer and Corcoran (1994 Vol.1 395–399), a thirty-six item instrument containing subscales of family conflict, family communication, family cohesion, directive leadership, and family health might be appropriate if the contents of the items are relevant to the worker's conception of family conflict. In the case of the SFI, there is evidence for internal consistency, reliability, and concurrent validity for the instrument's subscales. If it is clear that only certain subscales are relevant to the family, then just those subscales could be administered.

Choosing an Instrument

If the practice-researcher is considering an available instrument, it must be evaluated for its appropriateness. Criteria for selecting an instrument for practice research include the following dimensions: conception of the variable; bias; reliability and validity; availability of norms; direct or indirect use; and feasibility of implementation. These criteria are adapted from Tripodi and Epstein (1980).

First, the practice-researcher should determine how the authors of the instrument conceived of the variable in question and whether that conception is congruent with how the practice-researcher conceives the need of the client or client unit. This is a judgment of content validity and is enhanced by reviewing all of the items that comprise the instrument, checking to see whether they sufficiently represent the need variable. For example, an instrument for measuring family conflict may not be judged as representative if it does not include items pertaining to child management and discipline, family decisionmaking, intrafamilial relationships, family expectations, and chores. The more specific the practitioner can be about delineating the need variable, the easier it is to appraise the content validity of the instrument. Obviously, an instrument with low content validity should not be administered because the resulting information will be useless.

Biases, the second dimension of an instrument being judged, can occur in the contents of an instrument. These built-in biases typically reflect predisposing responses about the social, demographic, and/ or cultural characteristics of specific populations. For example, the contents of an instrument to measure social supports may be scored so that activities and behaviors of middle class whites are regarded as more favorable than those of working class, non-whites. Bias may be evident in relation to age, gender, sexual orientation, or other demographic characteristics. Biases also can be found in the way in which questions and possible responses are worded. Leading questions predispose the respondent to answer questions in a certain way. As an illustration, the statement "Indicate the last time you were depressed" presumes that the respondent was depressed in the past. Or, bias may be observable in the response possibilities provided to respondents. Suppose that a question asks "How many times did you drink more alcohol than you should have during the last month?" and the response choices are "one, two, or three or more times." By not including zero, the respondent is predisposed to indicate at least one episode of heavy drinking. The practice-researcher should carefully review the items in any test or instrument for potential biases. If some areas of bias are identified, it is possible to change the items in question and administer the revised version.

It is important to evaluate available intruments' reliability and validity. Employing the concepts of reliability and validity discussed in the previous chapter, the practice-researcher should appraise the evidence for reliability and validity. Content validity and some evidence of reliability, particularly of test-retest reliability (since the practice-researcher often is interested in assessing levels of need over time) are the most critical areas of reliability and validity to review.

Another dimension of available instruments that must be inspected is the availability of normative data. Normative data or norms represent average measures for specific populations. To be applicable, the populations should be standardized and representative of the clients with whom the social worker works. For example, an instrument which has its normative data based on the average scores of college psychology students is not likely to be appropriate for eighteen-year old homeless Hispanic men. The practice-researcher should look at descriptions of the populations on which the instrument was tested, and check for demographic variables such as gender, ethnicity, age, and social class that can indicate similarities or differences as compared to the practice researcher's client(s).

Instruments can be used directly or indirectly, and this constitutes another dimension to consider when examining an available measure. Direct use requires that the instrument be administered in the same format in which it is presented. In this way, information on psychometric properties such as reliability and validity can be regarded as appropriate. In many instances, however, the contents of the instrument may need to be revised. As an example, the instrument may have been written for people who possess greater reading skills than those of the social worker's client. In this case, it is important to determine whether the instructions and contents of the instrument are understandable by the client. An instrument can be used indirectly by modifying or adapting the contents to the language of the clients. Or, the instrument can be used as a stimulus for discussion in the context of an interview between the worker and the client. In either of these instances, it must be noted that data regarding norms, reliability, and empirical validity are no longer operative. This means that the worker will continue to make judgments about the instrument's content validity, and must obtain information pertaining to reliability. Suppose that a worker is working with one client with a problem of low self-esteem. The worker modifies an available instrument to assess self-esteem, so any known reliability estimates for that instrument become irrelevant. By establishing a baseline of repeated measurements of self-esteem using the modified self-esteem instrument, the practice-researcher can observe consistency over time (test-retest reliability), thus building a reliability estimate for that client as part of routine practice.

The final dimension on which available instruments should be critiqued is feasibility, and it is interrelated with the other dimensions discussed. The central question here is whether the instrument is feasible to use in practice. This includes the amount of time it takes to administer and score the test or instrument, as well as the cost of the instrument. Also important is the extent to which permission can be secured from the author of the instrument as well as the client for its use. An instrument that requires a great deal of time to administer or score simply may not be feasible in routine practice.

Developing Instruments

If available instruments are non-existent or deemed to be inappropriate, it may be necessary to develop instruments for assessing client needs. To assess the needs of individual clients or client units, three basic data gathering strategies typically are employed. These are self-rating scales, questionnaires, and interviews. The following sections offer guidelines for developing these tools.

Constructing Self-Rating Scales

Self-rating scales allow the client to indicate the existence and severity of a problem (Gottman and Leiblum 1974). In constructing self-rating scales, both the stimulus and the response alternatives must be considered. The stimulus consists of phrases, words, sentences, or questions to which the client is to respond. Response alternatives are the mutually exclusive response categories from which the client selects to indicate the level or severity of a problem. In the scale below, "severity of anxiety" is the stimulus, and the response alternatives are nine scalar points that range from 1, not anxious, to 9, severely anxious.

				Severity of Anxiety				
1	2	3	4	5	6	7	8	9
Not At All Anxious		Slightly Anxious		Moderately Anxious		Very Anxious		Severely Anxious

The number of points on self-rating scales typically range from two to eleven, and they can be presented in different formats. The worker must exercise judgment in selecting the exact number of points. Too few points may not provide enough detail about client need, while too many points may make it difficult for the client to distinguish between adjacent points. Figure 3.1 presents some examples, adapted from Tripodi and Epstein, of different formats for self-rating scales, with anxiety as the need to be measured (1980, 193–196).

To construct a self-rating scale for a client, the practice-researcher chooses a format for the scalar stimulus response system. It can be similar to one of those presented above or adapted to a form more suitable for the client. The most important principles to bear in mind are that the stimulus should be clear, and should attempt to rate only one dimension (for example, it should only rate anger, rather than anger and guilt). It should be ordinal, so that the categories of responses are ordered and are mutually exclusive and exhaustive. Numerical points should be anchored with clearly worded descriptions, at least at the two extreme ends of the scale and at the mid-point. Moreover, words and phrases used for anchoring the points should be distinct from each other and unambiguous, indicating different degrees of ranking on the ordinal scale. When anchoring scales for individual clients, it is possible (and desirable) to develop the anchors with some of the client's own words describing the need.

Self-rating scales are extremely flexible and can be developed to rate a range of client needs. For example, they can rate client moods, such as anger and depression, as well as attitudes toward self, such as self-image, or feelings of inferiority. To enhance the reliability and validity of self-rating scales, the scales should be constructed with the client, in the context of the interview. First, the social worker should identify the variable of need to be measured. Second, the worker should have in mind a scalar format that might be used. Third, the worker should present the scale format to the client, explaining the characteristics of ordinality, and mutually exclusive and exhaustive categories, and the dimension being rated. These need to be explained in language easily understood by the client. Analogies, such as that of a thermometer to indicate intensity of feelings or rungs on a ladder to indicate levels of difficulty, can be helpful. Next, the response stimulus and anchors are developed for the scale points, using the client's language as much as possible. Finally, a format for recording the ratings is developed, as are guidelines for scheduling the ratings.

FIGURE 3.1
Examples of Formats for Self-Rating Scales

1. Presence/Absence of Anxiety

Do you have symptoms of anxiety?

0 _____ no
1 _____ yes

2. Adverbial Frequency Scale

How often are you anxious?

1 _____ Very infrequently
2 _____ Infrequently
3 _____ Frequently
4 _____ Very frequently

3. Adverbial Severity Scale

How anxious are you?

1 _____ Not at all
2 _____ Slightly
3 _____ Moderately
4 _____ Strongly
5 _____ Severely

4. Percentage Frequency Scale

About what percentage of the time are you anxious?

0 _____ 0%
1 _____ 1–10%
2 _____ 11–20%
3 _____ 21–30%
4 _____ 31–40%
5 _____ 41–50%
6 _____ 51–60%
7 _____ 61–70%
8 _____ 71–80%
9 _____ 81–90%
10 _____ 91–100%

5. Frequency by Time Interval Scale

About how often are you anxious?

1 _____ Once a month or less
2 _____ Once every two weeks
3 _____ Once a week
4 _____ Twice a week
5 _____ Every other day
6 _____ Daily

FIGURE 3.1 (Continued)

6. **Likert Scale** (with or without neutral, "uncertain", category)

Indicate the extent to which you agree with the statement "I am anxious."

1 ____ Strongly agree
2 ____ Agree
3 ____ Uncertain
4 ____ Disagree
5 ____ Strongly disagree

OR

1 ____ Strongly agree
2 ____ Agree
4 ____ Disagree
5 ____ Strongly Disagree

7. **Bipolar Scale**

On a scale from 1 to 7, indicate the degree to which you are calm or anxious

1	2	3	4	5	6	7
Very Calm			Neither Calm Nor Anxious			Very Anxious

8. **Comparative Scale**

Compared to last week, how anxious you now?

1 ____ Much more anxious
2 ____ More anxious
3 ____ About the same
4 ____ Less anxious
5 ____ Much less anxious

9. **Goal Attainment Scale**

To what extent have you achieved the goal of reducing your anxiety?

+2 I'm completely free of anxiety. The goal is fully achieved.

+1 I have ocasional episodes of anxiety, but these do not interfere with social functioning.

0 I have episodes of anxiety that occasionally interfere with social functioning.

−1 I have frequent episodes of anxiety that interfere with social functioning.

−2 I'm anxious most of the time and find it difficult to function socially

By following this process, the worker ensures a high degree of content validity and sets the stage for reliability, to the extent that the worker specifies that whenever ratings are made by the client, they must be made with consistent definitions. Reliability is further enhanced if the worker and client agree on what types of information are to be considered for what periods of time when making the ratings. For example, a recently divorced client's rating of feelings of loneliness might focus on the feelings he has in the evening hours, after dinner, when he used to engage in family activities.

Two other procedures for enhancing reliability and validity with self-rating scales are possible, even though only one client is being rated. The first procedure, baselining, involves obtaining multiple measurements of the same phenomena over time *before* interventions are introduced. Suppose a client is on a waiting list to receive help in dealing with his anxiety about his pending retirement. When he is placed on the waiting list, however, he has an intake interview in which a five-point rating scale to assess his anxiety is developed as a part of that interview. Further, suppose the client is on the waiting list for three weeks, and that he provides a self-rating every week. In his own words, the anxiety is "nervousness," and a 5 on the scale indicates extreme nervousness while a 1 suggests that the client is not at all nervous. This can be depicted on a graph which registers the ratings for different points in time (see figure 3.2). In this case, let us assume that there was a rating of 4 at intake; 5 at week one; 4 at week two; and 4 at week three. Assuming there were no other factors affecting the degree of nervousness, there is evidence here of test-retest reliability, since there continues to be an expression of a high level of nervousness over time.

The worker could use the same rating scale to independently rate the client's degree of nervousness at intake and during the first interview after intake. By changing the response stimulus or anchors, the self-rating scale format is easily changed to a format for the worker to rate the client. For example, the stimulus "to what extent are you nervous" would simply be changed to "to what extent is the client nervous," and the same response system would be used for the worker's ratings of the client. If the worker and client agree in their ratings, then there is some evidence for concurrent validity.

Data from client self-ratings can indicate the degree to which there may be problems that should be addressed. Obviously, the existence and extent of a problem is evident at the high points on a scale. Moreover, if there is a baseline prior to treatment or intervention, the social worker can observe the extent to which the problem persists. The client who says he is "very nervous" one week but "not at all nervous" the following week has a less persistent problem than the client who says he's "very nervous" over two consecutive weeks. Persistence of a problem also can be noted while an intervention takes place. This is evident if there are no changes in the way in which the client perceives the problem over time, which indicates that the problem persists although an intervention has been introduced. Obviously, the practice-researcher will supplement the scale ratings with other information garnered in client interviews, in order to more fully understand the client need.

Suppose that this client was terminated from the active cases because he accomplished the goal of reducing his anxiety about his pending retirement. For purposes of maintenance, however, the worker may decide to request follow-up ratings at periodic intervals, such as every other week for two months after treatment is terminated. By reviewing these data, the practice-researcher can determine

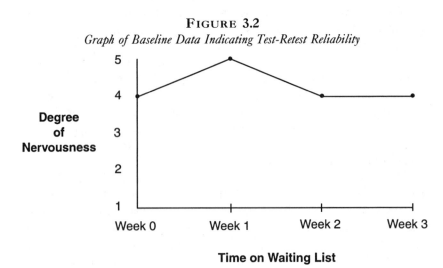

FIGURE 3.2
Graph of Baseline Data Indicating Test-Retest Reliability

Time on Waiting List

whether the client believes the problem is recurring. Such information may prompt the worker to suggest a follow-up interview to assess more fully whether the client would benefit from further intervention.

These analyses can also take place when the practitioner or significant others rate the client's condition without the client's rating. In these instances, however, it is an indication of a problem or need attributed to the client, not necessarily the client's expression of such a need. For example, a client's spouse may rate the client as persistently anxious, which also may be a sign that the spouse wishes the client to continue in treatment. This situation cannot be fully understood without carefully interviewing the spouse. Regardless of who completes them, rating scales provide a quick way to relay information. Their interpretation, however, becomes clearer within the context of more direct questioning.

Developing Structured Questions for Questionnaires and Interview Schedules

Structured questions are comprised of stimuli and response alternatives, similar to the self-rating questions we presented above. The stimuli consist of questions or phrases to which the client is asked to respond. The response alternatives are optional responses or answers, of which one or more must be selected by the client according to directions that are provided. Figure 3.3 contains examples of various types of closed-ended questions and response alternatives (adapted from Epstein and Tripodi 1977, 12–14).

Similar types of close-ended questions should be used in a questionnaire; if a questionnaire contains too many question formats, the respondents may become confused or fatigued. The stimuli (questions or phrases) should be clearly worded so the clients know what is being asked. In figure 3.3, respondents should know what is meant by nursing care. It may be helpful to provide a brief description of nursing care at the beginning of the questionnaire.

Each stimulus should contain only one thought. For example, "To what extent would nursing care and social work services be helpful to you" refers to both social work services and nursing care and should be changed to two questions. Stimuli should not bias the clients to select certain alternative responses. The vocabulary and syntax of the questions should be geared to the client's level of understanding, so that they make sense to clients.

FIGURE 3.3

Types of Closed-Ended Questions and Responses in Reference to the Need for Nursing Care

1. **Simple "Yes" or "No"**

   Would nursing care be helpful to you? yes _____ no _____

2. **"Agree"/"Disagree" Scales**

   Read the following statement and place a check next to the words that best describe the extent to which you agree with it.

   Nursing care would be helpful to me in dealing with my current family problems.

   Strongly agree _____ Agree _____ Disagree _____ Strongly diagree _____

3. **Frequency of Response Scales** (Adverb Modifiers)

   If they were available, how frequently would you use the service of a nurse?

   Very frequently _____ Occasionally _____ Never _____

4. **Frequency of Response Scales** (Numerical)

   If they were available to you, on how many days of the week would you need the services of a nurse?

   Seven _____ Six _____ Five _____ Four _____ Three _____
   Two _____ One _____ None _____

5. **Frequency of Response Scales** (Percentage)

   If a nurse were available to you, what percentage of your family's unmet health needs could be met?

   0–25% _____ 26–50% _____ 51–75% _____ 76–100% _____

6. **Comparative Response Scales**

   Compared to other needs that you currently have, how important is nursing care?

   Very important _____ Somewhat important _____ Unimportant _____

7. **Identification Response**

   Below is a list of ways in which a nurse could be helpful to you. Please check all those areas below in which you could use a nurse.

   _____ Help with dressing
   _____ Help with bathing
   _____ Help with following prescribed medical routine

_____ Help with preparing meals
_____ Help with going to the bathroom
_____ Help with exercise
_____ Other (Please specify) _____

To the extent possible, the responses should be likely to gather the type of information that is needed. Often the simplest choices are the most useful. In other words, do not use a more complicated response system when a simple "yes/no" response is sufficient. In addition, the instructions to the respondents should be clear. For instance, if they are to choose one alternative, the instruction "please check one" might be used. Or, if more than one response can be checked, this instruction might be "please check all that apply."

Structured questions can be used on questionnaires or forms or be read by the interviewer. When they are administered to only one client, the interviewer can clarify the questions, if necessary, but this process may change the meaning from that which was originally intended. On the other hand, this process provides a context for a high degree of content validity. If the questions are used with only one client, but at several points in time, it is important to standardize the questions over time after their contents have been modified in an interview.

The practice-researcher can provide the client with a questionnaire that contains questions about needs and client characteristics related to those needs. Generally speaking, questions that are relatively straightforward can be presented in a questionnaire prior to an interview. For instance, a questionnaire might collect basic information about client characteristics, like age, gender, and religion, and concrete information related to the client problem, such as other services the client has been involved with in the past, More complicated questions that require more thought or longer answers could also be included in a questionnaire, but might be delivered more effectively in the context of the interview where the worker can discern through observation, clarification, and probing whether the client understands the questions. For example, questions about circumstances surrounding the onset of a problem might be better dealt with in an interview.

Assessing Needs of Aggregated Clients

Aggregated clients refers to multiple clients or significant others grouped together, usually by an administrative arrangement. The caseload of a social worker, the combined caseloads of social workers assigned to a particular supervisor, and all the clients in an agency's adult day treatment program are instances of aggregated clients. Clients can also be aggregated for the purpose of determining needs in relation to specific characteristics such as gender, race, and religion. Thus, one might be interested in determining differential referral rates to specific social services for African-American, white, Hispanic, and Asian clients.

Instruments for collecting data from aggregated clients require more standardization than do devices for gathering data from an individual client. Because comparisons will be made across clients, each client should be presented the same stimulus and, when applicable, the same response categories. Once a questionnaire is designed and deemed ready for use, it is not changed or interpreted (as it might be for individuals) for different clients.

The two main procedures for assessing needs are: (1) survey procedures in which questionnaires, interview schedules, and rating scales can be used; and (2) analyzing agency data for trends in service usage, client characteristics, and demographic data that might be associated with particular needs. These procedures are discussed in the remainder of this chapter.

Survey Procedures

Conducting a needs assessment survey involves seven interrelated steps. They are:

1. Specify the population to which generalizations of need will be assessed.
2. Define need and develop an instrument to assess it. Typically, this is a questionnaire or interview schedule which might also include self-rating scales.
3. Select a representative sample of the population.
4. Contact the sample and administer the instrument.
5. Compile and tabulate the responses to the instrument.
6. Analyze the data.
7. If a need exists, develop and offer services or refer clients to appropriate agencies for services.

Each of these steps is discussed in more detail in the following sections.

Specify the Population

The population for study is an aggregated group of clients. These may be clients and significant others who are waiting for, arc receiving, or received services. The population may consist of all active cases for which a supervisor is responsible, or all inactive cases (those who have received services, but are not currently receiving them) seen by a particular social worker. Again, note that surveys often are used in communities to query persons who may have needs but have not received services from social agencies. Our intent here is to focus on survey procedures with finite populations that are relatively accessible to the practice-researcher; that is, populations of persons and their significant others who have had contact with the human service agency.

After defining the population, it is important to consider whether or not the population is accessible. That is, the practitioner should seek permission to access the clients according to the policies of the agency regarding the ethical conduct of practice research. For example, it may be permissible to seek out ex-clients for a follow-up study of need, but only if the clients are not personally identified and if their participation in the study is voluntary. In short, the practice-researcher must consider agency policies, possible agency constraints, and ethical standards in specifying a potentially accessible population. Ethical considerations outlined in chapter 2 also pertain here.

Develop an Instrument

The definition of needs will become manifest while the instrument is developed. The instrument should include an introduction that indicates the reason for data collection, the extent to which data are confidential, and how the data will be used. In addition, the questions should be related to the stated purpose of the needs assessment, and should be answerable in a relatively short period of time.

To illustrate, let us suppose that social workers and their supervisor in a children's hospital are considering offering groups for parents of terminally ill children. The hospital administration requires some documentation of the need for the groups, before the new service can be offered. In other words, do the parents have a need to discuss the illness and their feelings about it in group situations? In addition, suppose there are sixty terminally ill children in the hospital, all of whom have parents or guardians. The parents or guardians constitute the population. It is decided that a questionnaire can serve as the instrument. No available instruments appeared to tap this particular need. Figure 3.4 provides a draft of what such a questionnaire might look like. It is constructed by following the same principles as were discussed in the previous section on constructing questions to assess individual needs.

Once the questionnaire is constructed, it should be tested on a few parents, to ascertain whether the questions are clear. During testing, it is advisable to elicit suggestions for improving the instrument. This pretesting procedure enables the researcher to increase the content validity and the reliability of the questionnaire. If there are not sufficient time or resources to test for reliability prior to the use of a questionnaire in a survey, the reliability still can be enhanced by ensuring that the respondents are given standardized questions and responses and that the questionnaire is administered in the same way to all respondents.

The response rate (percentage of persons responding to an instrument) for mailed questionnaires typically is low, in the neighborhood of 50 percent. It can be increased by approximately 10–15 percent by making a second mailing (Dillman 1978). Mailed surveys can get expensive quickly: they require postage, duplication, and time for such tasks as preparing the mailing. A procedure that obtains a greater response rate, and is less expensive, is giving questionnaires to clients to complete while they are in the agency, or while they are in contact with an agency worker. Telephone surveys in which the questionnaires are read by the social worker to the respondent over the phone are an alternative to direct worker contact, and they usually provide a higher response rate than mailed questionnaires. Obviously, telephone surveys have expenses associated with staff time to administer the questions.

Select a Representative Sample

To be representative, a sample must have the same characteristics as the population. A sample should be a smaller replica of the population. For studies of need, as much of the population as possible should be studied. As a rough guide, the entire population should be studied if it is comprised of fifty or fewer individuals or client units. If the population is larger than fifty, samples of at least fifty should be obtained. To obtain representative samples from a larger population, the procedures of simple random sampling should be followed (Seaberg 1988).

FIGURE 3.4

Questionnaire for Parents or Guardians of Terminally Ill Children

Social workers at this hospital seek to provide appropriate, timely services for families and their children. To do this more effectively, we are asking for your cooperation in this brief survey. Specifically, we are interested in learning whether or not you would like to meet in small groups to discuss mutual concerns about your children and other family members. To help us answer this question, would you please complete this questionnaire and give it to your social worker after you have completed it? Your responses are confidential and will only be shared with the social work staff. Because you are not asked to sign this questionnaire, you will not be identified individually. In addition, the responses to this questionnaire will not affect any of the services that are currently provided to you and your child.

1. What is the illness that your child has? (Write in).

_____

_____

2. How long has your child had this illness? (Check one.)

    _____ 0–3 months   _____ 10–12 months

    _____ 4–6 months   _____ 1–2 years

    _____ 7–9 months   _____ Over 2 years

3. How long has your child been a patient in this hospital? (Check one.)

    _____ 0–3 months   _____ 10–12 months

    _____ 4–6 months   _____ 1–2 years

    _____ 7–9 months   _____ Over 2 years

4. a) Have you discussed your child's illness with any of the hospital staff?

    _____ yes   _____ no

   b) If yes, indicate which staff person(s). (Check all that apply.)

    _____ physician   _____ receptionist

    _____ nurse   _____ other (please specify) _____

    _____ social worker   _____ other (please specify) _____

5. To what extent are you satisfied with the information you have received about your child's illness? (Check one.)

    _____ Very satisfied   _____ Satisfied   _____ Neither satisfied nor dissatisfied

    _____ Dissatisfied   _____ Very dissatisfied

FIGURE 3.4 (Continued)

6. a) Is there other information you would like to receive from hospital staff?

    ____ yes   ____ no

  b) If you answered yes to the previous question, please indicate here what information you desire.

_____

_____

_____

7. Please place a check mark (√) next to the persons listed below if you have discussed your thoughts and feelings about your child's illness with them. (Check all that apply.)

    ____ physician   ____ family

    ____ nurse   ____ friends

    ____ social worker   ____ other (please specify) _____

    ____ receptionist   ____ other (please specify) _____

8. Please place a check mark (√) next to the persons listed below if you would like to discuss your thoughts and feelings about your child's illness with them, but have not yet done so. (Check all that apply.)

    ____ physician   ____ family

    ____ nurse   ____ friends

    ____ social worker   ____ other (please specify) _____

    ____ receptionist   ____ other (please specify) _____

9. a) If the social work department could arrange to have small groups of parents (5 to 6 parents in a group) meet with a social worker to discuss problems and concerns about terminally ill children, would you be interested in attending such group meetings?

    ____ yes   ____ no

  b) If you answered yes to the previous question, how often should the groups meet? (Check one.)

    ____ twice a week   ____ once a month

    ____ once a week   ____ other (please specify) _____

    ____ every two weeks

  c) If you answered yes to 9a, what times would be most convenient for you to attend meetings? (Check all that apply.)

Mondays: _ AM (9–12:00) _ PM (1–4:00) _ Evenings (6–9:00)

Tuesdays: _ AM (9–12:00) _ PM (1–4:00) _ Evenings (6–9:00)

Wednesdays: __ AM (9–12:00) __ PM (1–4:00) __ Evenings (6–9:00)
Thursdays: __ AM (9–12:00) __ PM (1–4:00) __ Evenings (6–9:00)
Fridays: __ AM (9–12:00) __ PM (1–4:00) __ Evenings (6–9:00)

10. What is your age in years? (Check one.)

____ 18 and under   ____ 36–45
____ 19–25   ____ 46 and older
____ 26–35

11. What is your race? (Check one.)

____ African–American   ____ Asian
____ white   ____ Other (please specify) _____
____ Hispanic

12. What is your marital status? (Check one.)

____ Married   ____ Divorced or separated   ____ Widowed
____ Never married

13. In addition to your child who is hospitalized, indicate how many children are living with you at home? (Check one.)

____ 0   ____ 3
____ 1   ____ 4
____ 2   ____ 5 or more

14. How much education have you had?

____ Less than high school   ____ Completed college
____ Completed high school   ____ Attended graduate school
____ Attended college   ____ Received one or more
                                         graduate degrees

Thank you very much for completing the questionnaire. Please remember to give it to your social worker. If you would like to give us any more information about your interest in attending a small group or other needs that you might have, please write on the back of this page.

We will illustrate random sampling procedures with a population of parents of terminally ill children. First, suppose all the families in the population of parents are listed in a column. Suppose that the population consists of 100 families and we wished to choose a representative sample of 50. Each family would be given a number, until all 100 were listed. The digits 00–99 could represent 100 families, with each family identified by a number (for example, Adams would be 00 and Zingerman would be 99). Now we are ready to choose a sample from a table of random numbers. If we choose a sample (n = 50) from a population of 100, we would consult a table of random numbers. (The following is excerpted from a table of Random Numbers in Monette, Sullivan, and DeJong 1990, 484).

<u>894</u>	920
<u>492</u>	974
<u>768</u>	450
<u>482</u>	379
<u>621</u>	422
<u>488</u>	005
<u>472</u>	782
554	576
333	797

Start at any point on the table and then proceed systematically, column by column, reading the numbers for each selection. Since all of the families in our population are identified by two-digit numbers (00–99), we would look at adjacent two-digit numbers within each column, choosing the first 50 different numbers that appear. For example, if we start with the upper left-hand corner in the table excerpt above, the first two-digit number in the first column is 89 followed by 49, 76, 48, 62, 47, and so on. Families with these numbers would be in the sample. Note that "48" was not repeated, as it already had been accepted into the sample. Selection of two-digit numbers would continue in this manner until 50 unique numbers had been selected. These numbers would represent the simple random sample.

Contacting the Sample

The sample can be contacted directly by the social worker, by mail, or by telephone, because the parents have children who are hospitalized and seen by the social worker. Clients who are on waiting lists, terminated clients, and clients who dropped out can be contacted by mail or phone. The first contact involves soliciting their participation, which is then followed by administering the questionnaire during an office visit, by telephone, or by mail. In such contacts, it is very important to convey to clients and significant others that the information is important for planning future services for clients and their families, but that their participation, nevertheless, is voluntary and that their particular responses will be held in confidence.

Compile Responses, Analyze Data, and Offer Services

Responses to open-ended questions are reviewed, and then placed into categories that are representative of the themes. Because they require much more time for analysis and because the information may not be easily categorized, it is unwise to include too many open-ended questions in a survey instrument. In our questionnaire for parents and guardians of terminally ill children, the first question asks parents to write in their children's illness. Answers to this item should be easily categorized. For example, categories might be brain tumor, leukemia, cystic fibrosis, don't know, and other. Having specified the categories, the practice-researcher then tabulates frequencies and percentages for each category. Out of fifty parents who identified the illnesses of their children, for example, 40 percent (n = 20) might have answered "cancer," 40 percent (n = 20) "cystic fibrosis," and 20 percent (n = 10) might respond "other." Already we can see that one possible analysis would be to compare responses from parents whose children have cystic fibrosis to those from parents whose children have cancer. Responses to closed-ended questions also are tabulated by frequencies and percentages.

Let us examine further hypothetical data from the questionnaire developed by the children's hospital social service staff. Questions 5, 6, and 8 relate to needs for information and discussion, and question 9 relates to the desire for group sessions as a social service. If responses occur something like the following, a need is clearly represented in the data.

In response to question 5, thirty out of fifty respondents (60 percent) indicated that they are either dissatisfied or very dissatisfied with information about their children's illnesses, while five respondents were satisfied (10 percent) and fifteen (30 percent) were neither satisfied nor dissatisfied. Moreover, forty-five respondents (90 percent) indicated they'd like to receive more information from hospital staff. In particular, they wanted to know more about the life expectancy of their child (70 percent) and how to maintain a high quality of life for the child during the illness (30 percent) (question 6). Respondents indicated that they would like to discuss their thoughts and feelings with friends (90 percent), family (80 percent), their social worker (80 percent), and their physician (50 percent) (question 8). Note that the percentages for this item can total to more than 100 percent because the respondents could check more than one answer. Responses to question 9 provide information that indicates whether groups should be offered. Group sessions were desired, with forty (80 percent) of the respondents saying that they would be interested in attending group meetings. The most popular schedule for the meetings was every two weeks (90 percent), and on Monday or Tuesday evenings (90 percent).

These data can be analyzed in more detail to provide information about needs. There might be differences in needs or preferred schedules for parents of different racial groups or marital statuses, or for parents whose children have different diagnoses. Clearly, the data presented here are simple to tabulate and analyze. Although hypothetical, they illustrate a clear need and a desire for services, which should be implemented by the social work department. Moreover, the data could be helpful in planning group sessions and in convincing hospital administrators of the need for this service.

Analyses of Existing Data

Analysis of data that already have been categorized and tabulated in the agency is more economical and efficient than is collecting and analyzing survey data. Of course, there may not be existing data to answer the particular questions of interest to the practice-researcher. Nonetheless, agencies often collect data for other purposes, such as reporting to governmental agencies or justifying requests for reimbursements from insurance companies. For instance, agencies often have data available that summarize client characteristics from face sheet information and that relate to the use of agency services. Here we present some examples of how such existing data can be analyzed.

Data about client characteristics can estimate a particular need when previous research is available to identify the client variables that are likely to be associated with that need. For example, previous research may indicate that persons who were abused as children are likely to abuse their own children when they become parents. Moreover, this abuse may be more likely to occur with low-income parents in large families. Thus, existing data indicate that previously abused, low-income parents of large families are *at risk* of abusing their own children. Yet this does not verify that they actually abuse their children. An *attributed need* for this at-risk group is the socially desirable need to prevent child abuse from occurring, a need that might be met in a number of ways such as offering child management skill training, informal social support groups, or respite care to these parents.

Accordingly, analysis of existing agency data on client characteristics may indicate whether or not there are clients who might be said to be at risk of abusing their children since their characteristics are highly correlated with a need category. Suppose 500 families were seen by a family service agency in a three-month period of time. Further, suppose that 150 of these families are low-income and, of that number, 100 families consist of one or more parents and one or more children. And, of those 100 families, fifty-five of the parents have indicated they were abused when they were children. Hence, these fifty-five parents are identified as a group of parents who are at risk of abusing their children. Agency staff could then determine if there is further information in their case records about actual abuse. Moreover, if some of the parents currently are being seen at the family service agency, their workers might explore the possibility of offering special services during regular sessions with the parents. Then, workers can consider whether or not there appears to be such a need and whether or not there seems to be a demand for that service from the clients. As this example illustrates, analyses of data may merely involve tabulating frequencies and percentages for identifying a potential population that is at risk. Similar analyses can be carried out for those at risk for substance abuse, suicide, and other problems, given available data. It must be emphasized, however, that this needs assessment procedure is indirect, and is only worthwhile if there is research suggesting very high correlations between client characteristics and the designated need category.

As another example, agency service statistics typically report the number of different services provided for agency clients. Categories of services might include face-to-face contacts with clients, telephone contacts with clients, group sessions, crisis intervention contacts, concrete services, and contacts with collaterals, as examples. These service statistics, along with data describing client characteristics such as age, race, gender, marital status, and family composition, can be analyzed to suggest possible needs. Waiting lists for home-maker services or respite care for caretakers of elderly relatives with health problems, for instance, suggest there are large numbers of families with practical needs and that those services, if possible, could be expanded. In contrast, low utilization of services suggests that there is little demand and, correspondingly, little need for service.

Agency statistics also can be analyzed for differential service usage, which may suggest either differences in needs or differences in services provided to different population groups. If differences are identified, further inquiry to discern whether there are problems in some aspect of the provision of agency services would be necessary. A chi-square (χ^2) statistic could be calculated to show whether or not there are differences in services. For illustrative purposes, we will describe how to use this statistic for the simple case of comparing dichotomous client characteristics with referrals to one of two services. There might be a question whether there are differences between African-American and white families' use of homemaker services. Because differential usage may be a result of income, the practice-researcher may decide to first obtain all clients at the same income level, say low income. Then the practice-researcher would need to determine how many African-Americans and how many whites did and did not receive homemaker services. These resulting numbers can be cross-tabulated as in table 3.1.

Table 3.1 depicts 100 clients (N = 100), of whom 50 are African-American and 50 are white. In addition, 50 clients used homemaker services and 50 did not. Whereas 40 white clients used homemaker services (C), 40 African-American clients did not (B). Correspondingly, 10 African-Americans used homemaker services (A), and 10 whites did not (D).

These data can be inserted in the following formula for chi-square (Hinkle, Wiersma, and Jurs 1988):

$$\chi^2 = \frac{N\,(AD-BC)^2}{(A+B)(C+D)(A+C)(B+D)}$$

Referring to the table above, the numbers can be substituted for the letters in the formula in this way:

$$\chi^2 = \frac{100[10(10) - 40(40)]^2}{50(50)(50)(50)}$$

$$\chi^2 = \frac{100(-1500)^2}{50(50)(50)(50)}$$

$$\chi^2 = 36$$

If the computed value of the chi-square statistic is greater than or equal to 3.84, the probability of the occurrence of that value is less than 5 times out of 100. When the probability is that low, it suggests that the populations of African-Americans and whites are probably different with respect to their use of homemaker services; this is a statistically significant difference (see Hinkel, Wiersma, and Jurs 1988 for discussion of uses of chi-square and of statistical significance). The probability level of .05, which was selected for this analysis, is a conventional one, although other probability levels with decision values for chi-square different than 3.84 could have been used.

As we noted, the results indicate there is differential usage of services. There might be different needs for African-Americans and for whites or there might be discrimination in the way the services are offered or provided. These questions cannot be answered with these data. The data suggest, however, that further inquiry should be pursued to determine whether there are need-service discrepan cies in the agency. Survey procedures could pursue this question further.

One can also use existing agency statistics to observe whether goals of treatment are realized. If goals are not achieved, the clients' needs still persist, and some other substitute service or referral might be offered. To illustrate this, suppose that a social work unit has fifty clients, all of whom received dual diagnoses for depression and alco-

TABLE 3.1

Cross-Tabulation of Ethnicity by Use of Homemaker Services

	Used Homemaker Services	Did Not Use Homemaker Services	Total Numbers
African-Americans	10 (A)	40 (B)	50 (A + B)
whites	40 (C)	10 (D)	50 (C + D)
Total Numbers	50 (A + C)	50 (B + D)	100 = N

hol abuse before treatment. All clients are receiving services to decrease their use of alcohol, but only half of the clients are receiving services to decrease depression. Further suppose that treatment is provided for six months, and alcohol abuse is substantially reduced for most of the clients. The social workers in the unit may be interested in obtaining information on depression after the six months of treatment for alcohol abuse to determine whether or not the problem of depression is continuing. Table 3.2 shows data for the fifty clients who show signs of depression before and after treatment.

From table 3.2, it can be discerned that 25 out of 50 clients showed signs of depression before treatment, while 40 out of 25 clients showed signs of depression after treatment. Moreover, 20 clients who showed signs of depression before treatment continue to be depressed after treatment (C), and 20 who showed no signs of depression before treatment are depressed after treatment (D). Clearly, there appears to be a persistent problem of depression and it appears to be worse after treatment. Is this indication of deterioration statistically significant at the .05 level of significance? In other words, are the results after treatment significantly different from those before treatment? The following formula for chi-square, the McNemar Test for the Significance of Changes, can be employed (Siegel 1956).

$$\chi^2 = \frac{(A-D)^2}{A+D}$$

where the letters for A and D are indicated in table 3.2, with $A = 5$ and $D = 20$. Hence,

TABLE 3.2
Signs of Depression Before and After Treatment

After Treatment	Before Treatment		
	Signs of Depression	No Signs of Depression	Total Number
No Sign of Depression	5 (A)	5 (B)	10
Signs of Depression	20 (C)	20 (D)	40
Total Number	25	25	50

$$\chi^2 = \frac{(5-20)^2}{5+20} = \frac{225}{25} = 9$$

Using the same decision rule as for the previous application of chi-square ($\chi \geq 3.84$, $r \leq .05$), it can be seen that the value of $\chi^2 = 9$, which is greater than 3.84. Consequently, the degree of post-treatment depression is statistically significant with a probability of less than 5 times in 100.

These are just some of the ways in which simple agency statistics can be employed to determine the persistence of a problem, as well as the possible existence of problems or needs. The use of such statistics is predicated on the maintenance of a viable information system within the human services agency. Without reliable and valid data and a system for processing those data, estimates of need could not be made in the manner shown. More direct estimates of need can be obtained by survey procedures, but it is costly if a new survey must be conducted every time information is needed, especially if that information can be routinely gathered and processed.

4. *Implementing Interventions*

Having assessed client needs, the practice-researcher next devises an intervention plan to meet those needs. When there are several needs or problems, the social worker and the client may prioritize them in order of their importance, thereby selecting those problems for immediate intervention (see Blythe and Tripodi 1989 for a discussion of procedures for developing problem hierarchies). In this chapter, we discuss intervention, implementation, and the use of research strategies for determining whether interventions are implemented as planned.

Intervention

An intervention is a set of activities designed to meet client needs and/or to ameliorate client problems. Because no single set of activities may be sufficient to address all the problems of a client, more than one intervention may be employed. Interventions may be complex, involving a theory of practice and a number of techniques designed to help clients achieve their goals. For example, a psychosocial intervention may be comprised of theory pertaining to the person in his or her environment which guides the deployment of a variety of techniques used in face-to-face interviewing such as exploration, clarification, and interpretation. In contrast, an intervention may be relatively simple, involving a single procedure to accomplish one particular sub-goal in working with a client. For example, the intervention may be a telephone call by the social worker to remind the client to keep an appointment with a job counselor. Thomas (1987) distinguishes among interventions by referring to an intervention method as a broad entity which is comprised of intervention techniques and a program format that provides a plan for focusing on one or more treatment goals. Similarly, Reid alludes to complex and simple interventions by referring to a specific intervention or a combination of interventions within a "larger intervention package" (1987:18).

In addition to differences in the complexity or number of interventions, interventions may be distinguished by such dimensions as structure, specificity, setting, amount, frequency, and duration. Structure refers to an arrangement of the physical environment as a context for interventions. Examples are the arrangement of chairs in a predetermined way for a group meeting, or the placement of persons in a family sculpting session. Specificity is the degree to which the details of the intervention are delineated, referred to as "proceduralization" by Thomas (1987), while the setting refers to the site where the intervention contents are to be employed, such as, home visit, office, or community. Interventions can also be distinguished by the amount of contact, the frequency of contacts, and the period of time in which contacts are made with clients.

The reader must bear in mind that words such as "treatment," "techniques," "technology," "practice," "intervention," and "methods" often are used interchangeably in the literature. When we use "intervention," we refer to a set of activities in which the social worker plans to achieve a treatment goal, bearing in mind that the activities may be simple or complex and may differ on dimensions as described above.

Sources of Interventions

Practice-researchers select interventions for use that ideally are based on demonstrated effectiveness. Hence, one source of interventions is the research literature. Two additional sources are based on practice. These are agency practices, that is, interventions that are typically employed in human services agencies, and practice experience of individual workers. Another source that generates a variety of interventions is the literature on practice theory. Finally, interventions can be generated on the basis of practitioners' hunches or hypotheses.

Interventions from sources other than the agency in which the practice-researcher is employed often cannot be applied without modification. Examples of necessary modifications might be the setting, the frequency of interventions, or the order of interventions. The practice-researcher will apply only those interventions that are possible within the agency context and that are deemed as ethically suitable. For example, the use of noxious stimuli such as negative reinforcers, marathon group therapy sessions, primal scream therapy, or rolfing, may or may not be adaptable in the context of particular agencies. Thomas's work on *Designing Interventions for the Helping Professions* (1987) articulates a variety of dimensions that can be employed for designing new interventions, while Blythe and Tripodi (1989), building on Thomas's work, specify several factors that are important in choosing interventions. These factors include the following: the relevance of the intervention to the clients' problem; the degree to which the worker and/or client possess the requisite knowledge, attitudes, or skills to implement the intervention; the compatibility of the intervention with the worker's and client's values, assumptions, and abilities; the degree to which the intervention is effective and efficient; the costs in time and money for implementing the intervention; and its empirical support from research.

Components of An Intervention

Another way to define or describe an intervention is to specify its components. A guide for specifying the components of an intervention is provided by a modification of a journalistic formula: *who* does *what* to *whom*, *where*, and *why*.

Who refers to the person or persons involved in providing the contents of the intervention. Most often it is the worker, but it may also be a client, a significant other, or another professional or paraprofessional helper who provides the intervention. For example, one particular intervention for a girl may involve a positive reinforcement such as praise given by her parents whenever she demonstrates positive behaviors at home such as completing homework for school or returning home at an agreed-upon time. The intervention may involve the social worker training the parents to positively reinforce their child's behavior.

What is the basic substance of the intervention—its contents. For example, it may refer to all those procedures involved in group work as an intervention, including the size and seating arrangements of the group, the length of meetings, the number and duration of meetings, the topics for discussion, and the worker's plans for focusing topics and clarifying discussion. Obviously, it is impossible to specify all of the contents that take place in an intervention. Those interventions that depend on worker-client interactions cannot be specified a priori to the *n*th degree; one may be able to discern the complete contents only by referring to tape recordings. On the other hand, modifications in the client's social, economic, or physical environment, initiated by the practitioner, may be observed more directly and easily. A substantial part of an intervention can be described by "proceduralization," which involves specifying an intervention in as much detail as possible so others can implement it (Thomas 1987). Obviously, some interventions are easier to specify than others. For example, one can articulate all the steps necessary to provide a didactic presentation on substance abuse, including the contents of the lecture along with slide presentations. For complex interventions, guidelines might be provided, as on the appropriate time for relating patterns of the past to present actions in psychodynamic therapy.

For all types of interventions, certain parameters can be provided that also specify the contents: the people involved in the interaction; the structure of the interaction, including its length of time and the format for its beginning and ending; the number of planned interactions; and the duration of interactions. To illustrate, an intervention may include the worker and a married couple, and there may be twenty planned sessions, one hour each, over six weeks. The worker may begin each interaction by focusing on the couple's difficulty in their marriage, not requiring either of the spouses to participate in any fixed order, but only in response to the interactions that occur. Depending on the theories that the worker uses to guide practice, these parameters can be specified in varying degrees.

Whom refers to the client. This may be an individual, couple, family, or group. The intervention may be further delineated by specifying the extent to which the client participates. One intervention may require that the worker and client develop a contract specifying mutual obligations and responsibilities. Another intervention may require that the worker help clients devise their own interventions for systems of social support in a self-help group. Still another intervention may focus only on the worker's provision of repeated instructions to assist individuals who are mentally challenged to cope in a limited environment.

Where is the place the intervention occurs. An intervention may be successfully implemented in one setting for particular clients but not in another setting for other clients. A home interview may provide an environment where a middle-class client feels sufficiently comfortable to discuss his problems, while that environment may be restrictive for a lower-class client who lives in a crowded apartment house.

Why is the purpose of the intervention. It refers to the goals of intervention that can be classified as those of change, maintenance, or prevention (Blythe and Tripodi 1989). Change goals focus on the resolution of clients' problems. The anxious client significantly reduces his level of anxiety; the drug abuser no longer takes drugs; the single father becomes better able to manage his children. Maintenance goals deal with the continuation of progress and avoiding relapse. Thus,the purpose of intervention in aftercare for patients discharged from a mental hospital may be to facilitate their adjustment to the community, and to avoid relapse to psychosis. Prevention goals concentrate on maintaining socially desirable behaviors. For example, a goal for a parent who was himself abused as a child may be to help prevent that parent from abusing his children.

Implementation

Implementation is the set of activities that provide the intervention, as formulated by the practice-researcher (Blythe and Tripodi 1989). This involves specifying the intervention as well as the attempts by the worker to apply the intervention in work with the client. Reid and Hanrahan (1988) discuss measurement for program evaluation and have similar conceptions regarding implementation as a process in which there are attempts to achieve goals.

Obviously, implementation is a basic ingredient of direct practice. It is extremely important to know whether or not the intervention(s) has been implemented for these basic reasons:

1. The worker must know what is actually taking place when the intervention is being applied. If it is not effective, the worker will need to change the intervention. Conversely, the worker will want to sustain it and possibly replicate it with other clients if it is effective.
2. If the intervention is employed because it has been demonstrated to be effective or efficient in practice and/or research settings, the practitioner must replicate the intervention to the degree that is possible. Otherwise, if there are deviations from the planned intervention, there is no assurance that the intervention will be effective and efficient since it would not be the intervention that was employed in previous practice situations.

Implementation Criteria

Many things may prevent interventions from being carried out as planned. The required activities in the intervention may not be understood by the worker or client, or there may be an insufficient amount of motivation to carry out required tasks. There may be extraagency influences that prevent implementation, such as sickness, transportation difficulties, or emergencies. There may be intraagency influences, such as changes in eligibility requirements, or cutbacks in funds that may alter the original plans. There may be special characteristics of the worker and/or the client that impede the planned delivery of services, such as their knowledge, attitudes, or skills.

There are two basic criteria that a practice-researcher can employ to analyze the implementation or lack of implementation of an intervention. These are intervention validity and intervention reliability.

Intervention validity can be regarded as "treatment integrity," the extent to which the intervention is implemented as it was planned (Peterson, Homer, and Wonderlich 1982) . An intervention is successfully implemented if there is a high degree of treatment integrity. Conversely, a low degree of treatment integrity indicates the lack of implementation. For example, if one specifies certain procedures, tasks, number of sessions, and time constraints as salient for implementing task-centered practice (Reid and Hanrahan 1988), then evidence must be presented that all of those specifications have been met in order for there to be a high degree of treatment integrity.

Intervention reliability is the degree to which the intervention is standardized and consistently applied in repeated applications of the intervention. This can be thought of as "procedural reliability" (Billingsley, White, and Munson 1980), which is the reliability of the ingredients of an intervention over time and across workers. Even if an intervention is initially applied as planned, this doesn't guarantee intervention reliability. There may be shifts in the worker, the client, agency policies, the client's environment, or other arenas. These shifts have been reported by McMahon (1987) and referred to as "treatment shifts," that is, intentional or unintentional changes in procedures. In short, the greater the degree of congruence between intervention procedures in different applications of the intervention, the greater the degree of intervention reliability.

Indices of Implementation

The act of implementing an intervention primarily involves the actions of the worker and of the client. In this context, note that "worker" is defined to include one or more workers, or a treatment team involved in providing one or more interventions. Besides the primary target of the intervention, "client" is expanded to include significant others, such as family and friends when they assist in providing interventions or engage in actions that are necessary for interventions to occur. The worker, for example, may teach a parent how to use a reward system to promote prosocial behaviors in his or her children. The children may be the primary clients, but the parent also is participating in providing privileges and consequences as an intervention. Clients need to accomplish basic tasks to implement an intervention. Obviously, they must keep appointments with the worker and participate in the intervention process.

Indices of the implementation of interventions are focused on the extent to which "workers" and "clients" comply with those actions necessary for the intervention. Therefore, two main sources for identifying whether or not implementation occurred are worker compliance and client compliance with the provisions of intervention. Having specified the components of an intervention by indicating *who* does *what* to *whom, where,* and *why,* the practice-researcher must next specify indices of worker compliance and of client compliance.

The supervisor, the field supervisor of students, the worker, and/ or the student worker are interested in whether or not interventions are implemented as planned. Field supervisors need to know whether there are problems in implementing an intervention so that guidance can be provided to their students. At the same time, all potential implementors of an intervention need to know if the planned intervention is appropriate for the particular client configuration in question.

Worker Compliance

The worker (practice-researcher) is defined as the person who is primarily responsible for implementing the intervention. This may include tasks such as: arranging for a meeting time and place; discussing such parameters of the intervention as frequency, duration, and number of sessions; enlisting the cooperation of the client; providing instructions that the client must follow; or focusing on specified topics of discussion.

Worker compliance is simply the accomplishment of those tasks. For example, a worker is compliant if she sets a meeting time and place, at a time convenient for the client and consistent with the intervention plan. A worker is compliant if the intervention specifies the discussion of certain topics and if those topics actually are discussed. A worker is compliant if he carries out these specifications: factual information is provided; the worker clarifies ambiguous information; and the worker avoids interpretations. In contrast, a worker is not compliant if the intervention is supposed to be eight weeks, yet the client receives services for fifteen weeks. Note that compliance only signifies the extent to which the planned actions were actually carried out. Implementation failures may be due to factors other than the worker's skills. Examples are environmental barriers, inappropriate interventions, and client characteristics.

Typically, compliance involves successfully completing several tasks relevant to the intervention. When that is the case, the practice-researcher must decide beforehand what will indicate compliance. If an intervention requires implementing all of the specified tasks, then compliance takes place only when all of the tasks are completed. Compliance is determined by the definition and specifications of the intervention. All of the tasks should be completed for compliance unless there is an a priori calculus that indicates how many or what combinations of tasks should be completed.

Some forms of intervention require contracts that contain provisions for the worker and the client. Those provisions must be adhered to in order for there to be worker compliance. Other forms of intervention may present guidelines for the worker's actions, rather than specifying behaviors that must be completed. For instance, in a child and family therapy clinic an intervention may specify that it is desirable to attempt to engage both the father and mother of a child in treatment. Hence, the worker may be regarded as compliant if either the father, the mother, or both parents participate in the intervention.

Client Compliance

The worker not only has responsibility for implementing the provisions of the intervention, but also must observe whether or not there is client compliance. As with worker compliance, client compliance occurs when the client and/or significant others successfully carry out prescribed tasks. These prescriptions include worker/client contacts, such as keeping appointments and following within-session prescriptions. In addition, there are those tasks that must be completed as part of the intervention, as well as those actions that must be completed when the client and/or significant other is providing interventions to other persons. For example, a client in drug treatment counseling may need to record the number of urges to use drugs and the antecedent conditions leading to those urges on a daily basis. A spouse of a person receiving an intervention for depression may be asked to monitor whether her husband takes his medication each day. In order to be compliant, a client may need to complete all the provisions of a contract. A parent of a child who has difficulty in school may agree to review the child's homework each night and to reward the child for attending school and for improving his grades.

Procedures for Assessing Compliance

Procedures for assessing compliance include developing or using instruments to collect compliance data that pertain to indices of implementation; collecting and analyzing data to determine the extent to which interventions are valid and reliable; and making decisions to further standardize the intervention, modify it, leave it unchanged, or discontinue using it. As Thomas (1987) indicates, a variety of quantitative and/or qualitative data can be employed for monitoring the implementation of interventions. Reid and Hanrahan (1988) discuss several methods for studying process in counseling programs. These methods essentially employ standard practice and research tools, such as observations, recording, interviewing, questionnaires, checklists, and forms. These research instruments can be constructed and adapted to assess client compliance with respect to implementing interventions. Although many types of instruments can be used in combination for studying the implementation of an intervention, we shall illustrate the process of assessing compliance by referring to only a few instruments. We believe, however, that the methods presented here can be generalized to many practice situations. To assess worker compliance, we focus on two basic procedures that supervisors and workers can easily use for assessing specific intervention prescriptions in the following sections. Before an intervention is applied, checklists can be used to record live observations. After an intervention is delivered, content analysis of records or tape recordings can be employed to determine the extent to which guideline prescriptions that depend on worker/client interactions were implemented. We further recommend that the practice-researcher assess client compliance by using interviewing techniques, live observations, and forms or questionnaires, depending on the specific clinical situation. The methods identified here also can be used for studying client compliance. Although we will be describing specific data gathering methods for studying the implementation of interventions, multiple methods can be used (Reid and Hanrahan 1988).

Gathering data is not sufficient for determining compliance. How the data are to be analyzed also must be specified. We shall consider the single case as the basic unit for determining compliance. After compliance data indicate that the intervention actually was implemented, the cases can be aggregated to provide information on whether or not an intervention can be implemented across clients as well as across workers.

Checklists to Assess Worker Compliance

A checklist is a form comprised of statements, questions, phrases, or words as stimuli and spaces to check ($\sqrt{}$) whether the stimuli occurred. To construct checklists for monitoring implementation of an intervention, the following steps are taken:

1. Translate the specifications of an intervention into behaviors whose occurrence must take place for the intervention to be implemented.
2. Select those behaviors that are observable by the practice-researcher prior to and during interventions.
3. Assemble the items in a simple format.

Development of a checklist follows principles of questionnaire construction. Each item should be clear and should contain only one thought. In addition, the checklist should contain identifying information, such as the specific case name and identification number, the worker, and the date and time of the recording (Epstein and Tripodi 1977). Other questionnaire items can be included to detect possible problems in implementation. And, open-ended questions can be included to record observations of implementation problems and other reasons why the implementation is not being implemented.

To illustrate a checklist, suppose group work is planned for eight teenage girls who are at risk for becoming pregnant. A package of interventions to prevent early, unwanted pregnancy in the teenagers will be provided by one school social worker two hours per week for ten weeks in a school classroom. The worker devises the following intervention plan.

1. The first fifteen minutes of each session involve a presentation by the worker including facts about birth control and birth control devices. This is followed by a ten-item quiz, after which there is a brief discussion of the factual contents.
2. The worker devises a role-play situation in which teenage girls may be at risk for unprotected sexual intercourse or are faced with the task of securing contraceptives, and role plays the situation with one of the group members. This is followed by the worker's attempts to engage all of the teenagers in a discussion of specific strategies for coping with such situations.
3. The worker repeats the role play, this time selecting two other teenagers. Discussion is again repeated, emphasizing things the teen did well to handle the situation and suggestions for improvement. The worker selects another situation and two teenagers to role play the situation, and again encourages similar discussion from each group member regarding coping strategies.
4. At the end of the session, programmed for 2 hours, the worker assigns homework such as having the group members get information about how to obtain contraceptives from various places in their community.
5. The tenth session ends with a review of what was discussed, and an evaluation of what group activities were or were not helpful to them.

With the intervention specified as above, an intervention checklist, as depicted in figure 4.1, could be used for each session and might look like this. This checklist is straightforward, easy to complete, and primarily pertains to worker actions. The worker may or may not comment on implementation successes or failures. The intent is to provide information that leads to possible facilitation or hindrance of the future intervention sessions. For example, students may be absent due to sickness, truancy, and the like; there may not be enough time to include all the planned interventions in the allotted time; the students may have indicated that one session on facts was enough; or the mechanical selection of each recipient to speak by the worker may hinder spontaneous group process.

The data are analyzed by first noting the number of check marks

FIGURE 4.1
Small Group Intervention Worker Checklist

Name of practice-researcher _____ Group identification number _____
Group session number _____   Recording date _____

Check (✔) whether the following intervention components occurred.

_____ Factual presentation

_____ Quiz administered

_____ Quiz discussed

_____ Homework discussed

_____ A situation was role-played

Attempts were made to include in group discussion the following group members:

    _____ A   _____ E

    _____ B   _____ F

    _____ C   _____ G

    _____ D   _____ H

_____ A second situation was role played

Attempts were made to include in group discussion the following group members:

    _____ A   _____ E

    _____ B   _____ F

    _____ C   _____ G

    _____ D   _____ H

_____ A homework assignment was given

Write in comments related to implementation success and failures.

  Successes: _____

_____

  Failures: _____

_____

and any items that did not contain check marks. For example, there may be check marks for 21 out of 23 items, with check marks not included for group member A in both role plays. A comment under implementation failures might note that group member A was absent because she got into a confrontation with a classmate before coming to the group and had to go to the principal's office. Hence, the intervention actions were followed for all those that were present; worker compliance is $21/21 \times 100 = 100$ percent. With respect to the total group, however, worker compliance is $21/23 \times 100 = 91$ percent. The worker and supervisor may decide that intervention is implemented as long as the following took place: factual presentation, quiz administered, quiz discussed, homework given, homework discussed, at least one situation role played and discussion solicited from three or more members of the group. Thus, there is worker-compliance if these seven items are fulfilled.

Remember, however, that the decision for what was to be included as intervention had to be made before the actual meeting. This is to maintain a standardized intervention. Suppose the same worker was providing the same intervention across groups (if the intervention was varied, statistics could not be aggregated). The same operational definition of compliance also must be selected—90 percent of all items must be checked in this example. If the worker has five groups and four of them meet or exceed the criteria for worker compliance, then there is $4/5 \times 100$, or 80 percent compliance across groups. The higher the percentage of worker compliance across groups, the greater the degree of standardization of the intervention. If there is a high degree of standardization, the worker need not make any changes. The worker can observe the degree of standardization for any of the ten planned group sessions.

Intervention validity can be assessed in these ways:

1. The content validity is adequate if the items in the checklist are representative of actions taken to implement the intervention. This judgment can be made by the worker and/or the supervisor.
2. Concurrent validity can be assessed by modifying the checklist so that the group members are asked whether the worker took those actions. The average score for all the group members could indicate the extent to which the group believed worker compliance occurred. If there is agreement between the independent assessments of worker compliance, there can be said to be concurrent validity.

Intervention reliability can be inferred by consistency in worker compliance. Hence, agreement can be assessed within groups by observing the extent to which there is standardization from interview to interview within groups as well as standardization between groups. The graph in figure 4.2 can easily be constructed to illustrate intervention reliability within the same group. The Y-axis represents the percentage of worker compliance on salient intervention items,

FIGURE 4.2
Graph of Intervention

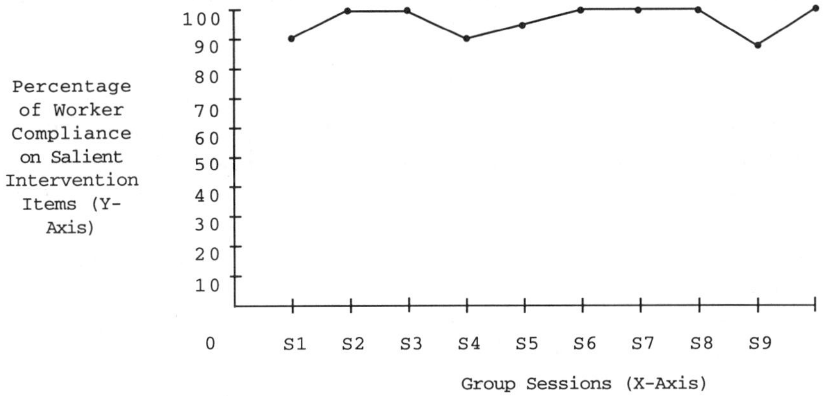

whereas the X-axis represents the group session number. The worker-compliance data for 10 sessions might look like this: Session 1, 88 percent; 2, 100 percent; 3, 100 percent; 4, 88 percent; 5, 94 percent; 6, 100 percent; 7, 100 percent; 8, 100 percent; 9, 85 percent; and 10, 100 percent. As shown on the graph, these scores would reflect a high degree of intervention reliability across sessions.

After data are analyzed, the practice-researcher must decide whether to increase intervention attempts or to modify the intervention. With reliable and valid intervention data, the worker may take no corrective action. With unreliable data, the worker tries to determine the source of the unreliability, deciding whether it can be corrected. For instance, it may take the worker more than two hours to implement all of the planned interventions. The worker can increase the session time, which might be too fatiguing for the group, or modify the intervention. The last item on the checklist, comments related to failures, might have worker observations indicating that the group members believed one role play was sufficient. Hence, the new intervention package might have fewer role playing sessions. This is obviously less of a problem than if the group members simply would not comply, or were inattentive.

Content Analysis to Assess Worker Compliance

Content analysis is a research procedure that can provide systematic descriptive information for analyzing tape recordings, case records, or other documents (Tripodi and Epstein 1980). When it is not possible to determine the extent to which there is worker compliance to planned interventions a priori, this research procedure can be employed. For example, a psychodynamic intervention with a psychotic client may specify that techniques of clarification, advice-giving, and exploration should be employed in interviews, but not interpretation in which connections are made between actions that represent different degrees of client awareness. The actual application of these intervention techniques can only be determined during or after the interviews take place, that is, by listening to a tape recording of the interview. Content analysis of the tape recording would reveal the extent of worker compliance.

Content analysis includes the following steps (adapted from Tripodi and Epstein 1980, 103–119):

1. The implementation requirements are specified. Returning to our previous example of group work for eight teenage girls, the worker may attempt to follow these prescriptions:

    A. The worker should not dominate group discussion, talking 40 percent or less of the time in the group session.
    B. The worker should initiate only planned topics, such as facts about teenage contraception and pregnancy, quizzes, role-plays, discussions about these role plays, and homework assignments.
    C. When group discussions stray from the planned topics, the worker should return the group to the topics.
    D. The worker should positively acknowledge statements by group members that are indicative of coping with situations regarding securing contraceptives or avoiding unprotected intercourse.

2. The documents to be used for content analysis must be identified. They should be relevant and consistently available. They should not be used if their validity is in question. For example, written process or summary recordings probably would not allow for accurate analysis of the proportion of time group members engaged in group discussion. Moreover, written recordings are less likely to contain an unbiased recording of worker-group member interactions. In analyzing the interventions as described in step number one, tape recordings would provide better information. Process and summary recordings might be preferable in other situations, such as in describing the workers' perception of the group's cohesion and in locating possible reasons for implementation successes and failures.

3. The unit of analysis, which further defines the document that provides the information for the content analysis is identified. In the above example, it is the tape recording of a group session. Since there are ten sessions, ten tapes should be available. Depending on the specification of the intervention, however, all of the tapes may or may not be used. If a sample of tapes is selected, it should be representative of the intervention for the ten sessions. Although analyzing all of the tapes would be more accurate, an inference of sufficient implementation can be made by analyzing every other tape. But, intervention corrections for subsequent sessions can only be made if the previous session is analyzed. For example, the worker can plan to focus more on the planned topics if content analysis of a tape of the previous session reveals a great deal of discussion about topics that are not relevant to the intervention. A supervisor may use the tapes for training purposes and, in so doing, might be interested in locating worker patterns across interventions for a particular group.

4. The analytic categories for the content analysis need to be identified and specified into measurement scales. The form in figure 4.3 illustrates the analytic categories, as well as measures of worker compliance with selected planned interventions for our case example of the group for teenage girls (see items 3, 6, 9, and 12 on the form).

   The variables of time, initiated topics by worker, group straying from planned topics, and re-focusing can easily be defined further to enhance reliability. Intervention D, coping and positive acknowledgement, would need further definition. A general defining statement and examples would further specify intervention D. For example, "coping" could be defined as any statement made by a group member in which she identifies a potentially effective behavior, interpersonal communication, and/or self-statement for helping her secure contraceptives or avoid unprotected intercourse. The teenager might suggest to a male partner that they engage in some other activity to avoid unprotected intercourse. She might ask her partner to first get some condoms. Positive acknowledgement is any statement made by the worker that acknowledges the teenager's attempt at "coping." The worker might say: "That's a good idea;" "You correctly identified the problem, and came up with a reasonable solution;" "Nice point;" or "You did a nice job of telling that guy to take some responsibility for his behavior."

FIGURE 4.3
Form for Content Analysis of Small Group

Name of practice-researcher _____ Group identification number _____
Group session number _____ Date of analysis _____

Intervention A
    1. Total time of tape (in minutes) _____
    2. Time worker speaks (in minutes) _____
    3. Percentage of time worker speaks (*#2 divided by #1 × 100* _____
Intervention B
    4. Number of topics initiated by worker _____
    5. Number of planned topics _____
    6. Percentage of initiated planned topics (*#5 divided by*
       #4 × 100 _____
Intervention C
    7. Number of times group strays from planned topics _____
    8. Number of times worker refocuses group efforts _____
    9. Percentage of refocusing efforts (*#8 divided by*
       #7 × 100 _____
Intervention D
    10. Number of coping statements _____
    11. Number of positive worker acknowledgments _____
    12. Percentage of positive acknowledgements (*#11 divided by*
       #10 × 100 _____

5. The next step in content analysis involves determining the reliability of the analytic categories. This can be done by testing for interrater agreement. In the above example, the extent of percentage agreement between two or more workers or between the worker and her/his supervisor could be compared. To illustrate, if the supervisor identified 10 statements the worker made that positively acknowledged "coping" by the teenagers, and the worker, in independently reviewing the tapes, identified 9 of these statements, there would be 90 percent agreement. Whether or not there is such a reliability test, the worker and/or supervisor should consistently follow precise definitions for each of the analytic categories.

6. Finally, the data must be collected and analyzed. The data can be analyzed after each group session, and transformed into indices of worker compliance, as shown on the form for content analysis. Intervention reliability can be analyzed in terms of consistency of responses across interviews. Intervention validity can

be approximated to the extent that the contents of the recording accurately reflect the dimensions of measurement. Empirical validity can be estimated by correlating responses of group members to questions about the worker's interventions with the results from the content analysis. Documenting empirical validity, however, might be a costly burden to add to the already time-consuming task of listening to the tapes. On the other hand, the process of content analysis is not especially costly if the practice-researcher and the supervisor include the use of tapes and their review as standard procedures.

Research Interviewing to Assess Client Compliance

Interviewing is comprised of a face-to-face interaction in which the practice-researcher asks questions of the respondent. Whereas therapeutic or treatment interviewing involves the client in the intervention, research interviewing is a systematic way of obtaining knowledge. When the practice-researcher is involved in providing intervention and carrying out research with a client, the distinctions between research interviewing and therapeutic interviewing become difficult to maintain. We recommend that research interviewing for assessing client compliance take no more than three to five minutes. Furthermore, we recommend that the interviewing be conducted at the beginning of the meeting with the client. Collecting the information at the beginning of the session allows it to be used immediately in the therapeutic encounter, rather than simply assuming client compliance.

Research interviewing ranges from structured interviewing, where the themes are predetermined and the questions are primarily closed-ended, as in questionnaires, to unstructured interviewing, in which the questions are open-ended and the themes are not known in advance. For gathering specific, predetermined information, structured interviewing or semi-structured interviewing in which the themes are specified but all of the questions are not, can be employed (Gochros 1988; Tripodi and Epstein 1980).

In suggesting the use of research interviewing to monitor client compliance, it is assumed that the intervention involves two or more meetings between the worker and the client, and that the research interviewing occurs in the second client contact, or in a client contact after specific intervention requisites have been discussed with a client. As indicated earlier, the client may be given one or more tasks to carry out. Once it is known what tasks the client is required to do and how often, the practice-researcher can develop an interview schedule which includes basic questions and response choices. It should include specific questions related to the tasks given to the client, and also may include a few unstructured questions that deal with possible reasons for the client's noncompliance in the event that the client does not complete the assigned tasks.

In the interview, the worker can ask for clarification of ambiguous responses via probes or follow-up questions that involve interviewer activities, such as repeating the question, repeating the answer, encouraging elaboration of a point by showing interest, pausing, or making comments such as: "Could you repeat that?" "I'm not sure I understand; could you clarify that?" and "Is that really what you mean?" (Gochros 1988). Social workers in direct practice have been trained in interviewing techniques, including establishing rapport and engaging clients. Hence, we assume that a primer on basic interviewing techniques is not necessary or appropriate in this context.

Suppose the practice-researcher is working with an unemployed, single mother who has a son in junior high school and a four-year-old daughter. The parent has a car that is in working condition, and she would like to find employment. Because she has not been successful in finding childcare, her employability is restricted. In addition, her son has been tardy to classes and has not been completing his school work. The practice-researcher is a school social worker. After an initial meeting, the worker and the mother decide to meet weekly to work on improving the son's school attendance and performance and to help the mother secure employment. After the first two interviews, the worker gives her tasks to carry out, the contents of which are specified on the interview schedule in figure 4.4. Prior to administering the interview schedule, the worker may give an introduction like this:

> If you will recall from our last meeting, we agreed that it's very important for you to complete certain tasks so that you can help your son and so that I can be helpful to you. To begin our work today, I am going to ask you some questions about these tasks.

The analysis of client information is relatively simple. In the preceding interview schedule, two basic interventions the parent is asked to do on a regular basis (from interview to interview) are monitored: (1) drive her son to school daily; (2) reward him weekly if he does his homework every night that week. The client's portion of the

FIGURE 4.4
Interview Schedule

Client identification number_____

Number of interview_____

Date of interview_____

Name of practice-researcher_____

Regular Interventions/Tasks

1. (a) Did you drive your son to school every school day during the past week? Yes _____ No _____
   [If yes, go to question #2]
   (b) If no, how many days did you drive him? _____
                                                    (write in)
   (c) If no, what prevented you from driving him to school?

   _____

   _____

2. Did your son do his homework every school night during the past week? Yes _____ No _____
   [If yes, go to question #3; if no, go to question #4]

3. (a) If yes to #2, did you reward him? Yes _____ No _____
   (b) Please elaborate. If yes, how did you reward him? If no, why didn't you reward him?

   _____

   _____

4. (a) If no to #2, how many nights did he do his homework? _____
                                                               (write in)
   (b) Were there any particular reasons why he didn't do his homework?

   _____

   _____

Special Interventions/Tasks (Only for this interview)

1. (a) Did you inquire about day care at the community center?
   Yes _____ No _____
   (b) If yes, what did you find out?
   (c) If no, what prevented you from inquiring?

   _____

   _____

intervention is implemented if the client completes both tasks and this provides an index of intervention validity. Moreover, if the client completes these tasks over time, intervention reliability is enhanced.

The open-ended questions about the failure to achieve tasks might be followed by probing questions to determine whether there are external barriers to accomplishing the tasks or any other problems the parent is experiencing. For example, the parent may not understand what "reward" means or may take away the reward if the son misbehaves, although his homework was completed each night. It may turn out that "reward" and the conditions for giving it need to be made more specific, so that the intervention can be more standardized. Corrective actions can take place in the context of the sessions and client compliance data for a specific interview may actually guide the session.

Live Observations to Assess Client Compliance

The practice-researcher is a participant observer when engaged in providing interventions by means of face-to-face contact. Observations can be made to monitor client compliance while interviews are taking place. What can be observed are physical and/or verbal behaviors of the client. Examples are the client's behavior toward the interviewer and significant others, verbal expressions, and responses to worker statements and questions.

The technique of observation involves recording structured or unstructured observations. Similar to structure in interviewing and in questionnaires, structured observations are those that are recorded on predetermined response systems such as scales, questions with response choices, or categories for counting the occurrence of particular behaviors or events (Tripodi and Epstein 1980). In contrast, unstructured observations are not predetermined. The practice-researcher observes a phenomenon, abstracts inferences from the observations, and develops concepts and hypotheses for further exploration and understanding of the phenomenon.

We recommend the use of structured observations, or systematic observation, to monitor client compliance, because it is less costly than unstructured observations, and can provide knowledge about the extent to which interventions are standardized in the context of worker-client interactions. To monitor client compliance, scales or categories that are pertinent to the task assigned to the client should be developed. Suppose that a client is very angry and dissatisfied with his partner, blaming many of his own problems on her. One indicator of the problem is that the client continually makes blaming, negative statements about his partner. As part of the intervention, the worker believes that the client must first change his behavior in the context of the interview situation with the worker. Thus, the client's task is to stop making these negative statements during sessions with the worker. If the client can comply with this in treatment, the worker will next help the man take some responsibility for his own problems. Thus, this is only one of many intervention strategies necessary to improve the client's relationship with his partner.

The process for making systematic observations requires the following:

1. The categories of observation must be operationally defined so they constitute levels of measurement in nominal, ordinal, interval, or ratio scales.
2. The units of observation must be specified. For verbal contents, the units might be the entire interview, segments of interviews, statements, or words. On the other hand, for physical events the units might be restricted to behaviors between the client and another person in the interview, or all persons in the interview at specified segments of time, and so forth.
3. The method for recording needs to be determined. Observations may be tallied during the interview, or at the end of the interview on measurement scales.
4. Interobserver reliability should be established. For example, a brief, five minute segment of an interview could be filmed or taped and independently coded by the worker and the client. The percentage agreement between the worker and the client or the supervisor and the worker could be calculated to indicate the degree of interobserver reliability.

As an example of this process of systematic observation, suppose a parent and her daughter are receiving treatment from a practice-researcher. In assessment interviews, the mother dominates discussion, interrupts her daughter whenever she talks, speaks only negatively about her, and even hits her during the interviews. The worker wants to determine if the mother can learn to control these behaviors during treatment sessions, when the worker is available to prompt, coach, and otherwise assist the mother. If so, they can attempt to generalize this to the family's real life. If not, a different intervention might be instituted. Figure 4.5 provides an example of an observation

FIGURE 4.5
Observation Form

Client identification number _____ Date of interview_____
Interview number _____ Name of practice-researcher _____
Comments: _____
_____

Physical Compliance (Hitting)

Hitting is defined as any physical action by the mother in which she forcefully uses any part of her body to make contact with any part of her daughter's body.

Tally the number of times hitting occurs _____

compliance = 0

Verbal Compliance

Interruption is defined as making comments or engaging in physical actions while the daughter is talking in an attempt to refocus discussion on the mother.

Tally the number of interruptions _____

compliance = 0

[After the interview is completed, make ratings on the scales below.]

Discussion

The daughter dominates discussion (Mother speaks 0% of time)	Daughter and Mother share equally in discussion (Mother speaks 50% of time)	Mother dominates discussion (Mother speaks 100% of time)

| 1 | 2 | 3 | 4 | 5 |

compliance = 3 or 4

Manner of Speaking

Manner of speaking is specified for the mother as positive, neutral, or negative when speaking about her daughter. "Negative" refers to disparaging remarks such as "She's always in trouble," "She's up to no good," "She never helps me," "I don't like her." "Positive" refers to supportive statements such as "She tries very hard," "I love her," "She's been very helpful."

When the mother speaks about her daughter, she usually speaks about her in the following manner:

Negative Manner		Neutral Manner		Positive Manner
1	2	3	4	5

compliance = 3, 4, or 5

form to assess client compliance on the part of the mother during family sessions.

With this observation form, hitting and interruptions can be tallied by the worker during the interview. The units of observation are each instance of those phenomena during the interview. The ratings are made at the end of the interview, with the units of observation identified as the statements of the daughter and her mother. If the units were smaller, say sentences, more precision would be obtained. The procedures would be impractical, however, requiring much more time and expense to complete and possibly interfering to a greater extent with the delivery of intervention.

Data from this form are easily analyzed for client compliance because there are specific behavioral standards to refer to: "compliance" is defined as no hitting, no interruptions, scalar points 3 or 4 for discussion, and scalar points 3, 4, or 5 for manner of speaking. Once there is intervention validity (that is, once client compliance is achieved), the practice-researcher can determine whether client compliance is consistent over time, thereby providing evidence of intervention reliability. In the *comments* section on the form, the practice-researcher can note any special or extenuating circumstances that might have impeded the implementation of the intervention or affected client compliance.

Forms and Questionnaires to Assess Client Compliance

Forms and questionnaires are constructed by following principles for obtaining reliable levels of measurement. Questions and/or statements should represent single thoughts, and be unambiguous, non-biasing, understandable to the respondent, and relevant to its major purpose; while response systems should be clear, mutually exclusive, mutually exhaustive, and logically related to the questions or statements. Our examples of a checklist, interviewing schedules, and an observational form in this chapter and a questionnaire in chapter 3 followed these principles.

Questionnaires and forms are especially well-suited for gathering information between sessions. Although other techniques, such as observations and interviews, will serve the same purpose, the extra costs would be prohibitive. Questionnaires can be given to the client at the end of one session to report on between-session activities and return to the worker at the beginning of the next session. Of course, whether or not the client completes this task also is an index of client compliance.

To illustrate the use of a simple form to examine client compliance, let us refer to a medical social worker's practice with a married couple. The couple has adult children who have families and who live within a radius of fifty miles from their home. The husband, who is older than the wife, is retired. The wife works part-time at the local library and is in good health. The husband has had a heart attack recently, and is an outpatient. At home, he has not followed his medical regimen and he and his wife have increased the frequency of their arguments. Since his heart attack, their social life has diminished, and they seem to be preoccupied by his physical condition and the fear of death. The social worker is seeing them both once every two weeks, and is focusing on their understanding of the illness, his compliance with the medical regimen, and their marital difficulties, which could aggravate his medical condition. The wife has been enlisted to aid in his compliance with the medical regimen. She is to dispense his medicine each day and watch him take it. In addition, she is to take a walk with him for thirty minutes each day. Every night, each spouse is to record the number of arguments they had with each other that day, and the reasons for arguing (see figure 4.6). Also, they each record any social contacts he or she had and what took place. The form depicted in figure 4.6 might be used for the wife. Questions 2 and 3 could be used for the husband as well as the wife. There is compliance with respect to the medical regime to the extent that check marks appear in the appropriate boxes. With seven days of recording, for example, there are 21 boxes to fill. The percentage of client compliance would be the number of boxes checked divided by 21, and this dividend multiplied by 100. For questions 2 and 3 there is compliance for recording a number (0 or higher) since this is regarded as compliance with the task of recording information. Hence for questions 2 and 3 combined, there are 14 possible compliant days and the percentage of compliance is the number of client days

FIGURE 4.6
Form for Determining Client Compliance

Name of client _____

Name of worker _____

Date form is completed _____

Interview number _____

1. Please place a check (✔) in the appropriate box for each day of the week if you give medicine to your spouse, observe him take it, or walk with him for 30 minutes.

	Sunday	Monday	Tuesay	Wednesday	Thursday	Friday	Saturday
Gave Medicine							
Observed him take medicine							
Took 30-minute walk together							

2. (a) During the past week, write in the number of arguments you and your spouse had. Please answer for each day, writing in "0" if you had no arguments.

FIGURE 4.6 (*Continued*)

Number of Arguments: Sun _____ Mon _____ Tues _____ Wed _____ Thurs _____ Fri _____ Sat _____

(b) If you had arguments with your spouse, what were the reasons for them?

_____

_____

3. (a) During the past week, write in the number of social contacts you had with persons other than your spouse. Please answer for each day, writing in "0" if you had no social contacts.

Number of
Social Contacts: Sun _____ Mon _____ Tues _____ Wed _____ Thurs _____ Fri _____ Sat _____

(b) If you had social contacts, what activities were involved?

_____

_____

checked divided by 14, and multiplied by 100. The qualitative and quantitative information in questions 2 and 3 can be used for further assessment as well as for some indication of progress, if there are desirable changes in the frequency of arguments and social contacts.

Forms such as this one must be carefully explained to clients, especially describing how they will be used in subsequent sessions. The analysis of these forms would be the same as analyzing compliance with other data-gathering devices. Hence, intervention reliability could be studied by examining the consistency of client responses over time. If there were several clients with similar objectives, say, dispensing medicine, interventions reliability across clients could be observed. Of course, validity is evident if there is, in fact, compliance.

5. *Designs for Monitoring Client Progress*

We believe that practice-researchers should monitor both client progress and the implementation of an intervention. Monitoring client progress refers to gathering and analyzing information while intervention is taking place, and to decisions about continuing, modifying, or ceasing the intervention. Although it is closely related to monitoring, evaluating an intervention is an analysis of the extent to which intervention goals are attained and, if they are attained, the extent to which goal attainment can be attributed to the intervention. Strategies for evaluating interventions are discussed in the next chapter. Here, our focus is on selected strategies and procedures for analyzing the extent of client progress.

The Monitoring Process

To monitor client progress, the following activities must be carried out:

1. Client goals must be specified;
2. Client progress must be defined;
3. Instruments for observing client progress must be selected or constructed;
4. Strategies for gathering and making inferences about data must be delineated;
5. Data must be gathered and analyzed.

Client Goals

There are three general types of goals in direct practice with clients: change, maintenance, and/or prevention (Blythe and Tripodi 1989).

Change goals are those that refer to changes in client problems or needs. For instance, a client may seek to eliminate his substance abuse. Maintenance goals are expectations about a steady state of behavior once change goals have been realized. Hence, the intervention goal for a client released from a psychiatric hospital to the community may be to maintain the reduction of psychotic symptoms and independent living in the community. Prevention goals also focus on maintaining a steady state of current behavior. For example, a client who had an abusive father may be assessed as being at risk of abusing his child. Although the client hasn't engaged in child abuse, an intervention may be designed to prevent the occurrence of child abuse.

Once the client goals are articulated, the practice-researcher should identify variables relevant to the client goals. This can be done by conceptualizing the relevance of any of the four types of client variables discussed in chapter 2 on measurement: (1) personal and demographic characteristics; (2) moods, feelings, attitudes, beliefs, and values; (3) knowledge, ability, and achievement; and (4) observable behaviors. For example, Type 2 variables related to attitudes toward using condoms and Type 4 variables related to actually practicing safe sex would be relevant to change goals for interventions with an HIV-positive client. Identified variables, as discussed in chapter 3, also can be further specified by appropriate levels of measurement as they pertain to client problems or needs. Thus, variables relevant to client goals can be specified in terms of problem existence, magnitude, duration, or frequency.

Intervention goals can then be delineated in relation to these variables. For example, it might be expected that a client change her behavior from criticizing herself 8 times per day to not criticizing herself at all. A client released from a mental hospital might be expected, with medication, to be free of auditory hallucinations. In essence, the practice-researcher's client goals specify the change (or lack of change, for maintenance and prevention goals) that is expected.

Client Progress

Obviously, client progress cannot be monitored unless the benchmarks of progress are indicated. First, the client goals that are expected are specified. When there are change goals, the expected degree of desirable changes may serve as a benchmark of goal attainment, if it can be determined with a fair degree of reason and accuracy. Workers should not state expected degrees of change if they have little or no information on which to base their expectations. With some client problems, however, the expected degree of change is clear. Sexual abuse, for example, must be eliminated. In contrast, for prevention and maintenance goals, goals are attained only when there are no changes.

Client progress occurs when data register the expected degree of change, or when changes follow the same direction as the expected degree of change. For example, the depressed client may be said to be making progress if his symptoms are eliminated, or if the number of episodes of excessive crying are reduced from 8 times weekly to once a week, so long as the episodes are equally severe. If the client's depression is eliminated, he may receive an intervention to maintain this state of emotional well-being. If the client reverts to depression, his state is said to deteriorate.

The concept of change is central to the notion of client progress or deterioration. We regard the change as a deviation from the current state of the problem or need variable being assessed. This deviation may be assessed by a predetermined degree of change regarded as clinically significant, or by a statistical criterion, such as a statistically significant change in measurements. For some problems, it is highly desirable that the problem be eliminated. Hence, clinically significant change might be said to occur if a supervisor eliminates his abusive, deprecating comments toward his staff when he originally made an average of twelve such comments per week. Or statistically significant change might be found, if there are changes in the patterns of data from a baseline of twelve abusive comments per week to four abusive comments per week.

It is important that the practice-researcher conceptualizes "change," clinically and/or statistically, and then defines progress in terms of that conception of change. This desire for change, of course, is the reason why interventions are implemented. It also provides a frame of reference for studying the degree to which progress is made regarding the ultimate attainment of client goals.

Instruments

In previous chapters, we presented criteria for selecting and developing instruments, along with examples of questionnaires, interview schedules, observation forms, and rating scales. The same principles apply for selecting or developing instruments for measuring progress.

Because it is preferable to obtain repeated measurements over the course of a case, it is important that the practice-researcher pay particularly close attention to test-retest reliability. If available, valid instruments that have good reliability, are efficient to administer, easy to use, and can be completed in short periods of time are preferable. These instruments, known as rapid assessment instruments, are available in the literature. An excellent source book is *Measures for Clinical Practice: A Sourcebook* by Fischer and Corcoran (1994). This book contains over 300 rapid-assessment instruments that can be used for adults, children, couples, and families for problems such as substance abuse, anxiety, family functioning, and interpersonal difficulties. As noted in chapter 3, if there are no standardized instruments that are pertinent to the monitoring of a client's progress, the social worker can develop relatively simple instruments that appear to have content validity and test-retest reliability.

Research Designs

Research designs are logical strategies employed for collecting data and for making inferences about levels of knowledge. When the practitioner is monitoring client progress, designs that will provide descriptive facts about variables related to client problems and/or associational knowledge between interventions and variables of client change (or lack of change) are of interest.

The designs presented here vary along three dimensions: single vs. multiple cases or client units; single vs. multiple measurements; and measurement(s) taken only during the intervention vs. measurements taken before (baseline) and during intervention. These designs are inexpensive to implement, and can determine whether progress is being made while the intervention is taking place. The same designs can analyze progress of one practice-researcher with one client unit (client, group, couple, family) or of one or more practice-researchers with more than one client, such as a caseload. Analysis of client change in a single case can be made if the same client variables are measured repeatedly at different points over time. With multiple clients, average change can be inferred if there is at least one measurement before and one during or after intervention. Research designs also provide the context for selecting procedures to analyze the information gathered about client variables.

Data Analysis

The monitoring process is completed after sufficient data are gathered and analyzed, and considered as inputs for making further decisions about the continuation of the intervention. Three basic strategies can be employed for analyzing data: qualitative matching, graphic analysis, and statistical methods. These relatively simple methods can be used with the four basic research designs for monitoring client progress. These methods incorporate all of the notions of monitoring we have presented. In particular, they are used with reference to intervention goals and client changes.

Basic Research Designs for Monitoring Client Progress

The four designs that we illustrate for the study of client progress with one or more client cases are: During-Intervention Measurement Design, $\overset{0}{X}{}^{1}$; Before/During-Intervention Measurement Design, $0\overset{0}{X}$; During-Intervention Time-Series Design, $\overset{000}{X}$; and Before/During-Intervention Time-Series Design, $000\overset{000}{X}{}^{2}$. Within the context of these designs, qualitative, graphic and statistical analyses will be discussed with respect to their relevance and their application, when appropriate.

Single Case Designs

During-Intervention Measurement Design, $\overset{0}{X}$

The simplest monitoring design for studying a single case is the During-Intervention Design, $\overset{0}{X}$, which consists of obtaining one observation or a set of measurements at one point in time after intervention has been initiated. As examples, there may be a measurement of drug abuse for a client when the goal is abstinence from drugs; an observation of family cohesion in a family that has a goal of staying together; or a measurement of group productivity for a group whose goal is to increase production.

The time measurement is taken should relate to expectations about the intervention and the worker's conception of progress for the client unit in question. If it is expected that progress will be made before the end of the third week, then measurement(s) should be taken at the end of that period. More than one variable might be measured if there are several objectives for the client unit. Suppose we have a family consisting of two parents and an adolescent. As a result of an intervention, it might be expected that family members' attitudes toward each other will be more positive, negotiations between parents and the teenager will increase, and family arguments will decrease after four months of intervention. Accordingly, after four months of intervention the practice-researcher would obtain measurements of family attitudes, communications indicating negotiations between the parents and the teenager, and family arguments.

Because this design takes measurement at only one point in time, there are insufficient data (not enough measurement points) to use graphic analysis or statistical methods. Qualitative matching, however, will provide some information about progress. In qualitative matching, the *actual* measurement is compared with what is *expected*. Hence, there would be an indication of perceived progress if the actual measurement coincides with what is expected. The client may be asked to give his opinion of whether progress has been made on a particular objective by comparing his or her state at the time of measurement with what he or she expected before intervention took place. At its best, this design provides information on the achievement of an expectation. But it also provides an opportunity for unknown response biases, particularly when obtained from self-reports of clients and/or workers. The information is less biasing when behaviors are matched with objectives. For example, one will receive more reliable information by matching an observation of the number of times per week a child hits his classmates during recess with an expectation of his hitting behavior than by asking the child's teacher whether the child has made progress in refraining from hitting other children. This, of course, assumes that the observational data are more reliable and valid than those from self-reports.

The weaknesses of this design are obvious. First, there are no empirical benchmarks; there are no comparable measurements. Moreover, the initial expectations may be too ambitious, especially if there is no clear empirical knowledge of the client's previous measurements on the variable in question. The heavy drinker who has ten drinks or more per day may, for example, reduce his drinking to two drinks per day, which clearly is a large improvement. If the objective is total abstinence and if measurement indicates the consumption of two drinks per day, no progress would be indicated by this design. There would be no way to say that two drinks per day is considerably less than ten drinks per day because that baseline information is not available. In contrast, the objectives may be set too low. For example, a client may exhibit understanding of the connection between her relationship with her father and her relationships with other men after one month of intervention. The actual behavior matches the expected behavior, and this may appear like progress. However, if the client possessed this insight before intervention occurred, it cannot be argued that progress occurred. Again, the practice-researcher can only know this if there is previous information regarding the variable being measured.

Before/During-Intervention Measurement Design, OX

This design has two time points for measurement of the same variable (or set of variables): before the intervention, X, and during intervention, when it is expected that progress will occur. When the goals relate to maintenance or prevention, change is not expected. For a client whose schizophrenia is in remission because of maintenance therapy, the goal might be that he will not relapse (as indicated by extreme agitation, distorted cognition, and auditory hallucinations). Furthermore, assume that he is not expected to relapse for six months. A measurement of agitation made before the maintenance therapy might reveal a low state of agitation. Suppose that six months after maintenance therapy has begun, a second measurement is taken. Employing qualitative matching as the mode of analysis, this design allows for the comparison of two measurements on the same variable, as well as a comparison of the measurement taken during intervention with preestablished expectations of progress. In the above example, if the measurement after six months indicates no relapse, then progress has been made.

Like any other design, the Before/During-Intervention Measurement Design depends on reliable, valid measurements. Test-retest reliability is especially important. If changes in measurement are due to unreliability, one cannot make any inferences about relapse or deterioration. Statistical methods and graphic analyses cannot be used for analysis in this design, because there are not enough data points. Nonetheless, this design allows for a more dependable estimate of progress than the During-Intervention Measurement Design, because there is a benchmark on the variable at baseline (before intervention) that is used for comparison.

With reliable, valid instrumentation, one can obtain a preliminary indication of an association between the intervention and progress toward goals. There simply are not enough data, however, to determine whether there is any stability in the observations. For instance, a client's mood swings may show a reduction comparing two data points. But more data points would be necessary to make reliable inferences of the stability of change.

During-Intervention Time-Series Design, X $\overset{OOO}{}$

The During-Intervention Time-Series Design is comprised of measurements taken at a series of points over time, using the same set of observations while the intervention is being implemented. Usually the points are at equal intervals, such as hours, days, weeks, or months. The minimum number of points required varies according to the type of data analysis employed. Qualitative matching requirements depend on the practice objectives and the preestablished expectations for progress at varying periods of time; a minimum of two or three points is recommended. Graphic analysis can be done with a minimum of three to eight points to estimate whether a visual pattern is linear or nonlinear and represents trends over time. While statistical time-series analysis, requiring up to fifty data observation points, is impractical for most practice research, other statistical procedures such as the C statistic for observing shifts in time-series requires only eight data points (Tryon 1982; Young 1941).

As an example of this design, suppose a school social worker is implementing an intervention to reduce a fifth grade boy's aggressiveness during recess. There were reports of hitting and other aggressive behaviors, but the practice-researcher (school social worker) had no precise data. Due to the need to ensure the safety of the other children, it is necessary to start intervention immediately. Hence, there are no baseline observations before the implementation of intervention. The major practice goal is to eliminate the hitting behavior by helping the boy

1. recognize his aggressive behaviors;
2. identify cues that he is about to become aggressive; and
3. develop better ways of communicating with the other children at recess.

Given the number of aggressive incidents during the first two weeks after seeing the worker, it was believed that the hitting must be significantly reduced after two months and be eliminated at the end of three months, if the child is to continue in this school setting. The worker employs a cognitive-behavioral intervention in weekly meetings with the boy. Instances of hitting are recorded on an observation form by the teacher at recess every day. The variable is the number of hits during a school week. Observations are recorded every week and are recorded in table 5.1. These data can be analyzed by qualitative matching, graphic analysis, or statistical analysis with the C statistic.

Qualitative Matching

In qualitative matching, as with other designs, the practice-researcher compares the data with the preestablished objectives. As assumed by the school social worker, the hitting behavior does occur and it persists for two weeks or more; for weeks 1, 2, 3, and 4, the number of hitting episodes are 10, 10, 9, and 10 respectively. At week 9, after two months, the frequency of hitting episodes has dropped to 4. Whether this is a clinically significant reduction depends on the perceptions or judgments of the worker, the boy's teacher, and the boy himself. It is clear, however, that the data show a reduction; and that could be regarded as a sign of progress. After 13 weeks, at three months, the boy

TABLE 5.1

Number of Hitting Episodes per Week by Fifth-Grade Client During the Intervention Phase

Week	Number of Hitting Episodes
1	10
2	10
3	9
4	10
[1 month] 5	8
6	6
7	6
8	5
[2 months] 9	4
10	3
11	2
12	0
[3 months] 13	0

no longer hits other children. At that point, the worker must decide whether to continue the intervention. The social worker may decide, for example, to continue observations for one more month, and focus on other practice goals. The worker may reduce the frequency of interventions, but continue making observations to determine whether the hitting behavior is permanently eliminated.

Graphic Analysis[3]

Graphic analysis involves graphing observations or data over time. The data from table 5.1 are plotted on figure 5.1 with the frequency of hitting as points on the Y-axis and the week in which the observation was made (time) on the X-axis. For example, for week 1, a line, BC, perpendicular to the X-axis and parallel to the Y-axis is extended until it intersects with a line, AB, that is drawn perpendicular to the Y-axis and parallel to the X-axis. The intersection of those lines is the first point on the graph, with 1 signifying the abscissa and 10 representing the ordinate following the same procedure, the second point is located at the intersection of lines DE and ABE (abscissa = 2; ordinate = 10), etc. After all the points are plotted, straight lines are drawn between successive points at weekly intervals to complete the graph as shown in figure 5.1.

FIGURE **5.1**

Graph of Client's Weekly Frequency of Hitting Other Children During the Intervention Phase

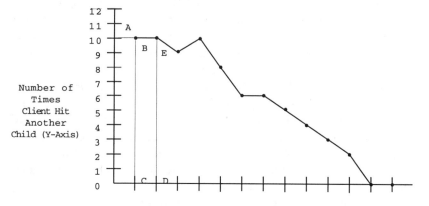

Time in Weeks (X-Axis)

The variable indicative of the client's problem is plotted on the Y-axis. This is the dependent variable that is subject to change during the intervention and can be expressed in units that illustrate problem magnitude, frequency, duration, or existence. The units between adjacent points should be equidistant. Time is plotted on the X-axis, and the units of time also should be equidistant.

Graphic analysis entails describing the visual pattern of the graph in relation to the data. Some typical visual patterns are displayed in figure 5.2. Acceleration indicates an upward change; deceleration, a downward change; horizontal stability indicates no change. Changes have mixed directions in cyclic and nonlinear patterns.

To analyze a graph of time-series data, the social worker should do the following during treatment:

1. Construct the graph;
2. Refer to the practice goals and expectations of progress to decide what data patterns (trends in the data) represent progress or deterioration;
3. Describe the graphic pattern in relation to the practice goals.

Following this process with the case example of hitting behavior for the fifth grade boy and referring to figure 5.1, a downward trend would represent progress, and the goal would be attained when there is no hitting behavior (0 incidents). An upward trend would signify deterioration while a horizontal stable line would represent no change. For figure 5.1, there is no change during the first 2 weeks, followed by a dip in the graph for week 3 and a return to the high point of 10 hitting episodes for week 4. This is followed by a decelerating pattern, indicating positive change, until the goal is accomplished at weeks 12 and 13. Qualitative matching can be combined with graphic analysis to indicate the goal is attained at 3 months (13 weeks). Moreover, at two months (9 weeks) there seems to be a clinically significant change: the number of hitting episodes has dropped from 10 to 4. Again, clinical significance would have to be defined a priori in relation to expectations for the particular client by the worker and possibly significant others such as the teacher. The graphed data depicting numbers and trends should provide information to assist in determining clinical significance. Other variables in the client's home and school environments that impede or facilitate progress may influence the worker's judgments of clinical significance.

FIGURE 5.2
Visual Graphic Patterns

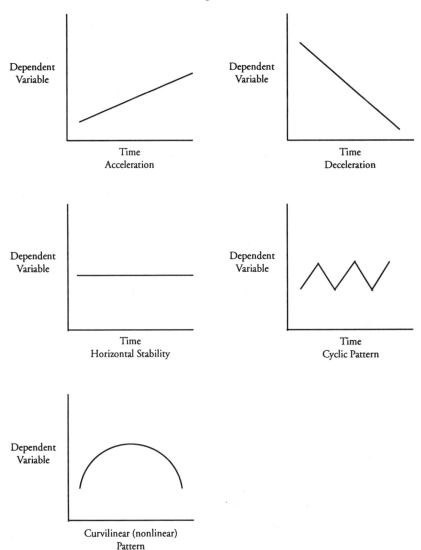

Dependent
Variable

Time
Acceleration

Dependent
Variable

Time
Deceleration

Dependent
Variable

Time
Horizontal Stability

Dependent
Variable

Time
Cyclic Pattern

Dependent
Variable

Curvilinear (nonlinear)
Pattern

Statistical Analysis

Statistical analysis can be used with the During-Intervention-Time-Series Design to determine whether there is a statistically significant change in time-series data. If there is a statistically significant change, it means that there are differences in the magnitude and/or slope of the data over time and these differences are not likely to have occurred on a chance basis at some designated level of probability. For example, a significance level of .05 indicates that a difference is not likely to occur by chance alone more than 5 times in 100.[4] Essentially, statistical analysis provides a criterion for determining whether there is a statistical change in the time-series. If through graphic analysis, one observes a trend suggesting change in a clinically desirable direction, then the achievement of statistical significance can be regarded as an indication of progress in the desirable direction.

The statistical procedure for the C statistic was first described by Young (1941). It was employed by Tryon (1982) for evaluating treatment interventions and by Fitz and Tryon (1989) for evaluating clinical programs. The procedures presented here are adapted from the presentation of Fitz and Tryon (1989). The C statistic requires a minimum of eight data points, and is converted to a Z statistic by dividing by the standard error of C.

To illustrate the use of the C statistic, return to our example of the young student having difficulty with his aggressive behavior in school. Suppose that the school social worker, observing a downward trend in a desirable clinical direction (that is, toward the ultimate goal of eliminating hitting behavior) at the end of 9 weeks wants to determine if the shift in the time-series is statistically significant. Table 5.2 contains all the data for making the necessary calculations to determine statistical significance.

Referring to table 5.2, statistical significance is determined by following these steps:

TABLE 5.2

Data for Calculating C, S_c, and Z Statistics for a Time-Series with 9 Data Points During Intervention

Weeks	Number of Hitting Episodes (0)	$(0_i - 0_{i+1})^2$	$(0 - \bar{0})^2$
1	10		$2.45^2 = 6.00$
2	10	0	$2.45^2 = 6.00$
3	9	1	$1.45^2 = 2.10$
4	10	1	$2.45^2 = 6.00$
5	8	4	$.45^2 = 0.20$
6	6	4	$1.55^2 = 2.40$
7	6	0	$1.55^2 = 2.40$
8	5	1	$2.55^2 = 6.50$
9	4	1	$3.55^2 = 12.60$
	$\Sigma 0 = 68$	$\Sigma(0_i - 0_{i+1})^2 = 12$	$\Sigma(0 - \bar{0})^2 = 44.20$

1. Record the basic data in columns 1 and 2. The data that are recorded for this example are the first nine points in the time-series because the social worker is interested in determining
whether there is statistical significance at 2 months.
2. Add all the observations (number of hitting episodes) in column 2 to obtain $\Sigma 0$ (68 in this case).
3. Calculate the average, or arithmetic mean ($\bar{0}$), of the observations. N refers to the number of observations, or data points.

$$\bar{0} = \frac{\Sigma 0}{N} = \frac{68}{9} = 7.55$$

4. Obtain the figures for column 3 by following this process. Start-
ing at the observation for week 1 in column 2 which is 10, subtract the next observation from it, which also is 10. $10-10=0$.
Then, multiply the result by itself, (that is, 0 times 0), to obtain the first figure (0) for column 3. Repeat the process using
the observations for the second and third week, $(10-9)^2 = 1$, to
obtain the second figure. Repeat the process again with the observations for the third and fourth weeks, $(9-10)^2 = 1$ to obtain
the third figure in column 3. Continue this process until the
last two observations have been manipulated in this manner.
5. Add all the figures in column 3 to obtain $\Sigma(0_i - O_{i+1})^2$, which is
12.
6. To obtain the figures for column 4, for each observation in column 1 subtract the arithmetic mean, $\bar{0}$, and multiply that result
by itself; that is, square it. Using the formula $\Sigma(0-\bar{0})^2$, for week
1, $(10-7.55)^2 = 6.00$ (rounded to the nearest hundredth). The
second figure for column 4 is also $(10-7.55)^2 = 6.00$. For the
third week, $(9-7.55)^2 = 2.10$. Continue this process for each of
the 9 weeks.
7. Add all the figures in column 4 to obtain $\Sigma(0-\bar{0})^2$, or 44.20.
8. Calculate C using the formula below.

$$C = 1 - \frac{\Sigma(0_i - 0_{i+1})^2}{2\Sigma(0-\bar{0})^2} = 1 - \frac{12}{2(44.20)} = 0.86$$

9. Calculate S_c, the standard error of C, using the following
formula.

$$S_c = \sqrt{\frac{N-2}{(N-1)(N+1)}} = \sqrt{\frac{9-2}{(9-1)(9+1)}}$$

$$S_c = \sqrt{\frac{7}{80}} = 0.30$$

10. Finally, convert the C statistic to a Z statistic.

$$Z = \frac{C}{S_c} = \frac{0.86}{0.30} = 2.87$$

11. Determine whether there is statistical significance. For any size of N (from the minimum of 8 on up), if Z is greater than 1.64, there is statistical significance beyond the .05 level of probability.

As a result of these calculations, the practice-researcher can state that there is a statistical shift in the time-series after 13 weeks of intervention and that the data are consistent with the goal of obtaining significant progress in the reduction of hitting behavior.

Before/During-Intervention Time-Series Design, 000 X^{000}

This design includes a time-series of observations made before the introduction of the intervention, 000, followed by the intervention and a time-series of observations during the intervention, X^{000}. Essentially, it adds a baseline to the During-Intervention Time-Series Design. This allows the practice-researcher to compare observations during intervention with those taken before the intervention, making it possible to suggest an association between the intervention and any observed changes in the time-series. The baseline, or time-series taken before the intervention, is an assessment period during which the extent and persistence of the problem can be determined, as indicated by the variable being measured. Ideally, an intervention is implemented only if the baseline provides evidence of a persistent problem. The desired number of baseline observations is three or more, with the exact number depending on the mode of analysis employed. In general, this design leads to clearer interpretations if the baseline has a graphic pattern that is horizontally stable.

Baseline data are extremely useful for judging progress in social work practice. Although it is not always possible to collect baseline data, there are many instances where such data may be available. Data might be gathered during a lengthy period of assessment when intervention is not introduced because it is not clear what the problem is or because a different problem is being addressed. Sometimes very good records are available from an agency which had previous contact with a client. Attendance records and grades in school settings or information on behavioral and emotional problems from residential facilities are examples. While clients are on waiting lists for services, it may be possible to collect data. When data are of an extreme nature, it may be possible to reliably reconstruct them by recall. Child abuse, battering, heavy alcohol or drug use, angry outbursts, and purging are just a few examples.

Let us return to the data in table 5.1, which contains a time-series of hitting behaviors per week by a fifth grade boy during intervention. To elaborate the Before-During-Intervention Time-Series Design, let us assume that there also are data at baseline for 9 weeks, as shown in table 5.3. Referring to tables 5.1 and 5.3, we shall illustrate how qualitative matching, graphic analysis, or statistical analysis can be employed with the Before/During-Intervention Time-Series Design.

Qualitative Matching

Recall that qualitative matching involves comparing the data with preestablished objectives. At baseline, hitting behavior ranges from 10–12 episodes over the 9 weeks. There appears to be no major shift in the data. During intervention, the data ranges from 10 to 0 at 13 weeks (see table 5.1).

If progress had been defined as a significant reduction at 5 weeks, then there is no progress during baseline. There is, however, progress at intervention. Compared to baseline, the time-series data during

TABLE 5.3

Number of Hitting Episodes Per Week by Fifth-Grade Client Before Intervention

Week	Number of Hitting Episodes
1	11
2	12
3	12
4	12
5	10
6	10
7	12
8	11
9	10

intervention show less undesirable behavior. Hence, it can be inferred that progress has been made During-Intervention. In comparison to the preintervention (preestablished) objective of eliminating hitting behavior, it is observed that the goal has been achieved at 12 weeks of intervention (refer to table 5.1).

Thus qualitative matching can be done in two ways with this design. The observations at intervention can be matched with those at baseline, with the notion that there is progress when desirable behaviors appear more often during intervention than during the baseline period. Likewise, the observations at intervention can be matched with the expectations of intervention, including when changes are expected to take place, if at all.

Graphic Analysis

In graphic analysis, the practice-researcher constructs a graph to represent observations at baseline and during intervention. The patterns at baseline and intervention are described. These patterns are compared and judgments of progress are made in reference to any apparent shifts in the time-series associated with the intervention.

To illustrate this, data from tables 5.1 and 5.3 are plotted to construct the graph shown in figure 5.3. Points are plotted in the same manner as for figure 5.1.

The pattern at baseline appears to be horizontal and possibly cyclic. It shows a high frequency of persistent hitting behavior. It is not clear whether the hitting behavior for weeks 8 and 9 (11 and

FIGURE 5.3

Graph of Client's Weekly Frequency of Hitting Other Children During Baseline and Intervention

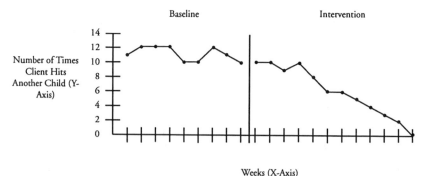

10 hits respectively) indicates a downward trend or simply is part of a cycle. During intervention, the pattern is clearly one of deceleration and of stability in so far as there is little variation from the downward trend. Comparing patterns at intervention and baseline, it clearly appears that more progress is made with intervention than without it.

Changes in time-series can be observed in magnitude as well as in slope (accelerating, horizontal, or decelerating patterns). The practice-researcher should look for possible similarities and differences in magnitude and slope between baseline and intervention time-series. Figure 5.4 represents comparisons between baseline and intervention that show no change. Line AB is decelerating with decreasing magnitude at the same slope during intervention and baseline. Line A_1B_1 is horizontally stable with no change in slope or magnitude in either phase. Line A_2B_2 is accelerating with increasing magnitude at the same rate during the baseline and intervention periods.

Illustrative changes in magnitude, showing change, are depicted in figure 5.5. At intervention, line AB is decelerating at the same rate as at baseline, but decreases in magnitude compared to baseline.

FIGURE 5.4

Graphs Showing No Change Between Baseline and Intervention

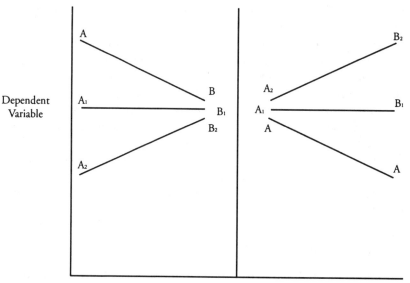

Dependent
Variable

Time

FIGURE 5.5

Graphs Showing No Change in Magnitude Between Baseline and Intervention

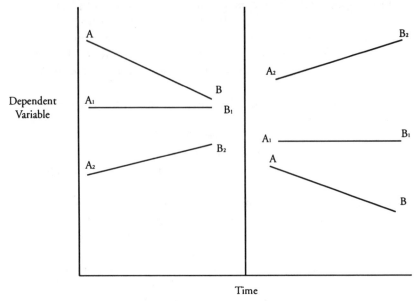

Time

Therefore, it signifies a change in the time-series at the point at which intervention was introduced. Line A_1B_1 is horizontally stable at intervention and at baseline, but it also has decreased in magnitude. In contrast, line A_2B_2 has increased in magnitude although it is increasing at the same slope at intervention and at baseline.

figure 5.6 shows possible changes in slope for horizontal, decelerating, and accelerating patterns. Obviously, depending on the treatment goals, some changes are not desirable and would indicate deterioration rather than progress. If at baseline, for instance, there is a horizontal stable pattern at magnitude X and during intervention then is an accelerating pattern that increases to 2X, then the magnitude has doubled. And if the dependent variable is undesirable, say suicidal ideation, then the graphic analysis would show increasing suicidal ideation appears to be associated with the intervention. The practice-researcher should then consider withdrawing or modifying that intervention.

Statistical Analysis

This section presents statistical techniques for analyzing data from the Before/During-Intervention Time-Series Design. The selection

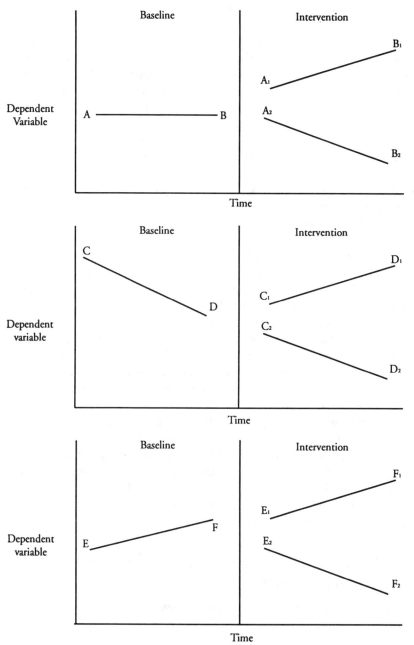

FIGURE 5.6
Graphs Showing No Change in Magnitude Between

of technique depends, in part, on whether the time-series in the baseline is horizontal. If so, the C statistic, along with the C_s and Z statistic, Shewart Chart Analysis, or the Binomial Test for Horizontal Baselines can be used. If there is no horizontal stability, the Celeration Line or a Modified C statistic can be employed. Each method is described in terms of the Before/During-Intervention Time-Series Design and an illustrative calculation is explained.

One method of determining whether there is horizontal stability at baseline is to use the C statistic to test for statistically significant changes. If there is statistically significant change, then there is no horizontal stability. If there is no indication of significant shifts in the time series, then horizontal stability can be inferred. The C statistic takes into account changes in both slope and magnitude. To compute the C statistic, follow the procedures illustrated in the text accompanying table 5.2.

Returning to the student who hit classmates at recess, both qualitative matching and graphic analysis suggest that progress is made with the intervention. Will statistical analysis suggest the same conclusion? First, it must be determined if the baseline is horizontal, so that a statistical technique can be selected. Table 5.4 provides the calculation for the C, S_c, and Z statistics for the baseline data presented in table 5.3. There, Z = .66, which is considerably less than the value of 1.64 that must be surpassed to achieve statistical significance at the .05 level of probability. Hence, the data in this example appear to have horizontal stability.

As indicated above, three different statistical procedures can be employed to determine whether the time-series in intervention is statistically different from the time-series at baseline when there is horizontal stability. If a statistically significant shift in the time series is observed, there is evidence of an association between the intervention and the changes observed in the dependent variable. These three procedures are discussed in the following section.

Methods for Inferring Changes in Time Series with Horizontal Baselines

The C Statistic and Its Associated S_c and Z statistics

The calculation for these statistics are carried out as above, using the intervention data (refer to table 5.2 and the calculations based on those data). If there is a statistical shift during intervention and not at

TABLE 5.4

Data and Calculations for C, S_c, and Z Statistics for a Time-Series with 9 Data Points Before Intervention (Baseline)

Weeks	Number of Hitting Episodes (0)	$(0_i - 0_{i+1})^2$	$(0 - \bar{0})^2$
1	11		$.11^2 = .01$
2	12	1	$.82^2 = .79$
3	12	0	$.89^2 = .79$
4	12	0	$.89^2 = .79$
5	10	4	$1.11^2 = 1.23$
6	10	0	$1.11^2 = 1.23$
7	12	4	$.89^2 = .79$
8	11	1	$.11^2 = .01$
9	10	1	$1.11^2 = 1.23$
	$\Sigma 0 = 100$	$\Sigma(0_i - 0_{i+1})^2 = 11$	$\Sigma(0 - \bar{0})^2 = 6.87$

$$\bar{0} = \frac{\Sigma 0}{N} = \frac{100}{9} = 11.11$$

$$C = 1 - \frac{\Sigma(0_i - 0_{i+1})^2}{2\Sigma(0 - \bar{0})^2} = 1 - \frac{11}{2(6.87)} = 0.20$$

$$S_C = \sqrt{\frac{N-2}{(N-1)(N+1)}} = \sqrt{\frac{9-2}{(9-1)(9+1)}} = 0.30$$

$$Z = \frac{C}{S_C} = \frac{0.20}{0.30} = .66$$

baseline, an association between the dependent variable and the introduction of the intervention is indicated. If the change takes a desirable direction, progress is indicated. Conversely, an undesirable change represents deterioration. To compute C, the minimum number of points in the time series is eight. This statistic cannot be computed when there is no variability in the observations; that is, the variance, $\Sigma(0 - \bar{0})^2/N - 1 = 0$. C reflects shifts both in slope and in magnitude. If there is no statistical significance, then there is no statistical evidence of change.

Previous calculations, based on the data on hitting episodes, found no significant shift in the baseline, but a significant shift in the intervention time-series. Moreover, the slope is in the desired direction, suggesting a reduction in hitting. Therefore, we have an indication of an association between the intervention and the reduction in hitting.

Shewart Chart Analysis

The Shewart Chart Analysis (Gottman and Leiblum 1974) involves determining limits based on the baseline data that, if exceeded by observations during the intervention phase, indicate statistical significance for those intervention observations. This procedure should be employed only when there is a horizontal baseline. Even then, Shewart Chart Analysis only provides a rough criterion of statistically significant changes, because there is no assurance that the time-series observations are independent from each other and are normally distributed, especially when a small number of data points form the time-series.[5] The procedure can be employed with baselines of five to ten data points, but with the understanding that this is a rough approximation to statistical significance.

The following steps should be taken to conduct a Shewart Chart Analysis:

1. Compute the arithmetic mean, $\bar{0} = \Sigma 0/N$, of the observations at baseline.
2. Compute the standard deviation, which is an index of variation. It is calculated by taking the square root of the variance of the observations, $\Sigma(0-\bar{0})^2/N-1$.
3. Multiply the standard deviation by 2.
4. Add the value obtained in Step 3 to the arithmetic mean. This is the upper limit.
5. Subtract the value obtained in Step 3 from the arithmetic mean. This is the lower limit.
6. Plot the upper and lower limits on a graph and draw horizontal lines parallel to the X-axis through each value. Extend the lines beyond baseline through the intervention phase of the graph. Any points that are outside of those limits are statistically significant beyond the .05 level of probability.

Turning again to the data on hitting episodes, table 5.5 uses the baseline data to calculate the limits for the Shewart Chart Analysis. Figure 5.7 presents the Shewart Chart Analysis on the graph of baseline and intervention data. Referring to figure 5.7, the limiting lines of $\bar{0}+2SD$ and $\bar{0}-2SD$ are extended from baseline through intervention. Any observations that occur below 9.25 indicate statistically significant progress at the .05 level. Thus, at the fifth week of intervention and beyond there are statistically significant changes in the desired direction and progress is clearly observable at 9 weeks in accordance with

TABLE 5.5
Computations for Shewart Chart Analysis Using Baseline Data on
Hitting Episodes

Weeks	Number of Hitting Episodes (0)	$(0 - \bar{0})$	$(0 - \bar{0})^2$
1	11	$-.11$	.01
2	12	.89	.79
3	12	.89	.79
4	12	.89	.79
5	10	-1.11	1.23
6	10	-1.11	1.23
7	12	.89	.79
8	11	$-.11$	.01
9	10	-1.11	1.23
	$\Sigma 0 = 10.0$		$\Sigma(0 - \bar{0})^2 = 6.87$

$$\bar{0} = \frac{\Sigma 0}{N} = \frac{100}{9} = 11.11$$

$$variance = \frac{\Sigma(0 - \bar{0})^2}{N-1} = \frac{6.87}{9-1} = 0.86$$

standard deviation $= SD = \sqrt{variance} = \sqrt{0.86} = 0.93$

$2\,SD = 1.86$

$\bar{0} + 2SD = 11.11 + 1.86 = 12.97$ (upper limit)

$\bar{0} - 2SD = 11.11 - 1.86 = 9.25$ (lower limit)

expectations that the client would improve by this time. Note that observations below the lower limit indicate progress because the treatment goal involves reducing or eliminating the occurrence of the dependent variable. If observations had been noted above the upper limit (12.97), these would have indicated statistically significant change in an undesirable direction or evidence of deterioration.

The Binomial Test for Horizontal Baselines

This test is a widely used statistic and requires fewer assumptions than does the Shewart Chart procedure, which is based on a normal distribution (Blythe and Tripodi 1989). For the Binomial Test, at least five observations must be collected during intervention. We also recommend that at least five observations be taken at baseline, although the procedure could be carried out with as few as three observations at baseline. The Binomial Test is based on the assumption that progress is equally likely at each observation point during intervention. During intervention, *progress* is defined as observations that occur during inter-

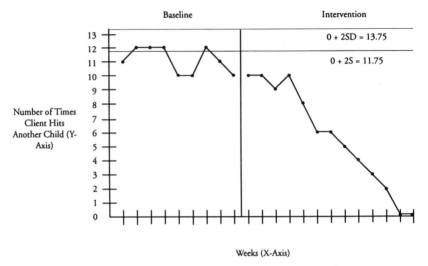

FIGURE 5.7

FIGURE **5.7**

Graph of Client's Weekly Frequency of Hitting Other Children During Baseline and Intervention: Shewart Chart Analysis

vention and are below the median of the observations at baseline (when *progress* is defined as deceleration). Conversely, no progress or deterioration is defined as intervention observations that take place above the median (that is, in an undesirable direction).

The Binomial Test is relatively easy to calculate, using the following steps.

1. Determine the median of observations at baseline. The median is the point at which 50 percent of the observations in a distribution lie above and 50 percent lie below. To calculate the median of the baseline, rank-order all the observations in the baseline. Referring to table 5.5, the observations are rank-ordered from the highest to the lowest as follows: 12, 12, 12, 12, 11, 11, 10, 10, 10. The median is the fifth observation, 11, since there are 4 observations above and 4 observations below it. If there are an even number of observations, the median is the average of the two middle points. In a distribution of four observations, 10, 9, 8, and 7, the median is the average of 9 and 8, or 8.5.

2. Draw a line through the median value parallel to the X-axis and extend it through the intervention period (see figure 5.8).

3. Determine the number of observations during intervention that are either above or below the median. Do not include observations that are exactly at the median. If the practice-researcher is interested in determining progress throughout the entire 13 weeks of intervention, then all 13 observations would be exam-

ined. If preestablished expectations about change taking place after 9 weeks of intervention were being studied, then nine observations would be involved.

4. Count the number of observations that show progress. Since all of the observations at interventions are below the median, there are 9 observations that show progress at 9 weeks, and 13 observations that show progress at 13 weeks.

5. Refer to table 5.6. Enter the first column at the number of intervention observations being considered (9 or 13 in this case). Read across to find the minimum number of observations which will indicate progress at a statistically significant level with $p \leq .05$. For 9 observations, 8 would show progress, while for 13 observations, 11 should show progress. If the number of observations on the desired side of the median is equal to or greater than the minimum number required for statistical significance, there is evidence of progress and of an association between the intervention and changes on the dependent variable. In our example, statistically significant progress is shown at 9 weeks as well as at 13 weeks.

Methods for Inferring Accelerating or Decelerating Changes in a Time-Series

The preceding statistical procedures should only be employed when there is horizontal stability. Without horizontal stability, they would indicate statistically significant results even though there were no changes between the slopes of deceleration or acceleration at intervention compared with the baseline time-series. Two procedures that

FIGURE 5.8

Graph of Client's Weekly Frequency of Hitting Other Children During Baseline and Intervention; Binomial Test

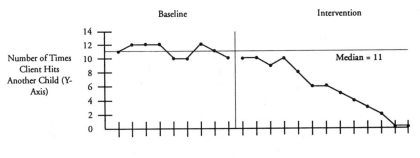

TABLE 5.6

Minimum Number of Observations Required to Show Progress at the .05 Level of Statistical Significance with the Binomial Statistic

Number of Observations During Intervention	Minimum Number of Observations That Must Show Progress
5*	5
6	6
7	7
8	7
9	8
10	9
11	9
12	10
13	11
14	11
15	12
16	12
17	13
18	14
19	14
20	15
21	16
22	16
23	17
24	17
25	18

*This is the smallest number of observations that can be used to evaluate statistical significance. (Derived and adapted from table 5.1 of Blythe and Tripodi (1989), *Measurement in Direct Practice*, Newbury Park, Ca.: Sage, p. 130, and from table IV.B of Walker and Lev (1953), *Statistical Inference*, New York: Holt, p. 48.

can detect shifts in slope or trends from baseline to intervention are the Celeration Line Technique and a modification of the C statistic.

The Celeration Line Technique

This technique (Blythe and Tripodi 1989) is a modification of the description provided by Gingerich and Feyerherm (1979). It applies the Binomial Test to accelerating or decelerating trend lines, following procedures similar to the Binomial Test for Horizontal Baselines.

Suppose that a practice-researcher is treating a client who has just escaped from Haiti to seek refuge in the United States after a dangerous journey over land and water. The client continues to experience anxiety attacks, months after reaching safety, particularly when she is away from her apartment or family. The anxiety attacks are so intense that the client is having difficulty attending English language classes and cleaning houses, which is an important source of income for her family. While the client was being treated for another problem, the social worker instructed her to collect baseline data on her anxiety attacks. The baseline is mildly decelerating and has the following frequency of anxiety attacks for weeks one through nine: 14, 14, 13, 13, 12, 13, 12, 11, 11. During a thirteen-week intervention, the client continued to record the frequency of the anxiety attacks. Initially, the attacks were fairly frequent, but they decreased over time. The frequency of the anxiety attacks during the thirteen weeks of intervention was: 10, 9, 10, 10, 9, 7, 7, 5, 3, 1, 1, 0, 0. The steps for calculating the celeration line are as follows.

1. Plot baseline and intervention observations as in figure 5.9.
2. Divide the baseline into 4 parts by dividing it at the median (½) and again dividing each half at its median (¼ and ¾) as shown in figure 5.9. The minimum number of baseline data points for which this procedure is possible is 5. But, 7–10 observations are preferable because it is difficult to observe accurate trends with fewer observations.
3. Calculate the means for each half of the baseline. Plot the computed mean value for the first half on the ¼ line and for the second half on the ¾ line. Connect these two points to form a straight line which is the celeration line.
4. Extend the celeration line into the intervention phase.
5. Count the number of observations during intervention that are not on the celeration line. Using the same logic as the Binomial Test for Horizontal Baselines, it can be assumed that observations subsequent to baseline are equally likely to occur above or below the celeration line. If there is a statistical change in the desired direction (below the celeration line in this example), this can be regarded as progress.
6. Count the number of observations that show evidence of progress. Figure 5.9 reveals 13 observations that indicate progress.
7. Refer to table 5.6 and locate the number of observations in column 1 and the corresponding minimum required number of observations that show progress in column 2. There is statistical significance at the .05 level of probability if the actual number of observations showing progress is equal to or greater than the number required. For this client, 11 observations are required to show statistical significance at 13 weeks. Thus, the degree of progress is statistically significant.

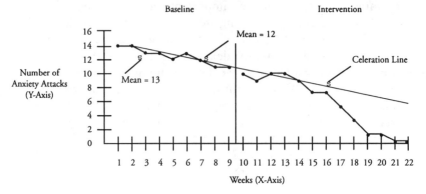

FIGURE **5.9**

Graph of Client's Weekly Frequency of Anxiety Attacks During Baseline and Intervention

The C Statistic for Comparing Trends

The C statistic can be used for comparing trends if there are the same number of observations at baseline as at intervention and if the slope or rates of celeration for the time-series at baseline and at intervention are not identical (Fitz and Tryon 1989). To determine whether slopes of baseline data and intervention data are the same, follow these steps:

1. Construct a celeration line for baseline time-series data.
2. Construct a celeration line for intervention time-series data.
3. Draw two sets of intersecting X- and Y-axes as below on graph paper. The units for time and the dependent variable should be equal.

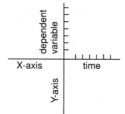

4. Plot the celeration lines on the intersecting X- and Y-axes.

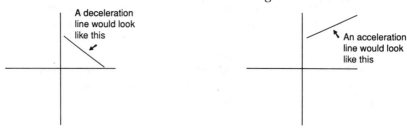

5. Extend the celeration lines to intersect the X- and Y-axes, forming a triangle ABC.

6. The ratio of AB to BC is the slope; it is the tangent of angle alpha and by referring to natural trigometric functions the angle alpha can be determined. For example, for AB/AC = 1, alpha $(\alpha) = 45°$; for 1.73, $\alpha = 60°$; and for .57, $\alpha = 30°$. It is not necessary to convert the slope to alpha, however, since they can be compared directly.
7. Determine whether the slopes are identical. They are not identical if they take opposite directions; that is, if one is accelerating and the other is descending. They are not identical if the ratios of AB/BC for the baseline time-series and the intervention time-series data differ. If the ratios differ by at least .05 (for instance, .55 vs. .60), they can be regarded as nonidentical since their corresponding alpha's will differ, in general, by at least 1 or 2 degrees.

If the slopes are not identical, the C statistic can be calculated. The procedure for using the C statistic is illustrated in table 5.7, using the data on the client's anxiety attacks before and during the first nine weeks of intervention. The method is similar to that presented earlier, except that 0 is calculated by subtracting the number of anxiety attacks for the first week of intervention from the number experienced in the first week of baseline (see the fourth column). This continues for each set of weeks. Since the Z value, 1.93, is greater than 1.64, the data indicate there is a statistically significant change from a mild rate of deceleration to a steeper one at intervention, thereby indicating progress at nine weeks.

Group Designs

Group designs involve more than one subject (client, group, or family) and are appropriate for monitoring progress when there are similar treatment goals for several clients. In this section, the same four

TABLE 5.7

Data and Calculations for C, S_c, and Z Statistics for Trend Comparisons at Baseline and at Intervention

Week of Observation	Number of Anxiety Attacks at Baseline O_1	Number of Anxiety Attacks at Intervention O_2	$O = O_1 - O_2$	$(O_i - O_{i+1})^2$	$(O - \bar{O})^2$
1	14	10	4		.61
2	14	9	5	1	.05
3	13	10	3	4	3.17
4	13	10	3	0	3.17
5	12	9	3	0	3.17
6	13	7	6	9	1.49
7	12	7	5	1	.05
8	11	5	6	1	1.49
9	11	3	8	4	10.37
			$\Sigma O = 43$	$\Sigma(O_i - O_{i+1})^2$ $= 20$	$\Sigma(O - \bar{O})^2$ $= 23.57$

$$\bar{O} = \frac{\Sigma O}{N} = \frac{43}{9} = 4.78$$

$$\frac{1 - \Sigma(O_i - O_{i+1})^2}{2\Sigma(O - \bar{O})^2} = C = 1 - \frac{20}{2(23.57)} = .58$$

$$S_c = \sqrt{\frac{N-2}{(N-1)(N+1)}} = \sqrt{\frac{9-2}{(9-1)(9+1)}} = 0.30$$

$$Z = \frac{C}{S_c} = \frac{0.58}{0.30} = 1.93$$

designs that were previously presented for monitoring progress with single cases are applied to groups of clients. Differences in the units of analysis and in data analyses are noted.

During-Intervention Group Measurement Design, X

This design consists of one observation or set of measurements during intervention for a multiple number of clients for whom there are similar practice goals. For example, a practice-researcher may have established a treatment goal to increase the self-concept of twenty fourth-grade children who appeared to be bored or disinterested in school and are judged as being at a high risk for delinquency. The intervention package consists of a planned series of small group discussions, films, field trips, and in-class group activities. After three months of intervention, it is expected that children will be interested in classroom activities and will have average self-concept scores as measured by Lipsitt's Self-Concept Scale for Children (Corcoran and Fischer 1987). The practice-researcher could specify what will indicate progress and when it is expected to occur. For example, after two months of intervention the worker might expect that at least 50 percent of the children will be judged by their teachers to be interested in classroom activities, and will have self-concept scores close to the norms of average self-concept scores.

Graphic analysis is not possible with this design because there is only one observation point. The measurements obtained at one period of time during intervention can be compared with an expectation of progress made before the intervention, using qualitative matching. In addition, the distributions of scores for the twenty children can be described statistically. As noted with single-case designs, the During-Intervention Group Measurement Design cannot be employed to infer associations between the intervention and client changes because client changes cannot be observed since there are no empirical bench marks or baseline measures.

Suppose that after two months of intervention, teachers judged that 40 percent of the children were interested in classroom activities. Empirical data for several clients, such as the array of self-concept scores, should be summarized with descriptive statistics. The interest in classroom activities is described by a simple descriptive statistic, the percentage of students interested. This was obtained by dividing the number of students interested, 8, by the total possible number of students receiving the intervention, 20, and multiplying the result by 100. Thus, $8/20 \times 100 = 40$ percent. This could also be expressed as a proportion, $8/20 = .4$.

By employing qualitative matching, it is apparent that the expectation of 50 percent interest was not attained. Unfortunately, the children's interest before intervention is not known, so progress cannot be inferred. Moreover, it is possible that there is unreliability in the teacher's judgments. With no knowledge of inter-observer reliability, possible inferences are further restricted.

Statistics commonly used to describe an array of data for small sample sizes (less than 30) are average measures and their variability, such as medians, means, ranges, variances, and standard deviations. For the array of data in this example, refer to table 5.8 where these measures are calculated for the scores on the Self-Concept Scale for Children. The first step in calculation is to arrange the observations

TABLE 5.8

Computation of Descriptive Statistics for Scores on the Self-Concept Scale for Children

Observations (0)	$(0-\bar{0})$	$(0-\bar{0})^2$
80	6.65	44.22
79	5.65	31.92
79	5.65	31.92
78	4.65	21.62
78	4.65	21.62
78	4.65	21.62
76	2.65	7.02
76	2.65	7.02
75	1.65	2.72
75	1.65	2.72
75	1.65	2.72
74	0.65	0.42
74	0.65	0.42
73	-0.35	0.12
72	-1.35	1.82
70	-3.35	11.22
68	-5.35	28.62
64	-9.35	87.42
63	-10.35	107.12
60	-13.35	178.22
$\Sigma 0 = 1467$		$\Sigma(0-\bar{0})^2 = 610.50$

$$median = mdn = \frac{75+75}{2} = 75 \qquad range = 80 - 60 = 20$$

$$\bar{0} = \frac{\Sigma 0}{N} = \frac{1467}{20} = 73.35$$

$$variance = \frac{\Sigma(0-\bar{0})^2}{N-1} = \frac{610.50}{19} = 32.13 \qquad SD = \sqrt{variance} = 5.67$$

or scores by rank order. The median can then be computed as that point which is the halfway point in the distribution. Here, the median is the average of the tenth and eleventh scores going down from 80 or $75+75/2=75$. The range is the difference between the lowest and the highest scores which is $80-60=20$ in our example. The mean is 73.35, the variance is 32.13, and the standard deviation (SD) is 5.67. The variance and standard deviation are indices of variation. The higher they are, the greater the variation. And, when the variance is zero, all of the scores are identical.

Having obtained these data, the practice-researcher can speak of the average self-concept scores among the 20 children. Moreover, the mean, 73.35, can be compared with the average score obtained when the Scale's author administered it to 498 children. This average was 86.75, with a possible range of 22 to 110, and lower scores indicating lower self-concept. After 2 months of intervention, the children in this classroom sample have a lower score than the average of those children for whom normative data are available.

Before/During-Intervention Group Design, $0\ X^0$

This design includes measurements for multiple subjects before intervention and at some point during intervention. In addition to qualitative matching of observations taken during intervention with preestablished expectations, the practice-researcher can statistically compare observations over two points in time. For the group of children described above, suppose that prior to intervention, 20 percent of the students were interested in classroom activities and their average score on the Self-Concept Scale for Children was 62.70. It can be observed that there is an increase in classroom interest (from 20 percent to 40 percent) and in self-concept from an average score of 62.70 to 73.35. Statistical analysis can determine whether the observed changes are statistically significant, as an indication of progress. This is the fundamental difference between single-case and group designs of this type. Change can be statistically analyzed with a group design since there are a multiple number of subjects, but not with the single case in the Before/During-Intervention Design.

McNemar's Chi-Square Test and Wilcoxon's Matched-Pairs Signed-Rank Test are two statistical tests that can analyze data from the Before/During-Intervention Group Design. Both are demonstrated here.

McNemar's Chi-Square Test for Change

This test can be used to determine changes in proportions in one sample (Hinkle, Wiersma, and Jurs 1988). To apply McNemar's Chi-Square Test, data are categorized as in table 5.9, which contains data for classroom interest for the 20 children before and after 2 months of intervention. We can see that 4 out of 20 children are interested and 16 (or 20 percent) are not interested before intervention. during intervention, 8 are interested and 12 (or 40 percent) are not. Notice

TABLE 5.9
McNemar's Chi-Square Test for Change for Analyzing Changes in Students' Classroom Interest

During Intervention	Before Intervention		
	Interested	Not Interested	Sum
Interested	4 (A)	4 (B)	8
Not Interested	0 (C)	12 (D)	12
Sum	4	16	20

$$\text{Chi square} = \chi^2 = \frac{(A-D)^2}{A+D} = \frac{(4-12)^2}{4+12} = \frac{64}{16} = 4.00$$

$\chi^2 > 3.84$, $p < .05$

that the table is constructed so that the sums of the columns represent interested and not interested children before intervention (4, 16); while the sums of the rows represent interested and not interested children during intervention (8, 12). The cells, A, B, C, and D represent possible changes in numbers before and during intervention. A signifies the number interested both before and during intervention, 4; B, the number not interested before but interested during intervention, 4; C, the number interested before but not during intervention, 0; and D, the number not interested before intervention and during intervention, 12. The chi-square statistic is calculated with the following formula: $\chi^2 = (A-D)^2/A+D$. If the calculated value of chi-square is greater than 3.84, there is statistical significance beyond the .05 level of probability. For our example, 4 of the 20 children who were not interested before intervention became interested, cell B; and this change is statistically significant, which is an indication of progress. With the McNemar Chi-Square Test for Change, the obtained chi-square value is always compared with the chi-square of 3.84. This test can be used with 20 or more subjects, if the data can be placed in categories.

Wilcoxon's Matched-Pairs Signed-Rank Test

This test can be used to ascertain changes in scores when the differences in scores before and during intervention can be ranked across cases. Table 5.10 illustrates the use of this test with the self-concept data for these 20 children. Each child's score before intervention is placed in column 3 and after intervention, in column 2. Column 4 contains the difference scores, obtained by subtracting scores in col-

TABLE 5.10
Wilcoxon's Matched-Pairs Signed-Rank Test for Testing Changes in
Students' Self-Concept

Child	During Intervention Score	Before Intervention Score	Difference	Rank of Difference	Ranks with Less Frequent Sign
1	80	60	20	18.5	
2	79	65	14	11.5	
3	79	70	9	9	
4	78	64	14	11.5	
5	78	63	15	13.5	
6	78	62	16	15	
7	76	69	7	8	
8	76	70	6	7	
9	75	70	5	6	
10	75	72	3	5	
11	75	73	2	3.5	
12	74	54	20	18.5	
13	74	53	21	20	
14	73	55	18	16	
15	72	53	19	17	
16	70	70	0	1	
17	68	70	−2	−3.5	−3.5
18	64	52	12	10	
19	63	48	15	13.5	
20	60	61	−1	−2	−2
					5.5 = T

umn 3 from those in column 2. The fifth column ranks the scores
from the least difference, 1, (see child 16) to the most difference, 20
(child 13). Note that the negative signs are retained in this column
(for children 17 and 20). Also, observe that when there are ties
(children 11 and 17, for example), the average of the ranks that would
have been assigned if there were not ties is calculated. For children
11 and 17 the ranks would have been 3 and 4, so their average is
3.5. The ranks with the less frequent sign are entered in column 6.
In this example, there are only 2 negative signs and 18 positive signs.
The T statistic is calculated by adding the ranks in column 6. This
statistic is then compared with the appropriate value of T for $N = 20$,
using table 5.11. If the obtained T value is less than the value in
the table (52 in this example), T is statistically significant. Thus, the
data in our example indicate that statistically significant increases
in self-concept occurred, and this could be regarded as a sign of
progress.

The T statistic can be computed with as few as 5 cases with
observations obtained at 2 points in time. If there are more than 25

TABLE 5.11

Critical Values of T in the
Wilcoxon Matched-Pairs
Signed-Ranks Test at the .05
Level of Statistical Significance

N	T
6	0
7	2
8	4
9	6
10	8
11	11
12	14
13	17
14	21
15	25
16	30
17	35
18	40
19	46
20	52
21	59
22	66
23	73
24	81
25	89

Source: Adapted from table C.15 of Hinkle, Wiersma, and Jurs (1988), *Applied Statistics for the Behavioral Sciences,* Houghton Mifflin, Boston, p. 673.

cases, T can be converted to the Z statistic by the following formulae (Hinkle, Wiersma, and Jurs 1988, 577):
where

$$Z = \frac{T - M_T}{\sigma_T}$$

and

$$M_T = \frac{N(N+1)}{4}$$

The calculated T is then compared against the value of 1.64. If it

$$\sigma_T = \sqrt{\frac{N(N+1)(2N+1)}{24}}$$

is greater than 1.64, there is statistical significance beyond the .05 level of probability.

$$\overset{000}{\textit{During-Intervention Time-Series Group Design, X}}$$

This design is based on the same logic for both single cases and for groups. Qualitative matching, graphic analyses, and statistical analyses can be applied to both situations. Group designs, however, summarize the data for all the cases at each point over time. Data might be summarized as means, percentages, or proportions. As with all group designs, the goals must be the same for all clients.

In qualitative matching, average measures obtained during intervention at specified points in time are compared with goals specified in terms of average measures. In addition to examining the entire group of clients, individual clients as well as subgroups that are of special interest can be analyzed. As examples, the practice-researcher might be interested in the relative progress of minority group clients compared to majority group clients, male versus female clients, or lower-class versus middle-class clients, given that they have the same goals and are receiving the same intervention.

To illustrate the analyses with average data, let us refer to our example with twenty fourth grade students. The ultimate goal is to increase self-concept, at least up to average scores as indicated on the Self-Concept Scale for Children. It is expected that at the end of two months (nine weeks) progress will be made. Suppose that measurements are taken every week for nine weeks after intervention begins. Each set of scores could be analyzed for individual children by the methods we have discussed previously, or, as indicated above, averages can be computed for subgroups. For purposes of illustration here, we will perform analyses for the group of twenty young people, although analyses for sub-groups would be performed in the same way.

To begin, average scores are calculated for the twenty children at each time point, weeks one through nine, after intervention is started. Suppose that the twenty children produced these measurements on Lipsitt's Self-Concept Measure for the first week: 67, 67, 66, 66, 65, 65, 64, 64, 63, 63, 63, 63, 62, 62, 61, 61, 60, 60, 59, 59. The mean of these observations is $\Sigma 0/N$ or $1260/20 = 63$. This process would be repeated for all nine weeks. Further suppose the resulting set of means is: 63, 63, 63, 60, 63, 65, 68, 71, and 73.

By qualitative analysis, it is apparent that the ultimate objective of 86.75, the average score Lipsitt obtained on a sample of nearly 300 fourth-grade children, was not been achieved by the children in this sample. Nonetheless, the average score of 73 at week 9 is higher than all the preceding scores and is, on the average, 10 points higher than at week 1. Graphic analysis shows a stable horizontal line for the first three weeks at 63, followed by a dip to 60 for the fourth week, and an accelerating trend line for the remaining weeks (see figure 5.10). It appears as if progress is being made, since the average scores are increasing. As for statistical analysis, using each average measure as an observation, computations of $C = 0.85$, $S_c = .30$, and $Z = 2.83$ indicate that there is a statistically significant shift in the time-series, which also indicates progress.

Since there are no baseline measures, it is not possible to look for statistical evidence of an association between observed progress and the intervention.

Before/During-Intervention Time-Series Group Design, 000 X
000

This design requires repeated measures over time at baseline and during intervention. Therefore, the intervention can be compared to both preestablished expectations of progress and the benchmark of time-series without intervention. With statistically significant shifts in time-series from baseline to intervention, there is evidence of an association between the intervention and shifts in the dependent

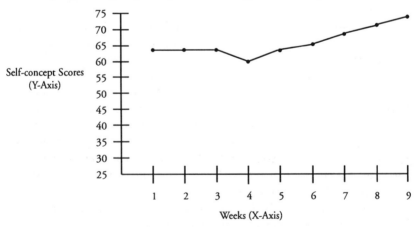

FIGURE 5.10

Graph of Average Self-concept Scores During Nine Weeks of Intervention

variable. We will continue with our case example of twenty children and refer, this time, to the expectation of increasing interest in classroom activities. After two months we expect 50 percent of the children will be interested. This time, however, we have teacher observations of children's interest in classroom activities for nine weeks during baseline and nine weeks during intervention. For this example, the average measure consists of the percentage of children interested in classroom activities each week. If, for instance, 4 children are interested in week 1, the measure would be $4/20 \times 100 = 20$ percent. The data (in percentages) for all children are described in columns 2 and 3 of table 5.12.

TABLE 5.12

Calculations for C, S_c, and Z Using Percentages of Children Interested in Classroom Activities During Nine Weeks of Baseline and Nine Weeks of Intervention (N = 20)

Week	Percentage of Children Interested in Classroom Activities During Baseline	Percentage of Children Interested in Classroom Activities During Intervention	0*	$(0_i - 0_{i+1})^2$	$(0 - \bar{0})^2$
1	20	20	0		79.03
2	20	20	0	0	79.03
3	20	25	5	25	15.13
4	20	30	10	25	1.23
5	20	30	10	0	1.23
6	25	30	5	25	15.13
7	20	35	15	100	37.33
8	25	40	15	0	37.33
9	20	40	20	25	123.43
			$\Sigma 0 = 80$	$\Sigma(0_i - 0_{i+1})^2 = 200$	$\Sigma(0 - \bar{0})^2 = 411.05$

$$\bar{0} = \frac{\Sigma 0}{N} = \frac{80}{9} = 8.89$$

$$C = 1 - \frac{\Sigma(0_i + 0_{i+1})^2}{2\Sigma(0 - \bar{0})^2} = 1 - \frac{200}{2(411.05)} = 1 - \frac{200}{822.10} = 1 - .24 = .76$$

$$S_C = \sqrt{\frac{N-2}{(N-1)(N+1)}} = 0.30$$

$$Z = \frac{C}{S_C} = \frac{0.76}{0.30} = 2.53, \ p < .05$$

*0 = Intervention Observation − Baseline Observation

These data are graphed in figure 5.11. By qualitative analysis, the ultimate goal of 50 percent interest had not been achieved after 2 months of intervention, but the children's interest had apparently increased. Graphic analysis indicates an accelerating trend during intervention compared to a relatively stable, horizontal baseline pattern, which indicates progress. With statistical analysis, it is clear that there are no statistically significant shifts in the time-series at baseline ($C = .26$, $S_c = .30$, and $Z = .87$, which is not statistically significant at the .05 level of probability). Using the C statistic for comparing time-series points for observations at baseline and during intervention, there is evidence for an association between increasing classroom interest and intervention (see table 5.12).

This design has an interesting feature: the data can be disaggregated to subgroups of special interest. As was shown for the total group of children, if one compares the time-series at intervention to that at baseline, there is a significant association between the intervention and the percentage of children interested in classroom activities. Suppose the practice-researcher is interested in determining whether this is the same situation for male and female children. The data for 20 children can be disaggregated for males and females by separating data on male from female children and providing data on the number of male children and the number of female children who are interested in classroom activities, calculating the percentages of males and females interested for all of the points in the time-series, and then analyzing the association between the intervention and the dependent variable separately for males and females. The data for this exercise are provided in table 5.13, and are graphed in figure 5.12.

FIGURE 5.11

Percentage of Children Interested in Classroom Activities During Baseline and Intervention

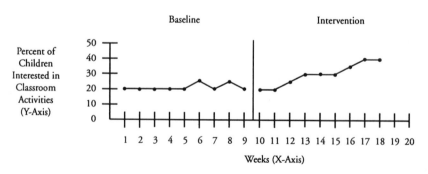

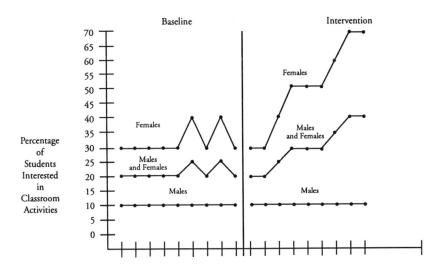

FIGURE 5.12

Graphs of Disaggregated Data for Males, Females, and Males and Females Combined

Referring to table 5.13, it can be observed that the percentage of males (column 3) and the percentage of females (column 5) interested in classroom activities provide the data for the graphs in figure 5.12. Note that each entry in column 6 is obtained by adding the numbers of males and females (columns 2 and 4). The data in column 7 are graphed in figure 5.10. In other words, data from column 6 were disaggregated into columns 2 and 4, and figure 5.12 shows the relationships between intervention and classroom interest for the 20 children disaggregated into 10 males and 10 females and for all of the children. Figure 5.12 indicates that there is no relationship for males, but there is a relationship for females. At intervention, there continues to be a stable horizontal pattern for males reflecting no change, an accelerating trend for both males and females indicating change, and an even steeper rate of acceleration for females, also indicating change. In essence, the relationship is specified to females. Statistical analyses can be done separately for males and females to confirm the graphic analysis. (The reader should do this as an exercise, using any of the statistical procedures we have discussed.)

The practice-researcher can explore other variables of interest by disaggregation. For example, the supervisor might disaggregate data (assuming there are equivalent treatment goals for clients) by super-

TABLE 5.13

TABLE 5.13

Numbers and Percentages of Males and Females Interested in Classroom Activities During Nine Weeks of Baseline and Nine Weeks of Intervention

	Week	Number of Males	(N = 10) Percentage of Males	Number of Females	(N = 10) Percentage of Females	Number of Males and Females	(N = 20) Percentage of Males and Females
	1	1	10	3	30	4	20
	2	1	10	3	30	4	20
	3	1	10	3	30	4	20
	4	1	10	3	30	4	20
Baseline	5	1	10	3	30	4	20
	6	1	10	4	40	5	25
	7	1	10	3	30	4	20
	8	1	10	4	40	5	25
	9	1	10	3	30	4	20
	1	1	10	3	30	4	20
	2	1	10	3	30	4	20
	3	1	10	4	40	5	25
	4	1	10	5	50	6	30
Intervention	5	1	10	5	50	6	30
	6	1	10	5	50	6	30
	7	1	10	6	60	7	35
	8	1	10	7	70	8	40
	9	1	10	7	70	8	40

visee. In our last illustration, 12 children may have been provided one type of intervention by social worker A, while the other 8 children received a different intervention from social worker B. Hence, this design is extremely useful for analyzing relationships for groups, subgroups and individuals, as long as the intervention goals are identical.

NOTES

1. This design notation was previously employed by Tripodi (1983). X represents the intervention; 0 represents one or more measurements on different variables at one point in time; 000 signifies a time-series of three or more observations on the same variable(s). When 0 or 000 are placed above X in this manner, $\overset{0}{X}$ or $\overset{000}{X}$, the observations or measurements occur during the intervention. Measurements that are taken before the intervention are placed to the left, like 0X or 000X.

2. This is the basic single-system design when used with one client (Bloom and Fischer 1982), It is similar to the interrupted time-series design used for studying groups; however, observations in the interrupted time-series design come after (rather than during) the intervention (Cook and Campbell 1979).

3. This section is derived from Blythe and Tripodi 1989.

4. In the remainder of the book, we shall refer to statistically significant differences only at the .05 level of probability. It should be noted that other levels might also have been employed, .10, .01, .001, etc. For the purposes of statistics presented in this book, we believe the .05 level is an adequate criterion of statistical significance.

5. Gottman and Leiblum (1974) propose a procedure to deal with noninde-pendent or autocorrelated observations. In their use of Bartlett's test to determine the statistical significance of autocorrelations, however, they assume the observations are independent (p. 148). Since observations are independent with horizontal stable baselines and zero or no variance, i.e., autocorrelation is equal to zero or close to zero, one can omit the computation of autocorrelation as long as one is satisfied with the Shewart Chart analysis as a rough criterion of statistical significance. With the data used in our example, the Gottman and Leiblum procedure for the test of significance of autocorrelation shows no statistical significance, which is due to the horizontal stability of the baseline time-series.

6. *Designs for Evaluating Practice Effectiveness*

Practice-researchers evaluate the effectiveness of their interventions for three basic reasons. The first reason is to generate information about the effectiveness of a specific intervention for a particular client so that they can be maximally helpful to the client. The second reason is to provide data about interventions that will facilitate the choice of relatively effective interventions for clients with different types of characteristics, problems, and settings. Finally, a more general reason for evaluating practice effectiveness is to enhance accountability to the agency, and its clientele, the profession, and the community.

Evaluation provides information about practice effectiveness (Blythe and Briar 1987). The degree of practice effectiveness can be defined in relation to three conditions: (1) goal attainment; (2) the association between a practice intervention and goal attainment; and (3) generality.

1. Practice effectiveness is the extent to which practice goals for a particular practice intervention are attained (effectiveness).
   When more than one intervention is involved, practice effectiveness is the extent to which one particular intervention is relatively more successful than another intervention in achieving practice goals (relative efficacy).
2. Practice effectiveness is the degree to which successful goal attainment is correlated with and/or causally related to the practice intervention(s).
3. Practice effectiveness is enhanced when the relationship between a practice intervention and goal attainment can be gener-

alized over time for a particular client, across clients for similar problems, and for clients with different problems in different environmental conditions.

The Evaluation Process

This process of evaluating practice involves the following steps:

1. Client goals are specified.
2. Conditions for effectiveness are defined.
3. Instruments for collecting data on goal attainment are selected or constructed.
4. Strategies for gathering data and for making inferences about goal attainment, correlation or causality, and generality are delineated.
5. Data are gathered and analyzed.

Client Goals

Client goals are specified in the same manner as discussed in chapter 5. In particular, variables that pertain to clients' problems or needs are delineated according to the problem's existence, magnitude, duration, or frequency. For change goals, the goal statement can suggest when change is expected to take place and for how long the change is expected to be maintained, if the practice-researcher has some basis on which to make such predictions. This provides information as to when measurements should be taken. When goals relate to prevention or maintenance, there may be no planned cessation of practice, as when a worker provides ongoing case management to a client with mental health problems who is living independently in the community. In this case, the practice-researcher may continue to monitor progress employing techniques discussed in chapter 5. When practice is terminated with prevention or maintenance goals, the social worker should decide on follow-up periods for observing the extent to which there is no change, that is, the attainment of maintenance or prevention goals at designated points in time.

Conditions for Effectiveness

As in the study of progress, the practice-researcher should conceptualize change clinically and statistically for variables that pertain to goal attainment. For example, a client goal may be to reduce drinking.

This might be conceptualized as a statistically significant reduction from ten drinks per day to some lower number, or a clinically significant reduction from ten drinks per day to a normative level of one drink per day. If the practice-researcher is interested in comparing the relative efficacy of intervention X and intervention Y for reducing drinking behavior, then that intervention which is relatively more effective may be defined as that which is associated with a greater reduction in drinking behavior. In addition to goal attainment, the practice-researcher should specify the kind of linkage (correlational or causal) that is expected between the intervention and goal attainment. Because it is more difficult to obtain evidence for causality, more rigorous, and often more complicated, research designs are required. Finally, the degree of generality should be indicated. Is the practice-researcher interested in goal attainment for one particular client at one point in time? Or, is it desirable to provide information about the generality of the intervention itself for other clients as well?

Instruments

Instruments should be selected or constructed to provide data relevant to goal attainment. Valid instruments with test-retest reliability are preferable for evaluating practice effectiveness. Again, principles for selecting and developing instruments have been discussed in previous chapters.

Research Designs

Research designs that allow the practice-researcher to make inferences about practice effectiveness are presented here. Both single-case and group designs are discussed. Within both types, we show how different designs are used to make inferences about descriptive facts, correlational and causal relationships about interventions, or the attainment of client goals. Moreover, the extent to which relationships are generalizable is discussed.

Data Analytic Techniques

The same categories of data analysis as were employed with monitoring client progress (qualitative matching, graphic analysis, and statistical methods) are discussed in reference to designs for evaluating practice effectiveness. These data analysis strategies, coupled with design features to control for internal validity threats, enable inferences about practice effectiveness to be made.

Monitoring Client Progress and Evaluating Practice Effectiveness

Monitoring client progress and evaluating practice effectiveness are closely related.[1] Similar variables are defined and measured in relation to client goals, the same instruments may be administered, and the same data analytic techniques are used. There are different emphases, however, in evaluation as compared to monitoring. Whereas monitoring focuses on descriptive and correlational data, evaluation seeks causal information as well. In addition to data obtained before and during interventions, evaluation emphasizes the collection of follow-up data after interventions are terminated. Hence, as used here, evaluation of practice effectiveness builds on and supplements information obtained in monitoring client progress. The primary function of monitoring is to provide inputs for making practice decisions while the practice-researcher is engaged in practice with the client. In contrast, evaluation yields information for making judgments about the effectiveness of practice as well as for making subsequent practice decisions, such as whether to provide additional or altered intervention(s) for a particular client.

Causality and Generality

Prior to presenting single-case and group designs for evaluating practice effectiveness, it is necessary to consider what type of evidence is needed for making inferences about causality and generality. To obtain knowledge about a causal relationship between an intervention (an independent variable) and goal attainment (a dependent variable), these types of conditions must exist (Tripodi 1983, 83–89; Blythe and Tripodi 1989, 140–143):

1. Independent and dependent variables are specified in measurable terms.
2. A correlational relationship exists between the independent and dependent variables.
3. Changes in the independent variable(s) (e.g., from no intervention to a specified amount of intervention) occur prior to changes

in dependent variable(s) (e.g., from the existence of a problem to no problem).

4. Changes in the dependent variable(s) are not due to variables other than the independent variable. These other variables have been termed internal validity threats by Campbell and Stanley (1966) and by Cook and Campbell (1979). For single-case designs and group designs, the following nine internal validity threats could bring about changes in the dependent variable and must be controlled or ruled out as possible explanations for observed changes.

   a. *History*—Events that occur between different measurements of the dependent variable over time. These can include any of a range of events such as loss of a job, marriage, or the onset of winter weather.

   b. *Maturation*—Physical changes within clients over time such as illness, developmental growth, or fatigue.

   c. *Initial Measurement Effects*—Subsequent responses to a measuring device that were affected by responses to the first measurement.

   d. *Instrumentation*—An unstandardized measurement and process that results in a change in the dependent variable. For instance, instrumentation effects might occur when a role-play test of social skill is administered with a male confederate on one occasion and a female confederate on another.

   e. *Statistical Regression*—The tendency for more extreme scores to regress to more average scores on repeated measurements of a dependent variable.

   f. *Multiple Treatment Interference*—Interventions from sources other than the one the social worker is evaluating which may be responsible for changes in the dependent variable.

   g. *Expectancy Effects*—Clients' expectations regarding the intervention, the social worker's skill, and other such factors may bring about change in the dependent variable.

   h. *Interactions*—The combined effects of any of the previous factors.

   i. *Other Factors*—These are other unknown variables that explain the occurrence of change in dependent variables.
(Blythe and Tripodi 1989, 142).

In addition to these nine threats to internal validity, two others are salient when practice effectiveness is evaluated with group designs. They are selection biases and experimental mortality. Selection biases refer to selection differences between comparison groups which could result in changes in the dependent variable. Experimental mortality refers to a differential loss or drop-out rate of participants in comparison groups.

Clearly, the list of potential threats to internal validity is formidable. Hence it is difficult to be absolutely certain that there is sufficient evidence to assert causality. To the degree to which internal validity threats are controlled, however, it is possible to make inferences about causal relationships.

Generality refers to the extent to which knowledge can be generalized across workers, clients, problems, and environments. It is obtained primarily by replicating interventions with consistent results for representative populations. Barlow and Herson (1984) discuss strategies for replicating single cases; Cook and Campbell (1979) discuss procedures for controlling external validity threats to enhance generality; and Yeskel and Ganter (1975) discuss the use of sampling techniques for obtaining representative samples. Essentially, three types of evidence are required to infer generality. First, the sample employed in each study must be representative of the population to which results are to be generalized. Second, when interventions are replicated and the results are to be compared for different administrations of the intervention, there must be evidence that the interventions are identical or at least very similar. Finally, the results of two or more administrations of the same intervention must be consistent.

Generality is based on cumulative knowledge acquired from practice research. As with causality, it can be inferred. When there is believed to be a low degree of generality, care should be taken to specify the limitations of the research. Most research designs provide relatively limited degrees of evidence for generality. Generality and its limitations will be further discussed in reference to each of the research designs presented in this chapter.

We selected five single-case and five group designs for evaluating practice effectiveness because they are representative of designs commonly employed to evaluate practice. These designs vary in the degree to which they can provide evidence for correlational knowledge and for causal inferences.

Single Case Designs

After-Intervention Measurement Design, X0

With the After-Intervention Measurement Design, measurements on one or more dependent variables are taken at one point in time, immediately after the intervention is terminated. As with the During-

Intervention Measurement Design used for monitoring progress, it is not possible to use graphic analysis and statistical methods because there are an insufficient number of data points. Qualitative matching can be used if the social worker expects certain results from the intervention. As described in chapter 5, these expectations can be compared with the obtained data.

To illustrate this design, two goals for a seven-year-old child might be to decrease his feelings of depression and to increase the time he plays with friends. Suppose the practice-researcher has no measurements of *depression* or *playing time* prior to intervention. Several strategies for collecting data on the dependent variables, depression and time spent playing with friends, are possible. A standardized instrument for assessing depression and an interview question in which the boy is asked how much time he spends with friends weekly would yield such data. If the client is not depressed and if he spends a considerable amount of time playing with friends, the worker might infer there is change, but there would be no empirical evidence to substantiate this. Questions might be asked of the boy about his perception of the extent of association (correlation) between intervention and change in the dependent variables. He might be asked: "To what extent have your feelings of depression changed since you first started to meet with me: increased ____, no change ____, decreased ____?" Or, "Compared to three months ago when you first started to see me, would you say that the amount of time you now play with friends each week is more ____, the same ____, or less ____?" Alternatively, the boy might be asked to rate the extent to which he currently is depressed and plays with friends after intervention; and then to make the same ratings on the same variables based on his situation before he engaged in intervention with the practice-researcher. Such data could provide evidence of a perception of change. Also, a follow-up question such as "what do you think led to this change?" might provide some indication that a perceived change is linked to social work intervention.

Although it can provide some evidence of a perception of change associated with intervention, this design does not provide any empirical evidence of a correlation between intervention and change in the dependent variable. Since there is no initial measurement, the internal validity threats of instrumentation, initial measurement effects, and statistical regression are not operative. By such means as observation, interviews with the parents, and available records, it might also be discerned that the boy did not receive intervention from other sources and that there were no marked changes in historical or maturational factors prior and subsequent to intervention. On the basis of qualitative data then, it can be inferred that there is a perception of change that could plausibly be attributed to treatment. But there is no empirical evidence to substantiate this speculation. This design provides no evidence of generality insofar as the perception of change is limited to the worker's intervention and the client receiving the intervention. It is the simplest and cheapest design to employ but it can be misleading about practice effectiveness, particularly if there are no efforts to verify the results with more empirical evidence with other clients.

Before-After Design, O_1XO_2

The Before-After Design involves measuring a set of one or more dependent variables, O_1 and O_2, before and after intervention, X. The practice-researcher can provide some qualitative evidence of an association between the intervention and the dependent variables by showing that no intervention (discerned by interviews and available case records) was given to the client before the first set of measurements, O_1, but that some change occurred between O_1 and O_2 after the administration of the intervention, X. In contrast to the After-Intervention Measurement Design, this design takes measurements of the dependent variables, depression and time spent with friends in the present example, before and after the intervention, eliminating the potential bias of retrospective falsification (perceptual distortions due to faulty memory). On the other hand, since there is measurement prior to intervention, initial measurement effects, instrumentation, and statistical regression are not controlled. The other internal validity threats also are not controlled but, as in the After-Intervention Measurement Design, qualitative information pertaining to history, maturation, and multiple-treatment interference can be obtained. This design provides descriptive information and some possible evidence of an association between intervention and changes in the dependent variable for one client. If no changes are observed, there is some evidence that there is no association or causal relationship. No evidence for generality is provided. Graphic analysis and statistical analysis procedures cannot be used since there are only two measurements. Qualitative matching can compare the observed change, $O_2 - O_1$, for the client with *a priori* expectations of clinical significance. For instance, a change in depression of 4 points, from 8 to 4 on a ten-point scale, and a change from three hours per week with friends, at baseline to ten hours per week after intervention may be indicators of clinical significance. If these criteria are achieved, the practice intervention for the boy may be regarded as effective.

Interrupted Time-Series Design, $000X000^2$

This design involves three phases: a baseline phase, an intervention phase, and a follow-up phase (Cook and Campbell 1979; Tripodi 1983). In each phase, a series of measurements on the dependent variable(s) are taken over time, preferably at equal intervals. The intervention phase measurements provide information about progress during intervention but are not necessary for the basic design which requires time-series before the intervention is instituted and after it is terminated. Ideally, the baseline time-series will have horizontal stability, with problem existence or a high degree of problem magnitude, duration, or frequency when the client goals describe change, and no problem existence or a small degree of problem magnitude when the goals are for prevention or maintenance. The intervention is introduced after the goals are clear to the practice-researcher, and is terminated when the goals are achieved or it is decided that the client will not benefit from continued intervention.

For the Interrupted Time-Series Design, variables must be specified and they should show evidence of test-retest reliability and validity. Referring to the example of intervention for a child to increase his playing time with friends per week, an ideal data pattern might look like that shown in figure 6.1. Measurements of playing time with friends are obtained weekly for eight weeks during baseline, eight weeks during intervention, and nine weeks during a follow-up period. The intervention is introduced after it is believed that the baseline is horizontally stable, intervention is terminated after it is believed the goal has been attained and follow-up measurements are obtained over a period of time that is comparable in length to the intervention, thereby providing a framework for easier interpretation of the data.[3]

Organizational Constraints and Ethical Considerations. The Interrupted Time-Series Design can only be implemented if a time-series at baseline can be constructed and if data can be obtained for the follow-up phase. This depends on the resources and priorities of the human service agency as well as on the willingness of the client to cooperate with data collection efforts.

To reduce costs during the follow-up period the practice-researcher may enlist the cooperation of significant others (such as the boy's family or teacher) to gather data. Mailed questionnaires or telephone interviews, instead of one-to-one interviews also will save time. The collection of follow-up data should be discussed and planned with the client prior to termination. Otherwise, the client may feel that it is an

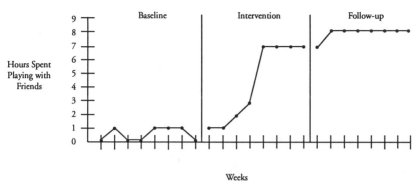

FIGURE 6.1

Graph of Interrupted Time-Series Design for Single-Case Data

invasion of privacy, and possibly unethical, to ask questions after intervention is terminated.

If data in the follow-up period indicate a reversal to a similar level of the problem as presented at baseline (in this illustration, suppose that the boy's playing time with friends reverts to zero or one hour per week), there are possible ethical implications. Such a situation requires that the agency offer continued intervention. Failure to do so could be regarded as unethical even if the agency doesn't have the resources for continued treatment. It is not justifiable to invade an ex-client's privacy by asking follow-up questions if treatment will not be provided when there are indications that client progress is seriously deteriorating.

Analysis. With this design, data can be analyzed by qualitative matching, graphic analysis, or statistical procedures. Qualitative matching involves matching *a priori* expectations (of the worker, the boy, or his family) of clinical significance with results obtained during follow-up. If it is believed that an increase of three or more hours of playing time is clinically significant, then it would be apparent that the goal has been realized (see figure 6.1). In the first two weeks of baseline, the boy had between zero and one hour of playing time, while his playing time increased to eight hours per week during the last seven weeks of follow-up.

Graphic analysis would be conducted in the same manner as discussed in the last chapter. Comparisons would be made between successive phases, that is, from intervention to baseline, and from follow-up to intervention, as well as from follow-up to baseline. Some possible patterns are depicted in figure 6.2. Graph A shows no change from baseline to intervention and from intervention to follow-up.

FIGURE **6.2**

Illustrative Patterns of Data for Interrupted Time-Series Design

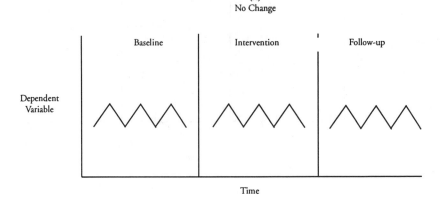

(A)
No Change

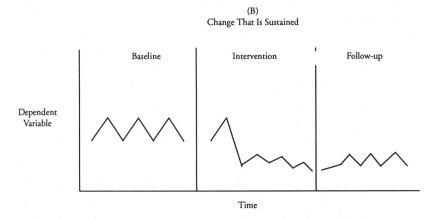

(B)
Change That Is Sustained

Graph B shows a stable, horizontal cyclic pattern at baseline, followed by a reduction in the values of the dependent variable at intervention, which is followed by a relatively stable change at follow-up and also when compared with baseline. If reduced values of the dependent variable indicate progress, then Graph A suggests progress that is maintained through the follow-up period. Graph C shows change in succeeding phases, from baseline to intervention and from intervention to follow-up. The greatest change is from follow-up as compared with baseline data. Graph D shows a change from baseline to intervention and a change in the opposite direction from intervention to follow-up. The data at follow-up, as compared with the data at base-

FIGURE **6.2** *(Continued)*

(C)
Continuing Change

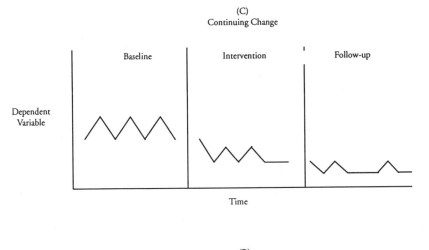

(B)
Change That Is Sustained

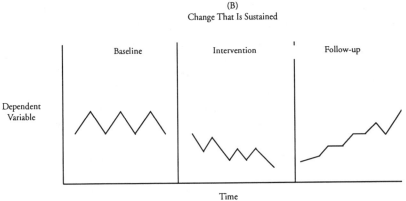

line, show no change. This pattern exhibits a reversal which is defined as a change from intervention to follow-up that is in the opposite direction of the change from baseline to intervention. In addition, the pattern of data at follow-up is similar to those at baseline, exhibiting no change.

The C statistic, the binomial, and other statistics for time-series analyses discussed in chapter 5 are applicable with this design. Statistical analyses can be made of the time-series itself within any of the phases (using the C statistic, for example) to determine whether there is horizontal stability. Statistical analyses are also made between phases in which intervention is compared with baseline, follow-up is compared with intervention, or follow-up is compared with baseline. The comparison of follow-up data with data at intervention has the purpose of demonstrating whether or not change achieved during intervention is maintained (as indicated by no statistically significant changes between intervention and follow-up), continued to occur (as indicated by a statistically significant change between follow-up and intervention in the same direction as a statistically significant change between intervention and baseline), or reversed (as indicated by a statistically significant change between follow-up and intervention in the opposite direction from a statistically significant change between intervention and baseline). Comparing follow-up data to baseline data allows the practice-researcher to examine whether practice effectiveness was achieved. Practice effectiveness is demonstrated when there is evidence of a statistically significant change in the desired direction and when the magnitude of change is consistent with that which is desired for clinical significance. Of course, when the practice goal relates to no change (maintenance or prevention), practice effectiveness is indicated when there are not statistically significant differences at a designated follow-up interval that is regarded to be lengthy enough to suggest clinically significant prevention or maintenance.

Control of Threats to Internal Validity. The Interrupted Time-Series Design provides evidence about the time-order of the intervention and the dependent variables. Evidence for correlation is provided if there are statistically significant changes between the time-series at follow-up and intervention phases. Since there are no comparison groups, experimental mortality and biased selection are not relevant. With evidence of a horizontal, stable baseline as determined by graphic and statistical analysis, the internal validity threats of initial measurement effects, instrumentation, and statistical regression are controlled. If they are operative, they would be suggested by accelerating or decelerating trends in the data. Multiple treatment interference, history, maturation, and expectancy effects are not controlled. If supplementary interviewing, observations, and available documents do not reveal the occurrence of such variables affecting the client, the practice-researcher may regard the relationship between intervention and outcomes as plausibly causal (even though he or she cannot be absolutely confident of this).

If the pattern of data is one that shows a reversal, as in Graph D of figure 6.2, there is some evidence that the factors of history, maturation, and multiple treatment interference are not as important as the presence or absence of the independent variable, the intervention. Despite the change between baseline and intervention, this pattern would indicate practice effectiveness at follow-up, because there is no statistically significant relationship between the follow-up and baseline time-series.

Generality. There can be evidence of generality over time with this design, but only for the client system being evaluated. There is no generality between workers, clients, or situations. If the design is replicated with the same results (say, for other clients with similar problems treated by the same worker or by other workers), evidence for generality can be obtained (Barlow and Hersen 1984).

Natural Withdrawal Time-Series Design, 000X000X000

This design, involving five phases, is an extension of the Interrupted Time-Series Design. The first three phases are identical to the Interrupted Time-Series Design. The fourth and fifth phases involve reinstating intervention and follow-up. This design can only be employed when there is a pattern of data that shows a reversal to baseline in the third follow-up phase.[4] figure 6.3 has the same data pattern for baseline and intervention as shown in figure 6.1, but in the third phase there is a reversal to the pattern initially exhibited in the baseline. This could be documented statistically by comparing phase

FIGURE 6.3
Graph of Natural Withdrawal Time-Series Design

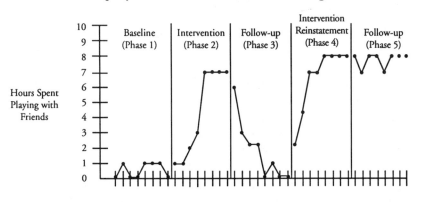

Weeks

1 to phase 3, showing no statistically significant differences, and by observing statistically significant differences between phases 2 and 3. When this reversal pattern occurs, it is possible to reinstate the intervention. Interventions might be naturally withdrawn by planned terminations or by events beyond the control of the social worker, such as extended illness or a lengthy vacation due to a school holiday. It is possible for the intervention to be re-instated. To use this design, the same intervention procedures must be employed and, of course, the client must be willing to return to treatment. Once intervention is reinstated (phase 4), measurements on the same dependent variable using the same time increments as in phases one to three must be obtained. An ideal data pattern is shown in figure 6.3 where phase 4 shows positive change (increased playing time) and phase 5 shows no reversal tendencies in the second follow-up period. Of course, the ideal pattern may not occur in which case the resulting design is basically an extended time-series design.

Organizational Constraints and Ethical Considerations. This design is more costly than an Interrupted Time-Series Design because it requires additional measurements and reinstating the intervention. Moreover, the practice-researcher may not be able to reinstate the intervention so that it is identical to what it was in phase 2. If this is the case, then additional evidence for the control of history, maturation, and multiple treatment interference cannot be obtained.

Ethical issues revolve around the timing of intervention, termination, and intervention reinstatement. Obviously, intervention implementation should not be delayed if it will harm the client. Correspondingly, interventions should not be purposely withdrawn unless it is believed that clients will continue to achieve or maintain their goals. In short, follow-up procedures should be a routine feature of practice, following termination of treatment.

Analyses. The same methods of analysis as used for Interrupted Time-Series Designs can be applied in this design. Additional graphic and statistical analyses are necessary for interpreting the data obtained in phases 4 and 5. Phase 4 is compared with phase 3. The direction of differences is observed in the graphic pattern. For example, in figure 6.3, phase 4 shows increasing hours of playing time, which is compatible with the intervention goal, while phase 3 shows decreasing hours of playing time. Statistical analysis would show statistically significant differences between phases 3 and 4. After the goal is achieved (beginning in the third week of phase 4) there should be no statistically significant differences between phases 4 and 5, indicating maintenance of the change goal.

Control of Threats to Internal Validity. This design controls for initial measurement effects, instrumentation, and statistical regression when the baseline produces a pattern of horizontal stability showing no statistical trends in the time-series. Experimental mortality and biased selection are not relevant. Interviews, case records, or observations might provide information on the potential influence of expectancy effects, history, maturation, and multiple treatment interference. When the ideal pattern for this design is obtained, there is some evidence that changes in the dependent variable are under the control of intervention rather than historical, maturational, or other treatment factors. In other words, data in both intervention phases 2 and 4, must be statistically significant when compared with phase 1 baseline, and the follow-up phase 3 must be statistically significantly different from phases 2 and 4, but not from baseline. If historical, maturational, and other treatment factors were operative, phase 3 would not have shown a reversal pattern to baseline.

Generality. This design provides additional evidence of generality over time for one person, but no new evidence for generalizations across clients, workers, situations, or problems.

Multiple Baseline Design Across Clients, $\begin{matrix} 000X000\ 000 \\ 000\ 000X000 \end{matrix}$

Technically speaking, the Multiple-Baseline Design Across Clients is not a single-case design because it involves comparing two or more clients' Interrupted Time-Series Design data.[5] In order to compare clients, they all must be dealing with identical problems; they also must be treated with the same intervention. This design provides additional control for historical, maturational, or other treatment factors. It also provides some evidence of generality across clients with the same practice-researcher. As with the Natural Withdrawal Time-Series Design, it depends on the occurrence of data patterns that conform to the idealized design. The Multiple-Baseline Design, depicted in figure 6.4, involves the following:

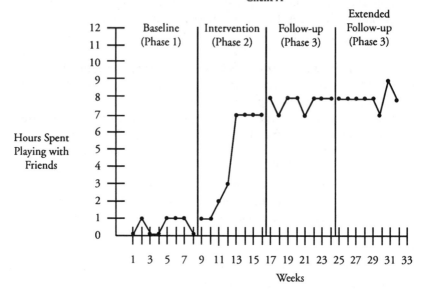

FIGURE 6.4
Graph of Multiple-Baseline Design

Client A

Hours Spent Playing with Friends

Weeks

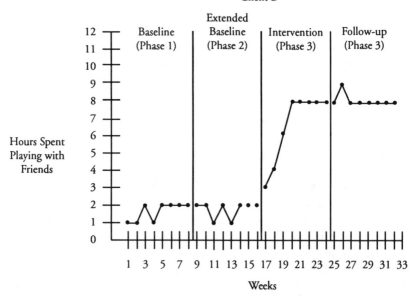

Client B

Hours Spent Playing with Friends

Weeks

1. There must be two or more clients having identical problems. To continue with our example, there would need to be another boy who also has limited playing time with friends, leading to a treatment goal to increase the number of hours of playing time.
2. A baseline must be established for each client, such that there is horizontal stability and evidence of a problem (in this case, little or no playing time).
3. An intervention is administered to one client, but not to the other(s). At the same time, the baseline is extended for the other client(s) (see extended baseline for client B in figure 6.4).
4. If the intervention goal is achieved for client A, the intervention is terminated. Follow-up data are then obtained to provide evidence for persistence of treatment effects. Meanwhile, intervention is implemented for the second client, assuming that the extended baseline continues to provide evidence that there is a problem.
5. The intervention is terminated for client B if the intervention goal has been attained (this occurred following week twenty-four for client B). Follow-up data are then obtained for client B, (phase 3) to show maintenance of treatment effects. In addition, further maintenance data are provided for client A in extended follow-up. This extended follow-up period shows continued similarity in the data patterns during the same period of time.

If there are more clients, the same process is repeated, so that the intervention is administered successively but with increasing time lags for each client after the intervention goal has been achieved for the preceding client. For three clients, the pattern would be like this:

Client A	Baseline	Intervention	Follow-up	Follow-up	Follow-up
Client B	Baseline	Baseline	Intervention	Follow-up	Follow-up
Client C	Baseline	Baseline	Baseline	Intervention	Follow-up

Organizational Constraints and Ethical Considerations. This design is only feasible in those agencies that have many clients with similar problems. The requirement of extended baselines and follow-up periods means that additional agency resources must be expended. Moreover, the practice-researcher must spend more time and energy in comparison to that required by Interrupted Time-Series Designs.

The use of extended baselines for clients other than the first client to receive the intervention might be regarded as unethical, because it can be construed as an unnecessary delay in treatment. The ethical issues are minimized when clients on waiting lists are used for extended baselines, when the problem is such that undue harm or discomfort would not be manifest for the client if some delay in treatment or if part of the baseline can be reliably reconstructed. More serious problems exist when changes do not occur in a desirable direction for client A, but client B might realize positive results if he or she received treatment. If the practice-researcher is aware of this in advance, it is not ethical to withhold treatment. The ethical posture for the practice-researcher using the Multiple-Baseline Design is to specify expected times in which goals are to be achieved as accurately as possible and to persistently monitor progress in all phases of the design.

Analyses. Qualitative matching, graphic analysis, and statistical analysis can be employed, using the same methods as previously discussed. To demonstrate that the conditions for ideal data patterns are realized, the following analyses should be conducted, using the design in figure 6.4 as an example.

1. The time-series for client A at baseline is compared with that for client B. If there are no statistically significant differences, this demonstrates problem similarity. In addition, data during the extended baseline for client B should not differ from other phase 1 baseline data for both clients A and B.
2. Data collected during intervention for client A should be compared to that client's baseline data. Statistically significant differences provide evidence of an association. Further, no change for client B, comparing data at extended baseline (which occurs at the same time as the intervention for client A) to client B's phase 1 baseline, provides evidence suggesting that change realized by client A is not produced by historical, maturational, and other factors.
3. Intervention data for client B should show statistically significant changes when compared with data at baseline.
4. Follow-up data should be compared with data at intervention and at baseline for both clients. No statistically significant changes between follow-up and intervention show maintenance of treatment effects, whereas statistically significant changes between follow-up and baseline provide further evidence of goal attainment and practice effectiveness.

Control of Threats to Internal Validity and Generality. With the ideal patterns, the internal validity threats controlled by the Interrupted Time-Series Design also are controlled by the Multiple-Baseline Design Across Clients. Replications with two or more clients with the same findings increase the social worker's confidence in the degree to which factors such as statistical regression, standardization, and the influence of previous measurements are controlled. Obtaining statistically significant changes in the dependent variable with one client while observing no significant changes during the same period of time for the other client who is not receiving treatment provides some evidence for the control of expectancy effects, maturation, history, and multiple treatment interference. This is strengthened when it is followed by a statistically significant change for client B after the intervention is introduced. Of course, this is only true to the extent that the assumption of problem equivalence for the clients is tenable and that the intervention given to both clients is identical. This becomes feasible by paying close attention to the implementation of the intervention. Moreover, evidence of generality across clients (with the same worker and the same problem) is obtained if the results are consistent for both clients.

Group Designs

Group designs, involving more than one client, can provide information about the practice effectiveness of the caseload of one social worker or of several social workers. Information can also be obtained to facilitate a supervisor's evaluation of one or more workers, and to conduct an agency evaluation. Results can most easily be combined and interpreted across clients when their problems are similar, when the intervention applied to alleviate their problems is similar, and when the practice goals are operationalized in the same manner. Clients may receive interventions in a group or individually, by the same or by different social workers. Dependent variables in group designs cover the range of possible variables, with an emphasis on observable, reliable, and valid variables obtained by means of standardized instruments. Examples of such variables include indices of self-concept, symptom reduction, communication shifts, positive interpersonal interactions, violent behaviors, abuse, delinquent acts, weight loss or gain, medical compliance, substance abuse, moods, self-care skills, and independent living. In short, the same dependent variables can be employed in single-case designs and in group designs.

After-Intervention Measurement Design, XO

One set of measurements on one or more dependent variables, 0, is obtained after the intervention, X, is terminated with the After-Intervention Measurement Design. The practice-researcher must provide evidence of implementation of the same intervention for each client included in the study. When the intervention is a group intervention, such that all of the clients being evaluated receive the same intervention, evidence of the standardization of intervention for each client is readily available. When all of the clients are seen individually, support for the standardization of intervention is more difficult to obtain. The practice-researcher can keep notes, logs, recordings, or checklists on the contents of the interventions, the practice objectives, and other intervention parameters, as discussed previously in chapter 4. The practice-researcher also must exercise caution in using the same procedures for obtaining measurements from each of the clients.

This design is the simplest design available to evaluate the effectiveness of practice for a group of clients. Unfortunately, it also provides the least amount of information. To illustrate this design, imagine that ten female clients are receiving group intervention once a week for ten weeks. The group is for women who are extremely critical of themselves. Included in the intervention are lectures and discussions about the effects of self-criticism, cognitive strategies for identifying and modifying self-criticisms, role-play practice, and homework assignments to reinforce group experiences. At the end of ten weeks each client is asked to record the number of self-critical statements she made during a particular day. Further, let us suppose that the number of self-critical comments by the ten clients at the termination of the ten-week group intervention is as follows: 20, 20, 18, 20, 13, 10, 10, 14, 10, 15.

Organizational Constraints and Ethical Considerations. There are few organizational constraints affecting this design. The only possible constraint might be the use of too much time and resources if too many dependent variables are measured. Because the clients are not coerced into providing data, data are confidential, and the dependent variables are relevant to the practice goals, there are not significant ethical problems. With the example of self-critical statements as the dependent variable, there do not appear to be major problems related to agency resources or ethics.

Analysis. Because measurements are taken at only one point in time, graphic analysis cannot be used. Descriptive statistics can be presented to show the distribution of the ten clients with respect to self-criticism, but analysis of statistically significant changes is not possible since there are no measurements of the dependent variable before the treatment group began. Qualitative matching can determine effectiveness by matching the obtained data with what was expected.

The data of the ten clients may be described statistically by computing these statistics: mean, median, range, variance, and standard deviation. To do so, the number of self-critical statements is ordered from the most to the least, as shown in table 6.1, to simplify computation of the median. Because 15 and 14 are the points above which (and below which) half of the cases fall, the median is 14.5. The computations for the other statistics are shown in table 6.1. The mean is 15, the range (20–10) is 10, the variance is 18.22 and the standard deviation is 4.27.

TABLE 6.1

Descriptive Statistics for Ten Clients Receiving Group Intervention for Self-Critical Behavior

Client	No. of Self-Critical Statements (0)	$0 - \bar{0}$	$(0 - \bar{0})^2$
A	20	5	25
B	20	5	25
C	20	5	25
D	18	3	9
E	15	0	0
F	14	−1	1
G	13	−2	4
H	10	−5	25
I	10	−5	25
J	10	−5	25
	$\Sigma 0 = 150$		$\Sigma(0 - \bar{0})^{22} = 164$

$$median = \frac{15 + 14}{2} = 14.5$$

$$\bar{0} = \frac{\Sigma 0}{N} = \frac{150}{10} = 15$$

$$range = 20 - 10 = 10$$

$$variance = \frac{\Sigma(0 - \bar{0})^2}{N - 1} = \frac{164}{9} = 18.22$$

$$standard\ deviation = \sqrt{variance} = \sqrt{18.22} = 4.27$$

If the goal is to reduce the number of self-critical statements for each client, goal attainment cannot be discerned from these data. As with the single-case After Intervention Measurement Design, the practice-researcher might gather additional data. In this example, the worker might ask each client whether she is now more self-critical, the same, or less as compared to the beginning of intervention. Then, the practice-researcher could describe the proportion or percentage of the clients who achieved the goal of reducing self-critical behavior. If eight clients report that they are less self-critical, then 80 percent of the clients indicate they have attained the goal. Again, note that this is a perception based on retrospective and self-reported data, and is subject to falsification and/or error.

On the other hand, suppose the goal is set at some number, say fifteen. Clients A-E (or 50 percent) would have attained that goal, while Clients F-J, would not have done so. In terms of the group average, the mean of 15 indicates goal attainment, while the median of 14.5 does not. For this example, the proportion or percentage of clients assessed by qualitative matching as attaining the goal provides a clearer and more accurate picture of effectiveness than does the mean or median. Care must be taken to select the descriptive statistic(s) that best represents, not misrepresents, the data.

Control of Threats to Internal Validity. Experimental mortality, selection bias, statistical regression, and initial measurement effects are not relevant because no initial measurements were taken and comparison groups were not used. Instrumentation can be controlled if the practice-researcher follows the same measurement procedures for all clients. History, maturation, multiple treatment interference, expectancy effects, and other factors are not controlled, although some information on their influence or lack of influence might be obtained from observation, interviews, or case records. For example, clients may report that they have not been ill, have not experienced major life changes, and have not received other interventions during the time which they attended group sessions.

Generality. Results cannot be generalized to other workers, clients, or problems from this design. Assuming that the clients are representative of the entire caseload, the worker *can* generalize the results to his or her caseload. Since the group of clients was not selected through random sampling, however, there is no way that the practice-researcher can be completely assured that this smaller segment of cli-

TABLE 6.2

Number of Self-Critical Statements Before and After Group Intervention

(1) Client	(2) Before Intervention	(3) After Intervention	(4) D	(5) D²
A	20	20	0	0
B	21	20	1	1
C	22	18	4	16
D	25	20	5	25
E	26	13	13	169
F	24	10	14	196
G	24	10	14	196
H	23	14	9	81
I	30	10	20	400
J	28	15	13	169
			$\Sigma D = 93$	$\Sigma D^2 = 1253$

$$\overline{D} = \frac{\Sigma D}{N} = \frac{93}{10} = 9.3$$

$$\Sigma d^2 = \Sigma D^2 - \frac{(\Sigma D)^2}{N} \qquad t = \frac{\overline{D}}{\sqrt{\dfrac{\Sigma d^2}{N(N-1)}}}$$

$$\Sigma d^2 = 1253 - \frac{(93)^2}{10}$$

$$\Sigma d^2 = 1253 - \frac{8649}{10} = 388.1 \qquad t = \frac{9.3}{\sqrt{\dfrac{388.1}{10(9)}}} = \frac{9.3}{\sqrt{\dfrac{388.1}{90}}} = \frac{9.3}{\sqrt{4.31}} = \frac{9.3}{2.08}$$

Since $t = 4.47 > 2.262$ (degrees of freedom $= 9$), $p < .05$

ents is representative of the entire caseload. Random sampling would ensure with very little error, that each client in the caseload had an equally likely chance of being included in the sample, but such a procedure seldom is ethically or practically possible in routine social work practice.

Before-After Measurement Design, 0_1X0_2

The Before-After Measurement Design includes a set of measurements for more than one client on one or more dependent variables, 01, prior to the introduction of the intervention, X, and another set of measurements for the same clients on the same dependent variable(s) after intervention is terminated, 0_2. Since there are before and after measurements for more than one client, empirical evidence of a statistical correlation is possible. Returning to our example, table 6.2 reports the number of self-critical statements before and after intervention for the ten clients who received the group intervention. Calculations also are provided for computing a t statistic for matched pairs, which can indicate whether there is a statistically significant association between the intervention and the dependent variable, the number of self-critical statements. These calculations will be described in the forthcoming section on analysis.

Organizational Constraints and Ethical Issues. The Before-After Measurement Design requires sufficient resources to obtain measurements before and after the intervention. If the intervention lasts for an extended period of time, there could be a loss of data due to client dropout. Given informed consent, confidentiality, and voluntary participation on the part of the clients, there are no major ethical problems. Ethical problems could occur if the measurement process is noxious, although this is not the case with the example presented here.

Analysis. When using this design, graphic analysis is not meaningful, since there are only two points in which data are gathered. Qualitative matching and statistical analyses can be conducted following procedures discussed in chapter 5 for the Before-During Intervention Group Design. Statistical methods outlined there to compare "during" measurements to "before" measurements also could compare "after" measurements to "before" measurements in this design. Hence, McNemar's Chi-Square Test for Change can analyze nominal data and Wilcoxon's Matched Pairs Signed-Rank Test can analyze ordinal data, as discussed in chapter 5. For dependent variables on interval or ratio scales, such as the number of self-critical statements, the matched pairs t-test is another statistic that can be employed. Referring to the data in table 6.2, this statistic is calculated and interpreted as follows (Pagano 1981):

1. Enter the data for each client before and after intervention as shown in columns 2 and 3. Client B, for example, is shown to have made 21 self-critical statements before intervention and 20 after intervention.
2. Subtract the numbers in column 3 from those in column 2 to

give the difference, D, in column 4. Add up these difference scores to produce the sum of the differences, or ΣD.

3. Square the D score for each client. For example, for client C, $4 \times 4 = 16$ and for client D, 5 times $5 = 25$. These results are placed in column 5. After they are calculated, add the squared differences to produce the sum of the squared difference scores, ΣD^2.

4. The statistical formula for the *t* statistic is

$$t = \frac{\overline{D}}{\sqrt{\dfrac{\Sigma d^2}{N(N-1)}}}$$

where

$$\overline{D} = \frac{\Sigma D}{N},$$

and

$$\Sigma d^2 = \Sigma D^2 - \frac{(\Sigma D)^2}{N}.$$

Calculate D, Σd^2, and *t* by substituting the appropriate numbers as shown in table 6.2. The *t* statistic provides an indication as to whether there are statistically significant changes in the data before and after intervention for the same group of clients. Associated with each *t* value is a probability value that indicates the frequency of its occurrence. If the probability value is low, generally considered to be less than 5 times out of 100 (written as $p < .05$), then the *t* value is statistically significant. This means that there are statistically significant differences in the distributions of data before and after intervention. A statistically significant *t* statistic provides empirical evidence of a significant correlation between the intervention and the dependent variable. In our example, the *t* value is 4.47.

5. Determine the appropriate degrees of freedom (df) for the *t* statistic. Degrees of freedom refer to "the number of scores that are free to vary in calculating the statistic" (Pagano 1981, p. 292). For the matched-pair *t* statistic, the degrees of freedom is the number of matched pairs minus one. Thus, $df = N - 1$ or $10 - 1 = 9$ for these data. Degrees of freedom must be determined because there are different probability distributions for different degrees of freedom. In other words, there are different

t values associated with the .05 level of probability, and these *t* values vary in relation to the degrees of freedom. Table 6.3 indicates *t* values for the .05 level of statistical significance for varying degrees of freedom.

6. Referring to table 6.3, locate the *t* value associated with the .05

TABLE 6.3

Critical t Values for Matched-Pairs t-test at Various Degrees of Freedom[1]

Degrees of Freedom	t Value for .05 Level of Statistical Significance
1	2.706
2	4.303
3	3.182
4	2.776
5	2.571
6	2.447
7	2.365
8	2.306
9	2.262
10	2.228
11	2.201
12	2.179
13	2.160
14	2.145
15	2.131
16	2.120
17	2.110
18	2.101
19	2.093
20	2.086
21	2.080
22	2.074
23	2.069
24	2.064
25	2.060
26	2.056
27	2.052
28	2.048
29	2.045
30	2.042
40	2.021
60	2.000
120	1.980
∞	1.960

[1]Adapted from Pagano, R. (1981). *Understanding statistics in the behavioral sciences.* St. Paul, MN: West Publishing Company, Table D, 53.

level of statistical significance. For 9 degrees of freedom, the *t* value is 2.262.

7. Compare the calculated *t* value with the *t* value obtained from table 6.3. If the calculated *t* value is greater than or equal to the tabled value, the calculated *t* value is statistically significant. If the calculated *t* value is less than the tabled *t* value, it is not statistically significant. Since the calculated value of *t*, 4.47 in our example is greater than 2.262, (*t* > 2.262), *t* is statistically significant. Stated differently, the associated probability of obtaining a *t* statistic this great is less than 5 times out of 100 (p < .05).

For our example, the statistically significant *t* value provides evidence of a significant association for the group of clients. While it indicates that, on the average, there is change for the group, it does not indicate how many of the ten clients actually changed. To determine this, one would go back to the data for each client in columns 2 and 3 of table 6.2. Here, it is observed that nine out of ten clients (90 percent) reduced their self-critical behavior and the average reduction is the mean of the difference scores listed in column 4, which is 9.3. Data such as this can be used in qualitative matching, as previously illustrated, to determine whether or not there is goal attainment.

Control of Internal Validity and Generality. No internal validity factors are controlled with this design. Experimental mortality and biased selection are not relevant because there is no comparison group. Because measurements are taken before the intervention, it is possible that statistical regression and/or the effect of previous measurements are responsible for the observed change in self-critical statements. In addition, there is a greater possibility of error due to lack of standardized measurement since the measurement procedures must be identical for all clients prior to and after intervention. Additional data might provide information about the influence of other factors such as history and maturation. In itself, the design does not control for these factors. Without random sampling, the degree of generalizability is not known. Therefore, the results cannot be generalized to other workers, clients, or client problems.

Interrupted Time-Series Design $_{OOO}X_{OOO}$

The Interrupted Time-Series Design involves taking several measurements spaced at equal time intervals during three sequential phases: baseline, intervention, and follow-up. Two or more clients having the same goals and the same dependent variables are administered measurements at baseline until their averages (means, percentages, or proportions) are horizontally stable. The intervention is then implemented and measurements are continually taken during intervention. At termination, the intervention is withdrawn, but measurements on the dependent variable continue. The intervention must be identical for all of the clients. For purposes of interpretation, the amount and length of intervention also should be equivalent. The design can be employed for multiple clients receiving the same intervention from the practice-researcher. This design is more feasible when the intervention is a group intervention following a prescribed set of procedures and fixed in terms of length and number of sessions. Examples of this type of intervention might be group interventions to train clients in parenting skills, to alleviate undesirable behaviors such as substance abuse, or to teach safe-sex practices.

A planned intervention to reduce self-critical behavior for a group of ten clients may be administered for eight weekly, one-hour sessions after an eight-week horizontal baseline is established, as depicted in figure 6.5. Subsequent to termination, the same number of measurements over the same time period (8 measurements over eight weeks) are taken in the follow-up period. Ideally, the number of measurements in each phase is identical. Before shifting phases from baseline to intervention and from intervention to follow-up, however, the most important consideration is that there is stability in the graphic pattern.

FIGURE 6.5

Graph of Interrupted Time-Series Design for Group Data

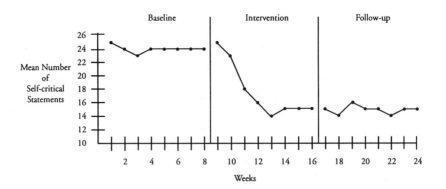

Organizational Constraints and Ethical Considerations. If the length of the intervention is not prescribed, the design may be difficult to carry out. Intervention for one client may last one month; for another, five months. Averaging results across different intervention periods distorts the data to a great extent. It is preferable to use single-case designs separately for each client, rather than combining interventions of varying lengths in the same group design. A more difficult problem emerges if there are varying lengths of time for each client before there is horizontal stability at baseline. This leads to the delayed introduction of intervention for some clients, which in turn may have ethical ramifications unless there is a substantial waiting list for the agency's services.

Analysis. All the analyses that have been discussed for the Interrupted Time-Series Design with a single case can be employed in this group design. With the group design, however, each point on the graph represents an average measure (mean, proportion, or percentage) for the group of clients. Thus, the information presented represents the group rather than any one individual client. Moreover, the data can be disaggregated to form single-subject designs for each client as was shown in chapter 5.

Qualitative analysis, graphic analysis, the C statistic, Shewart Chart Analysis, the Celeration Line Technique and the Binomial Test can be used for purposes of analysis. Referring to figure 6.5, follow-up data are compared to baseline data to analyze the changes associated with the intervention. To observe trends in data patterns, data at follow-up are compared with those at intervention and data at intervention are compared with those at baseline. The data pattern at follow-up is statistically significant when compared to baseline data but not in comparison to intervention data.[6]

Qualitative matching, graphic analysis, and statistical analysis can be combined. Suppose that the goal of group intervention for ten clients is that after eight weeks of intervention 50 percent or more of the group will make fewer than ten self-critical statements per day (or seventy per week). Again, referring to figure 6.5, it is obvious that the group mean, although showing a statistically significant reduction, does *not* show that the goal is accomplished. Because the mean averages extreme differences, it is possible for some clients to achieve the goal even though it is not shown by the average measure. For example, an average of 20 might reflect all clients scoring 20 (that is, making 20 self-critical statements per day. Or, an average of 20 could be obtained if five clients scored 40 each and five clients scored 0 each, or if two clients scored 100 and each of eight clients scored 0. Table 6.4 contains the calculations for these 3 distributions, all with a mean of 20. Note that in two of these situations (Distributions B and C) one-half or more of the clients made fewer than the group average of 20 self-critical statements per day.

When the goal is specified in terms of a percentage for the entire group to achieve, the indicator for the dependent variable should be directly relevant to the goal. Figure 6.6 shows a graph for baseline, intervention, and follow-up, for which the dependent variable is the percentage of the group making fewer than twenty self-critical statements per week. For illustrative purposes, suppose the group is comprised of ten clients. The graph is relatively easy to interpret. At baseline, which is horizontally stable, no client met the goal of making fewer than twenty self-critical statements per week. During the first week of intervention, one client (10 percent) achieved the goal of fewer than twenty self-critical statements. At the thirteenth week, four clients (40 percent) achieved that goal and at termination, week 16, six clients achieved the goal, which was maintained during weeks 17, 18, 19, 20, 22, 23, and 24. The C statistic could have been employed to show statistically significant differences between follow-up and baseline.

TABLE 6.4
Three Hypothetical Distributions, Each with a Mean of 20

Distribution A	Distribution B	Distribution C
Number of Self-Critical Statements	Number of Self-Critical Statements	Number of Self-Critical Statements
20	40	100
20	40	100
20	40	0
20	40	0
20	40	0
20	0	0
20	0	0
20	0	0
20	0	0
20	0	0
$\Sigma 0 = 200$	$\Sigma 0 = 200$	$\Sigma 0 = 200$
$\bar{0} = \dfrac{\Sigma 0}{N} = \dfrac{200}{10} = 20$	$\bar{0} = \dfrac{200}{10} = 20$	$\bar{0} = \dfrac{200}{10} = 20$

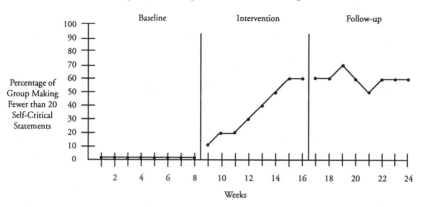

FIGURE 6.6

Graph of Interrupted Time-Series Design

Control of Internal Validity Threats and Generality. As with the Interrupted Time-Series Design for single cases, history, maturation, multiple treatment interference, expectancy effects, and interactions are not controlled. Information can be obtained for each client from observations, interviews, and available case records, but with several clients it is more difficult to show that these factors have little influence on changes in the dependent variable. Variables such as illness, fatigue, and stress probably vary greatly among clients.

Initial measurement effects, instrumentation, and statistical regression can be controlled with evidence of a horizontal baseline. It is especially important that the measurement process be standardized, so that all clients are measured in the same way. If this is the case, the practice researcher has further confidence that instrumentation is not affecting the study's internal validity. Since there are no comparison groups, experimental mortality and biased selection are not relevant. The practice-researcher should take care to include the same number of clients at all measurement points in this design, particularly since average measures can be distorted by extreme values, even if reported for only one client. Moreover, an extreme score causes greater distortion as the total number of clients decreases.

There may be some evidence of generality to the extent that the clients have similar characteristics, problems, and goals. The social worker would have to show that the clients in the study were representative of other clients that he or she typically encounters in practice. Still, there is little basis for generalizing to clients in other agencies, or with other workers. The results are applicable only to the workers delivering the same intervention to clients similar to those in the study and employed in the human service agency where the research occurs.

Generality can be built into the design by including a large number of clients with different characteristics and other social workers and their clients. To demonstrate generality across workers and clients within the human service agency, the practice-researcher would first present the results for all clients and workers combined. Then, the data would be disaggregated so that individual time-series designs are constructed for each worker and that worker's clients. Further disaggregation would be by type of client (say males only and females only). All the separate time-series would be analyzed in the same way. To the extent that results are consistent across clients and across workers, there is some basis for generality across workers and clients. Nevertheless, the workers and clients may or may not be representative of other workers and clients in the agency.

Nonequivalent Control Group Design, $\dfrac{O_1 X\, O_2}{O_3 X_0 O_4}$

In the Nonequivalent Control Group Design, an experimental group receives an intervention, X, while a comparison group does not, X_0 (Tripodi 1983). Measurements (O_1 and O_3) on the dependent variable are made for both groups of clients before the intervention (X) is delivered to the experimental group and again (O_3 and O_4) after the intervention is delivered. Differences between the experimental and comparison groups are compared with respect to their relative degrees of effectiveness. The comparison group controls for the possible effects of history, maturation, and multiple treatment interference. The two groups are regarded as potentially non-equivalent because possible selection bias is not controlled, as in the randomized Before-After Control Group Design, which will be discussed subsequently. Biased selection means that the clients in the experimental and comparison groups probably are not comparable on relevant variables (variables that are either theoretically or empirically related to the dependent variables). Three different strategies can approximate control of selection biases: control by definition, control by individual matching, and control by aggregate matching (Rossi, Freeman, and Wright 1979; Tripodi 1983). To illustrate these strategies, suppose ten high school students are at risk of being sent to a more restrictive school placement because they frequently exhibit disruptive behavior in the classroom. They receive an eight-week intervention consisting of a token economy and daily group sessions. A comparison group of ten clients is selected from a list of students who also are at risk of removal from this school setting due to their disruptive behavior. A school secretary collects information from the teachers of both experimental and comparison group members indicating how often they disrupted class during the previous week. The same data are collected after the experimental group receives eight weeks of treatment.

To determine which variables are relevant, the practice-researcher reads empirical research and conceptual papers related to disruptive behavior in high school. Variables potentially related to this problem might be age, gender, and number of previous school placements. Older students are apt to be more disruptive than will be younger students, males more disruptive than females, and students who had more previous school placements more disruptive than those who had fewer placements.

Control of selection biases is a simple procedure. The practice-researcher selects one or more variables and specifies the levels of the variable to be included in the research. For example, gender has two aspects or levels, male and female. It is controlled by definition if only males (or only females) are included. Hence, the ten clients selected could all be male, in which case the ten clients in the comparison group would also all be male.

Control of selection biases by individual matching of subjects is a procedure by which pairs of individuals are identified with respect to one or more relevant variables and each individual is arbitrarily assigned to the experimental or comparison group. For example, there may be two age groups for the prospective clients: an older group of seventeen- and eighteen-year-olds and a younger group of fifteen- and sixteen-year-olds. The practice-researcher identifies pairs of younger students and pairs of older students and assigns one member of each pair to the experimental group and the other to the comparison group.

The third strategy for controlling selection biases is aggregate matching. This involves identifying the percentage or proportion of experimental group clients who have a particular characteristic on a relevant variable. Then a comparison group is constructed such that its members have the same percentage or proportion of the particular characteristic as do the members of the experimental group. For example, 70 percent (seven) of the clients in the experimental group may have one or more previous school placements, and 30 percent (three) may have had no previous placements. Thus, the comparison group should also have these same proportions to control for previous school placement by aggregate matching.

Aggregate matching and control by definition are the simplest procedures for dealing with selection biases. When control is by definition, the homogeneity of the research samples is increased, but the degree of generality is reduced. For instance, one cannot generalize to female clients on the basis of intervention with male clients. More than one strategy can be used, but it is impractical to attempt to control more than a few variables, especially with samples as small as ten to thirty clients. In any case, Rossi, Freeman and Wright (1979) advocate selecting a small number of variables for control based on the argument that variables specified as relevant are usually highly correlated.

Organizational Constraints and Ethical Considerations. The problem with the Nonequivalent Control Group Design rests primarily on the selection of a control group. There may not be a waiting list, and it might be regarded as unethical to withhold treatment from some clients who need it. Sometimes a control group can be constructed of non-clients who exhibit the target problem and who have characteristics similar to the experimental group but, at best, they represent an approximation to a control group since they may not have the desire or motivation to seek treatment for the problem. For agency research, this design is most feasible when there is a list of clients waiting to receive the intervention or an available population of potential clients who would be willing to receive an intervention and who would like to change in a way that is consistent with goals of the experimental clients. If a group of subjects is employed as a comparison group, it is ethically imperative that the practice-researcher offer intervention to those subjects after the comparison period has elapsed. The longer the period of comparison, from when pre- to post-intervention measures are taken on the dependent variable, the greater the chances that subjects will drop out of the research and that the ethical ramifications will be more pronounced.

Analysis. Analysis of data yielded by this design centers on obtaining information of the relative effectiveness of the experimental group to the comparison group. For practice effectiveness, there obviously should be a greater degree of effectiveness for those clients who receive an intervention as compared to those who do not receive it. Qualitative matching involves the practice-researcher comparing changes for both groups in relation to *a priori* goals. For example, the worker might set a goal that 50 percent of the clients will disrupt their classes two times or less per week. The degree of goal attainment could be examined for both experimental and comparison groups. If the goal is too easily attained (say ten or fewer disruptions per week), it may not be sufficient to demonstrate practice effectiveness because both experimental and comparison groups may achieve it. If the comparison group subjects attain the goal, this can hardly be regarded as practice effectiveness since they did not receive any intervention. Indeed, it might even be a sign of non-practice effectiveness! Another type of *a priori* goal would be to specify the degree of relative efficacy between the experimental and comparison groups. For example, it might be specified that a greater percentage of clients will achieve the goal in the experimental group, as contrasted to the comparison group. Or, it might be asserted that the goal attainment in the experimental group will be greater and statistically significant as compared to that of the comparison group.

Graphic analysis is not too informative, since there are only two points for comparison for the experimental and control group, but it could be used to illustrate observed changes before and after intervention. As illustrated in figure 6.7, there was 0 percent of goal attainment for both groups before intervention. After intervention, 60 percent of the experimental group attained the goal, whereas only 20 percent of the comparison group did so.

Finally, a simple statistical procedure to test for statistically sig-

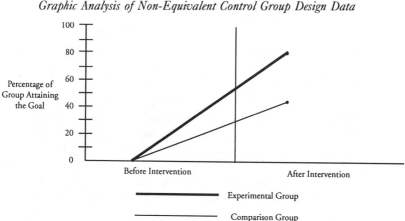

FIGURE 6.7
Graphic Analysis of Non-Equivalent Control Group Design Data

nificant differences between the experimental and comparison groups is the chi-square test for independent groups (McNemar 1957). The chi-square statistic for independent groups can be used when there are two comparison groups (such as experimental and control) and when goal attainment can be operationally defined. Goal attainment can be thought of as success or effectiveness, as specified by the practice-researcher prior to introducing the intervention. For the example of school disruption, goal attainment could be considered to be achieved when students disrupt class two times or less per week.

table 6.5 illustrates the general format and the formula for this statistic. *A* refers to the number of clients in the experimental group who have attained the goal and *B* denotes the number of clients in the comparison group who have attained the goal. Similarly, *C* indicates the number of clients in the experimental group who have not attained the goal and *D* the number of clients in the comparison group who have not attained the goal. Accordingly, A + C is the number of clients in the experimental group and B + D is the number of persons in the comparison group while N is the total number in the experimental and comparison groups. Note that this statistic should only be used when there are ten or more persons in each group.

To apply this chi-square statistic, these procedures should be followed:

1. Define goal attainment in specific, quantifiable terms.
2. After data are obtained for all subjects in the experimental and comparison groups, put the data in tabular form as in table 6.5.
3. From the table, obtain the necessary values to make substitutions in the following formula:

$$Chi\ square\ (\chi^2) = \frac{N\,(AD - BC)^2}{(A+B)(C+D)(A+C)(B+D)}$$

4. Compare the computed value of chi-square (12.8 in the example in table 6.5) with 3.84 (3.84 is the value of chi-square associated with a probability level greater than or equal to .05). If the value is greater than or equal to 3.84, there are statistically significant differences between the proportions or percentages of those achieving goal attainment in the experimental group and the comparison group, thereby indicating that the experimental group is relatively more effective. Referring to the example in table 6.5, we see that 90 percent (nine out of ten) of the experimental group attained the goal, while only ten percent (one out

TABLE 6.5

	Experimental Group	Comparison Group	Total
Number Attaining Goal	A	B	A+B
Number Not Attaining Goal	C	D	C+D
TOTAL	A+C	B+D	$\sqrt{N}$

$$\text{Chi square } (\chi^2) = \frac{N(AD - BC)^2}{(A+B)(C+D)(A+C)(B+D)}$$

If chi-square is greater than or equal to 3.84, the probability associated with that value of chi-square is less than or equal to .05 ($\chi^2 \geq 3.84$, $p \leq .05$)

EXAMPLE

	Experimental Group	Comparison Group	Total	
Number Attaining Goal	9(A)	1(B)	10(A+B)	$\chi^2 = \dfrac{20(81-1)^2}{(10)(10)(10)(10)}$
Number Not Attaining Goal	1(C)	9(D)	10(C+D)	$\chi^2 = 12.8$, which is statistically significant since it is greater than 3.84.
TOTAL	10(A+C)	10(B+D)	20(N)	

of ten) of the comparison group did. Not surprisingly, the chi-square tests suggests that the progress realized by the experimental group is statistically significant.

Control of Internal Validity Threats and Generality. The Nonequivalent Control Group Design provides some control for history, maturation, and multiple treatment interference, to the extent that the experimental and comparison groups can be regarded as having similar exposures to the environment. This control is stronger if the groups have similar characteristics on relevant variables. The chief problem with this design is the possibility of bias entering the selection of the groups. These potential biases can be reduced with such strategies as matching and control by definition, as previously discussed.

Regression effects are not controlled when individual subjects have extreme scores, but their effects are reduced if the pretest scores for the experimental and comparison groups are equivalent, and if there is change at the posttest for the experimental group, but not for the comparison group. Although experimental mortality is not controlled, the practice-researcher can observe whether or not it occurs. It is less likely to be a problem when interventions are time-limited. Instrumentation and effects of previous measurements are controlled to the extent that there are no changes from pre- to post-test measurements for the comparison group.

The samples for these designs are accidental or convenience samples so the extent to which they can be generalized to other clients or workers is unclear. Generalization attempts should be limited to clients and workers within the agency. Generality is increased to the extent that evidence documenting the similarity of clients and workers in the study to other clients and workers in the agency can be produced.

Randomized Before-After Control Group Design, $\dfrac{RO_1X\,O_2}{RO_3X_0O_4}$

The Randomized Before-After Control Group Design is the classical experimental design. It involves specifying a pool of subjects (clients) who are eligible for the intervention. These subjects are randomly assigned (R) to either an experimental group, RO_1XO_2, or to a control group, $RO_3X_0O_4$. Both groups are measured at the same time intervals, before and after the intervention, on one or more dependent variables. The experimental group (X) receives the intervention, while the control group (X_0) receives no intervention. The changes in the dependent variable for the experimental group, $O_2 - O_1$, reflect influences of the intervention, history, maturation, and effects of measurement; while dependent variable changes in the control group, $O_4 - O_3$, are due to changes in history, maturation and measurement effects. Assuming the influencing factors are additive (hence, subtractive) in the same way for both experimental and control groups, the difference between $O_4 - O_3$ and $O_2 - O_1$ [or, $(O_4 - O_3) - (O_2 - O_1)$] indicates the influence or contribution of the independent variable, X, to the observed changes.

The basic difference between this design and the Nonequivalent Control Group Design is the use of randomization in assigning clients to the experimental or control groups. Randomization is based on probability theory, which allows each client in the subject pool an equally likely chance of being assigned to the experimental or the control group. The practice-researcher can flip an unbiased coin or use a table of random digits (for example, odd digits represent assignment to the control group and even digits represent assignment to the experimental group) to assign clients. This procedure eliminates experimenter bias, controlling for the factor of selection bias.

Organizational and Ethical Constraints. When there is a large waiting list, randomization is not necessarily unethical, particularly if all of the clients waiting for the intervention have the same magnitude of problem severity. (Note that we assume that an agency will screen clients before placing them on a waiting list, so that clients who might harm themselves or others are not allowed to wait for treatment.) On the other hand, when there is a sufficient amount of available intervention for all clients, it may be regarded as unethical to deny the intervention for any of the clients. This is particularly a problem if the intervention is expected to lead to a desirable outcome, based on knowledge about its effectiveness.

Because it provides greater control over internal validity threats than do the other designs discussed in this chapter, the experimental design is most useful when there is a desire to obtain causal knowledge and when the extent to which an intervention is effective is unknown. Since it is costly to maintain an experiment, it is most feasible when interventions are of relatively short duration, or time-limited. Moreover, after the experiment is completed, intervention can then be offered to those clients who are in the control group.

As with any type of social work practice, interventions may have undesirable or deleterious effects on clients, resulting in negative change or deterioration. Hence, it is unethical to administer an intervention to clients, especially repeatedly, without some knowledge about the consequences of the intervention.

A potential problem with the control group is that control group members may seek interventions elsewhere if they are available. Therefore, the practice-researcher should obtain information from clients in both experimental and control groups about their receipt of other interventions. This, of course, requires more agency resources.

Analysis. The same techniques for analysis as described for the Nonequivalent Control Group Design can be employed. Another statistical technique that can be used with the classical experimental design is the *t*-test for independent groups (Pagano 1981). This statistic indicates whether or not the group means of the experimental and control groups are statistically significantly different. The statistic is based on the assumption that the sampling distribution of the differences between the group means is normally distributed (in a bell-shaped curve) and that the population variances for both experimental and control groups are equivalent. The procedure of randomizing clients from the same subject pool makes these assumptions plausible, whereas there is no evidence to support these assumptions with the Nonequivalent Control Group Design.

Let us return to the example of an eight-week group intervention to reduce disruptive behavior in high school students. For this design, let us suppose randomization is employed which results in the assignment of ten students to the experimental group and ten students to the control group. To calculate the *t* statistic, the following steps must be taken.

1. Record the data for the experimental and for the control group as in columns 1, 2 and 3 of table 6.6. This indicates the before and after measurement scores for each client. Hence, client I in the experimental group disrupted class 30 times per week prior to intervention and ten times per week after intervention, while client R in the control group disrupted class 26 times per week both before and after the intervention was given to the experimental group.

2. Calculate the means and variances of the difference scores for the experimental and control group as follows:

   a. For each group, subtract the score for each client in column 3 from the score in column 2 to obtain the difference scores, denoted as X_1 for the experimental group and X_2 for the control group (column 4).

   b. Obtain the arithmetic means for the difference scores of experimental ($\bar{X}_1 = \Sigma X_1/N_1$) and the control groups ($\bar{X}_2 = \Sigma X_2/N_2$) which are 9.3 and 0.2, respectively.

   c. For the experimental and the control groups, subtract the mean from each difference score ($X_1 - \bar{X}_1, X_2 - \bar{X}_2$) as shown in column 5.

   d. Square the values in column 5 to obtain column 6.

   e. Calculate the variances for the experimental group ($S_1^2 = \Sigma(X_1 - \bar{X}_1)^2/N_1 - 1$) and for the control group ($S_2^2 = \Sigma(X_2 - \bar{X}_2)^2/N_2 - 1$), which are 43.12 and 0.40 respec-

TABLE 6.6
Data and Calculations for t-test for the Randomized Before-After Control Group Design

Experimental Group

(1)	(2)	(3)	(4)	(5)	(6)
Client	Before Measurement Score	After Measurement Score	Column 2– Column 3 X_1	$(X_1-\bar{X_1})$	$(X_1-\bar{X_1})^2$
A	20	20	0	−9.3	86.49
B	21	20	1	−8.3	68.89
C	22	18	4	−5.3	28.09
D	25	20	5	−4.3	18.49
E	26	13	13	3.7	13.69
F	24	10	14	4.7	22.09
G	24	10	14	4.7	22.09
H	23	14	9	−.3	.09
I	30	10	20	10.7	114.49
J	28	15	13	3.7	13.69
			$\Sigma X_1 = 93$		$\Sigma(X_1-\bar{X_1})^2 = 388.10$

$$\bar{X_1} = \frac{\Sigma X_1}{N} = \frac{93}{10} = 9.3$$

$$S_1^2 = \frac{\Sigma(X_1 - \bar{X_1})^2}{N_1 - 1} = \frac{388.10}{9} = 43.12$$

Control Group

(1)	(2)	(3)	(4)	(5)	(6)
Client	Before Measurement Score	After Measurement Score	Column 2– Column 3 X_2	$(X_2-\bar{X_2})$	$(X_2-\bar{X_2})^2$
K	21	21	0	−.2	.04
L	23	22	1	.8	.64
M	22	23	−1	−1.2	1.44
N	22	21	1	.8	.64
O	26	25	1	.8	.64
P	25	25	0	−.2	.04
Q	24	24	0	−.2	.04
R	26	26	0	−.2	.04
S	28	28	0	−.2	.04
T	29	29	0	−.2	.04
			$\Sigma X_2 = 2$		$\Sigma(X_2-\bar{X_2})^2 = 3.60$

$$\bar{X_2} = \frac{\Sigma X_2}{N} = \frac{2}{10} = 0.2$$

$$S_2^2 = \frac{\Sigma(X_2 - \bar{X_2})^2}{N_2 - 1} = \frac{3.60}{9} = 0.40$$

$$df = N_1 + N_2 - 2 = 10 + 10 - 2 = 18$$

$$t = \frac{\bar{X_1} - \bar{X_2}}{\sqrt{\frac{S_1^2}{N_1} + \frac{S_2^2}{N_2}}} = \frac{9.3 - 0.2}{\sqrt{\frac{43.12}{9} + \frac{0.40}{9}}} = \frac{9.1}{\sqrt{4.79 + 0.04}} = \frac{9.1}{2.20} = 4.14$$

Since t = 4.14 is greater than t = 2.101 with 18 degrees of freedom (see Table 6.3), probability associated with t is less than .05.

tively. Note that $\Sigma(X_1 - \bar{X}_1)^2$ and $\Sigma(X_2 - \bar{X}_2)^2$ are the sums of column 6 for the experimental group (388.10) and for the control group (3.60).

3. Calculate the degrees of freedom (df) by using this formula $df = N_1 + N_2 - 2$.
4. Calculate the t statistic for independent groups by using this formula:

$$t = \frac{\bar{X}_1 - \bar{X}_2}{\sqrt{\dfrac{S_1^2}{N_1} + \dfrac{S_2^2}{N_2}}}$$

5. Refer to table 6.3 to obtain the value of t associated with a probability level of .05 for 18 degrees of freedom. This value is $t = 2.101$.
6. Compare the calculated value of t (4.14) with the tabled value (2.101). If the calculated t is greater than or equal to the tabled value, the difference between experimental and control group means is statistically significant at or beyond the .05 level of probability. If the calculated t is less than the tabled value, the difference between the means is not statistically significant. For our example, the mean difference is statistically significant. Hence, there is change in the dependent variable that is associated with the experimental group over and beyond any changes that might have occurred in the control group by chance alone.

Control of Threats to Internal Validity and Generalization. This design controls for all internal validity threats except for their possible interactions and experimental mortality. To further support the control of internal validity threats, the practice-researcher should show whether experimental and control group clients have received interventions from other resources or have experienced other unusual events that might be related to possible changes on the dependent variable(s). If there are no extraneous interventions or events or if they are distributed equally between experimental and control groups, it is plausible that the groups are equivalent and are experiencing similar phenomena except that the control group did not receive intervention.

Further evidence that there are no changes due to history, maturation, regression, measurement effects, and unstandardized measurement can be obtained by showing that there are no statistically significant differences within the control group, comparing before and after measures (columns 2 and 3 of table 6.6) using the matched pairs *t*-test. The basic data and calculations are in table 6.7, where it is observed that the calculated value of *t* is less than the tabled value of 2.262 and is thus non-statistically significant indicating no changes due to those potential internal validity factors.

To the extent that the subject pool is a representative sample of the potential client population, the results can be generalized to that client population. This is possible if each member of the subject pool is randomly drawn from a larger population. If not, the results are generalizable only to the clients in the subject pool. The results are not generalizable to other workers unless random sampling is obtained from a larger population of workers; each of which applies the intervention to a randomly selected group of clients. Because this is not the case in this experiment, generalization to workers is not possible.

TABLE 6.7
Data and Calculations for Matched Pairs t-test for Control Group Scores

Client	Before Intervention Score	After Intervention Score	D	D²
K	21	21	0	0
L	23	22	1	1
M	22	23	−1	1
N	22	21	1	1
O	26	25	1	1
P	25	25	0	0
Q	24	24	0	0
R	26	26	0	0
S	28	28	0	0
T	29	29	0	0
			$\Sigma D = 2$	$\Sigma D^2 = 4$

$$\overline{D} = \frac{\Sigma D}{N} = \frac{2}{10} = 0.2$$

$$\Sigma d^2 = \Sigma D^2 - \frac{(\Sigma D)^2}{N} = 3.6$$

$$t = \frac{\overline{D}}{\sqrt{\dfrac{\Sigma d^2}{N(N-1)}}} = \frac{.2}{\sqrt{\dfrac{3.6}{90}}} = 1$$

Since 1 is less than t for 9 degrees of freedom (N−1), which is 2.262 (see table 6.3), t is not statistically significant.

NOTES

1. The relationship between evaluation and monitoring discussed here is similar to notions of summative and formative evaluation (see Scriven 1967).

2. The three "O's" before and after X, the intervention, refer to three or more measurements.

3. The Interrupted Time-Series Design does not call for a specified length of time for each of the phases, but the measurements should be obtained at equal intervals of time across all of the phases, if possible.

4. See Barlow and Hersen (1984) for a discussion of reversal designs. We do not present other designs in which the practice-researcher deliberately creates experimental conditions to reverse the data patterns since we regard this as an unethical practice.

5. See Barlow and Hersen (1984) for other types of multiple-baseline designs.

6. As an exercise, the readers should verify this using statistical procedures discussed in chapter 5.

7. *Summarizing and Reporting Results of Practice Research*

In previous chapters we discussed strategies and procedures for assessing client needs, determining the extent to which interventions are implemented, monitoring client progress in achieving practice goals, and evaluating effectiveness of interventions with individuals and groups. Information obtained from such efforts are the results of practice research. This information can be kept in case records and used as the basis of reports to interested consumers. But why should records be kept? And, how can they be most useful?

We believe that the fundamental reason for maintaining records of practice research is that practice can be improved by the information obtained from practice research. Maintaining information on the results of research on an individual case (individual, group, or family) within cases enables the practice-researcher to do the following:

1. Ascertain the extent to which a client's needs or problems were met or reduced;
2. Provide a reference point of the client's needs and their resolution if the client should relapse and/or return to the agency for additional help;
3. Determine the degree to which one or more interventions appears to be effective or ineffective for a particular case, client problem, and treatment goal;
4. Furnish data that might be used during the course of intervention to discuss progress or lack of progress with clients and significant others, with the practice-researcher's supervisor, and with treatment teams or individual practice consultants, and to make practice decisions.

Information about cases is especially valuable while practice is taking place, for it is the essence of that which can be fed back to clients as they participate in the intervention process. Moreover, it satisfies the ethical and professional requirements of accountability. Preserving information from single cases provides a basic source of data that has several potential applications. By making comparisons across cases, it is possible to determine the types of problems frequently dealt with by the practice-researcher. Aggregating single-case data allows the worker to estimate which interventions were implemented for what problems and with what degree of effectiveness. For example, a practice-researcher might have used intervention X for ten clients. Evidence of effectiveness might have been obtained for eight clients, all of whom had relationship problems with their partners, while two clients who had relationship problems with their colleagues did not respond to the intervention. Such information also could help determine the extent of need and problem difficulty among clients in the worker's caseload. Finally, these data could provide evidence about factors that facilitate or impede the implementation of interventions.

Obviously, data from practice research across cases (such as needs assessments of agency clients or results from the use of group designs for monitoring progress and for evaluating effectiveness), like the aggregation of results from single cases, can be very informative. These data may provide estimates of training and supervisory needs. For instance, if interventions are ineffective for a particular practitioner, and not for others, the practitioner may benefit from more intensive supervision to effectively implement that intervention. Or, if an intervention is unsuccessful for a particular type of client, this may lead agency staff to explore why the intervention is unsuccessful and to implement training regarding how the intervention is best instituted. These data may indicate the need for new agency policies. For example, a practice-researcher's data may suggest that interventions may be more successfully implemented if home visits and/ or transportation are included. Needs assessments, surveys, client satisfaction studies, and effectiveness studies can help agency staff be accountable to its board. Information regarding the extent to which the agency is meeting client needs, providing services, or delivering effective interventions all would be of interest to agency board members. Certain data across cases might indicate staffing needs. For instance, data indicating an increase in substance abuse problems among new referrals coupled with less positive outcomes for these clients might lead an agency to recruit staff with expertise in working with substance abuse problems. Finally, data on groups of clients served by the agency might serve as public relations material for potential funders such as United Way. These are just a few of the ways in which data across clients can facilitate and enhance various agency tasks and functions. In our experience, agencies that devote the resources to producing such data, even of a very elementary variety, find a multitude of ways to use it, both inside and outside the agency.

Consumers of Practice Research

Within the agency, the primary consumers of practice research concerned with individual cases and/or caseloads are the client, the practice-researcher, and the supervisor. Outside the agency, referral sources and social service professionals working with the same client population will find practice research on both individual cases and caseloads informative. Agency colleagues and administrators may also be potential consumers. Practice research that is devoted to aggregating across programs is of prime interest to the agency board, administrators, and supervisors. Information regarding new and important information about the agency's programs, practices, and policies is potentially useful for the profession, the community, and for the board and agency colleagues. Publications in the form of brochures, technical reports, monographs, or articles for professional journals enhance the public image of the agency, and are helpful for public relations and fund raising.

These potential consumers can realize a wide range of benefits from the results of practice research. Following are suggestions about just a few of the ways in which each of the potential consumers of practice research might use the information derived from practice research.

The *client* might observe and discuss with the practice-researcher graphs showing change or lack of change and other data that are indicative of goal attainment. In our experience, such graphs motivate and secure continued client cooperation and participation in treatment. Involving clients in decision making about interventions while examining client data not only respects clients as self-determining individuals but also results in better treatment plans.

The *practice-researcher* can build knowledge about differential effectiveness with various types of clients and client problems by examining records of effectiveness. Moreover, information can be developed about problems in implementing certain interventions and which strategies were more or less effective and efficient. Basic data can be provided for case presentations to supervisors, consultants, and treatment staff for purposes of making decisions about interventions within the confines of agency functions and policies. Finally, just as with the client, a graph indicating some client progress can be very motivating to a social worker, particularly when dealing with some extremely challenging client problems.

Supervisors might examine data from one of their workers' caseloads to identify potential problems in the delivery of social services and gaps in the knowledge and skill of their staff. It may indicate the need to secure training from external consultants about implementing particular interventions or assessing certain client variables, and/or it may suggest the need to focus supervisory sessions on particular topics.

While applying appropriate measures to insure client confidentiality and appropriate access to case records, *colleagues* within and outside the agency need to have access to detailed case information regarding assessment, implementation of interventions, client progress, and effectiveness. Sometimes, workers become ill, transfer from the agency, or are away for extended periods of times. In these instances, new or backup workers need to know something about the status and progress of cases to provide services that are consistent with those provided by the original workers. Well-documented case information from a social worker in one agency may help a worker in another agency who is dealing with another aspect of a client's life make a more appropriate, better informed decision for that client.

Administrators are interested in aggregated (group) results of needs surveys and interventions. Information about need can be used to justify requests for grants and other types of financial aid to better serve clients. The likelihood of securing additional funding increases as the administrator can show that the agency practices and policies are effective in accomplishing client goals of maintenance, prevention, and change.

Information about agency effectiveness and efficiency is important for *agency board members,* many of whom are engaged in raising funds for agency operations and are concerned about appropriate fiscal management.

Academicians, such as social work researchers and social scientists, can benefit from knowledge about agency effectiveness and problems in implementing interventions. This type of information may stimulate them to work with agency staff in developing, refining, and evaluating agency interventions. Such joint activity may also stimulate social work education, particularly by providing more examples of client needs, facilitators and barriers to interventions, and knowledge of effectiveness and ineffectiveness.

Through presentations at public fora (forums) and professional conferences, and in the literature of the profession, information about agency practices can be disseminated and discussed with other *professionals*. Such discussions may lead to further improvements in agency practices.

Ethical and Organizational Considerations

The maintenance and accumulation of records requires an expenditure of agency resources. All agencies have some type of recording and information systems. The degree to which additional recording from practice research is affordable and feasible depends upon the agency's priorities, its resources, and upon its existing information systems. Some agencies employ computerized systems for keeping track of client demographics and eligibility data, as well as fiscal and service information. At the opposite extreme, some agencies keep minimal, hard copy records but do not have routine information systems in which the data can be easily accessed.

Practice research data can be recorded and easily transformed for information systems. It does not require additional work beyond that which the practice-researcher engages in when working with clients to maintain records on a case-by-case basis, or to maintain the results of group research. To computerize such information requires more time, and it also relies on the commitment of financial resources and time in its initial phases. Over the long run, however, a computerized system is cost-efficient, because data about cases can be accessed or aggregated instantly.

Therefore, administrative supports, financial backing and the desire of practice-researchers are critical to recording and maintaining records of practice research. Barriers are the lack of time, resources, and skills needed to erect a good record-keeping system.

The ethical issues of confidentiality, identification of clients, informed consent and information-sharing among agencies are important to consider. Permission must be obtained to collect and use data from clients. This is generally not a problem in the use of data between clients, workers and supervisors; and reports to clients and supervisors do not need any additional assurances for confidentiality. However, sharing information with others in the same agency or between agencies requires informed consent. Informed consent is usually obtained by indicating that no individuals will be identified. Results are fictionalized for single cases, and are aggregated for groups. Moreover, the agency and its location are also not identified in the release of information.

The practice-researcher should be aware of agency practices and policies about the exchange of information about clients, and she or he should adhere to them. This should be done in reports at conferences as well as in written documents. Even when information is derived from other sources, such as agency demographics obtained from intake interviews, the practice-researcher should determine what provisions of informed consent and confidentiality were made. If there are no clear provisions on record, the practice-researcher should obtain permission from the client, specifying the nature of the report, who will use the information, the extent of client identification, and the notion that his participation is voluntary and does not affect her/his right to further treatment.

Computers and Practice Research

As suggested above, there are several advantages to computerizing client data. When entered into a well-designed information system, client data can easily be accessed, updated, and manipulated. More importantly, these data can be reported in various ways to answer a range of questions—questions that may be of interest to any of the potential consumers of practice research.

Procedures for developing computerized information systems have been outlined in great detail (Grasso and Epstein 1989; Pardeck and Murphy 1990). Both the information systems and computers and software, in general, can enhance practice at all levels. In our opinion, it is extremely important that the needs and interests of all potential consumers of practice research be considered in the design of an information system and the introduction or expansion of computer facilities in a human services agency. All too often, these information systems are designed to accomplish routine monitoring or reporting needs for agency administrators, and nothing more (Briar and Blythe 1985). Unfortunately, this represents a gross underutilization of the potential of computerized data bases. Moreover, this narrow application typically relies on considerable data-collection and sometimes input by practitioners. In essence, the computerized information system may require that much effort be expended by certain segments of the agency, while primarily meeting a few needs of other agency staff. Moreover, computers have several other uses beyond the information system applications.

Computerized client records offer the agency many advantages. While the potential applications are still being developed and tested, even clients may benefit from the computerization of agency information. Some computer applications facilitate sharing information with clients and giving them immediate feedback. For example, Hudson (1982) designed a computerized data base that allows clients to use a computer keyboard to complete standardized measures that assess client problems. Upon completing a measure, the client receives his or her score, a clear interpretation of the score, and an updated graph of all of the client's scores to date. This is just one example of the ways computers might provide clients with information.

Computerized information systems can help practice researchers in many ways (Briar and Blythe 1985). When practitioners routinely specify client problems and goals, identify specific treatment techniques, and monitor their progress toward goals, all of this information can form a data bank to inform decisions with the current client and with future clients having similar difficulties. Paperwork also can be facilitated by computers, as routine but required forms asking for the same information, but in a different format each time, can be at least partially completed by the computerized information system. Computers also can remind practice researchers of deadlines, follow-up intervals, and the like. Simple statistical packages to support practice research efforts are available to simplify data analysis activities.

Supervisors, administrators, and agency board members all can reap benefits of computers and computerized information systems. When individual practice-researchers enter information about the types of client problems being handled and treatment outcomes, the information can be aggregated across clients and practitioners to inform program planning and decisionmaking. For instance, certain data patterns may suggest that supervisors should more closely supervise certain client presenting problems, seek in-service training on specific topics, or recruit staff with particular areas of expertise. Administrators and board members will also benefit from such information to the extent that they are involved in these types of decisions, at some level.

Preparing Reports about Needs Assessments

The basic contents of needs assessments for individuals and aggregates of clients were presented in chapter 3. Recall that we suggested that the practice-researcher should consider such dimensions as the type of client population (active, waiting list, or discontinued), the operational definition of need, whether the need is for an individual client or for groups of clients, and the procedures for gathering and analyzing need data. To be of maximum benefit, the results of needs assessments should be communicated to other persons who can use or take action on the findings. Here, we provide the basic criteria for producing written and oral reports about the results of needs assessment studies.

The first criterion is to specify the consumer of the report, which, among other things, suggests whether it should be written, presented orally, or both. Generally, reports for clients and supervisors are made orally and with less detail than are reports written for administrators, the community, and the profession. An oral presentation is more likely to emphasize the results and possible implications, while written reports usually include the methodological details of the needs assessments as well as the results. The practice-researcher should consider whether or not there will be more than one type of consumer. The report, written or oral, detailed or summarized, should be appropriate for the consumers. To obtain an estimate of what is appropriate, the social worker might present an outline of all that could be included in a report and discuss it with the consumer. The practice-researcher also should have some sense of the desired content and length of the report. For example, administrators are primarily interested in the results. This does not mean, however, that the methodology would not be presented. Enough of the methodology should be transmitted to provide a context for interpreting the conclusions, and additional methodological details might be included as an appendix to a written report or as a written supplement to an oral presentation. For instance, conclusions about needs based on intake data for all active clients are not necessarily the same as are conclusions based on an accidental sample of clients.

Another consideration that affects the format of the report is whether the needs assessment is for an individual client or for a group. For individuals, there is less necessity for a written report than an oral report when the consumer is the client, supervisor, and/or the worker. However, some written materials might be helpful, such as the instrument used for gathering data and simple tables or graphs that succinctly summarize the data. Reports of aggregated needs of clients can be more easily presented and discussed when the data are in graphs and/or tables.

In addition to the format of the report, the practitioner also needs to consider the content of the report. The needs being assessed should be clearly defined by specifying relevant variables and their operational definitions. Hence, the data-gathering instrument, along with evidence of its reliability, validity, and possible normative data should be included in the report. Although the details of instrumentation might be located in an appendix, it is important to provide some specific, albeit brief, answers to the following questions about the instruments:

1. Why was the instrument selected or developed?
2. Does the instrument provide a clear picture of the need being assessed?
3. Are there other instruments and/or indices of need that might have been used? If so, why weren't they?

The target population should be identified, and the practice-researcher should indicate the extent to which the sample actually is representative of the population. Of course, if the report is about one client, this is not necessary. For more guidance, refer back to the discussion of representative sampling in chapter 3.

The report should include information on the data collection process and any observations about limitations of the data. Potential limitations include low response rates, over-or under-estimates of need, and possible biasing conditions in the data collection itself.

Data analyses should be presented in graphic or tabular form, as appropriate. Supplementary descriptive information should indicate the type of analyses as well as report the conclusions about individual or average measures of need in a straightforward manner. For example, using simple percentages, it might be reported that 60 percent of the clients on the active caseloads live in substandard housing, and 90 percent of those clients are Asian (see table 7.1).

Last, but certainly not of least importance, the report must discuss the implications of the findings for the agency in relation to its resources. Recommendations might be made to provide increased services or to make referrals to other agencies if appropriate services are not available in the agency. For example, in the report about housing, administrators, board members, or others may want to find out exactly

TABLE 7.1

Percentage of Active Clients Living in Substandard Housing By Ethnic Status
($N = 100$)

Conditions of Housing	Ethnic Status				
	Asians	Blacks	Hispanics	Whites	Total
Standard	3	4	3	30	40
Substandard	54	3	3	0	60
TOTALS	57	7	6	30	100

where the clients live, noting whether there are any similarities in the living conditions. If all of the clients live in a housing project, they may inquire further from the housing project on substandard conditions. Moreover, they may advocate for better conditions for those clients or contact other agencies or organizations that have the resources to deal with the housing project, such as a housing authority or tenants rights organization.

figure 7.1 lists the components to include in oral and written reports about needs assessments.

Preparing Reports on Implementing Interventions and Client Progress

Recall chapter 4 on implementing interventions and chapter 5 on designs for monitoring client progress. In chapter 4, we presented concepts and procedures for assessing worker compliance and client compliance as indices of implementing interventions. And, we discussed a process for determining the extent to which there is client progress toward attaining specified goals in chapter 5.

Reports on implementing interventions and on client progress often are made while the work is "in progress" and, therefore, tend to be brief, oral presentations. For practice with individual cases, the primary consumers are the client, the worker, and the supervisor. When work with a client is presented for consultation or for a case presentation to other workers and/or supervisors, written and graphic materials also may be included. When there are several clients who have common goals and for whom a program of interventions is designed, the primary consumers of a report on intervention implementation and client progress are practitioners, supervisors, and administrators. Again, written and graphic materials may add to the oral presentation.

FIGURE 7.1

Ingredients of Reports About Needs Assessments

Type of client need
Definition of target population
Sampling procedure
Representativeness of sample and its limitations
Definition of need
Specification of instrument
Data about reliability, validity, and norms
Response rate and possible limitations in data collection
Data analyses
Conclusions and implications for program planning and further interventions

These reports should be less formal than reports of intervention effectiveness after cases have been terminated. For the most part, they are presented in the context of worker-client and supervisor-worker interactions when dealing with individual clients. For example, a graph may illustrate progress in achieving a goal and information pertaining to worker and client compliance with intervention plans may be presented and discussed. Results or conclusions should be emphasized with brief descriptions of the client(s), goals, interventions, and instruments employed to measure implementation and progress. Since the work is in progress, the reports should be geared as much as possible to practice decisions that might need to be made about interventions or programs, such as modification or substitution.

In making a report, the practice-researcher will find it helpful to keep in mind the ingredients of a complete report, even though the practitioner may not necessarily refer in detail to all of these ingredients in an oral communication. When reports are written for consultants, supervisors, or administrators, they should be brief. Instruments, methodological assumptions, and tables should be presented as appendices.

The basic ingredients of a complete report include the concepts and procedures discussed in chapters 4 and 5 organized in a logical manner. To begin, the practice-researcher should identify the *target of intervention*, which may be a client system, such as a family or may consist of aggregated cases, such as many different families who receive an intervention from several different practice-researchers. The client system should be briefly described with respect to variables such as age, gender, school or occupational status, family composition, income, and presenting problem. Descriptions of aggregated clients should focus on their similarities and differences in terms of relevant variables. For example, twenty clients may be the target of intervention aimed at preventing unwanted teenage pregnancy. All of the clients may be female, between the ages of thirteen and fourteen, Catholic and Hispanic, but they may vary in terms of family income, school attendance, and grades in school. Workers should also be briefly described by characteristics that are relevant to intervention implementation such as training and experience with the intervention and population, and demographic characteristics that might influence clients beyond the intervention. It is especially important to describe similarities and differences among workers when there are two or more practitioners delivering the intervention.

The goals for intervention should be specified so that they are in the form of variables that indicate the degree to which change, maintenance, or prevention is occurring. In addition, problems that are not the foci of intervention should be briefly described if it is believed that they might influence the attainment of the primary practice goals. For example, the primary goal may be to prevent pregnancy by means of didactic presentations and group discussion. Yet, family relationship difficulties may be another problem that could affect the achievement of the primary goal even though these are not be the target of the intervention.

The intervention should be described so that its contents and parameters are clear. Obviously, when reporting feedback to a client, it may not be necessary to indicate what the intervention is (was). A case presentation to a supervisor or a consultant should include some detail about the intervention, particularly about what the worker actually did. This is necessary so that the professionals can speculate about possible modifications when data indicate difficulty in implementing interventions and/or lack of client progress.

Client and worker compliance as indices of intervention implementation should be defined. For example, as previously discussed in chapter 4, client compliance may include the completion of homework-type assignments between sessions with the practice-researcher, while, worker compliance may be evidenced by discussing those assignments with the client at the beginning of each session. These definitions can be brief and provided as a context for interpreting indices of compliance. To illustrate, client compliance may be defined as the number of days during a week that a client gives medication to his wife. Over a period of four successive weeks, the client may have complied three out of seven, four out of seven, five out of seven, and six out of seven days, indicating increasing compliance over a period of one month, a sign of intervention implementation.

To present information about progress, it is important that the consumer of the report know how progress is defined. In this regard, the practice-researcher takes care in specifying clinical and/or statistical definitions of progress. For example, to obtain progress when the goal is abstinence from drug use, the clinical definition of progress may be no change of any magnitude from the onset of intervention to a later time such as two months, while the statistical definition might be no statistically significant changes from the onset of intervention to observations made two months later. These definitions need not cover such lengthy periods. They also might indicate the measuring instrument, which can be appended in a formal report or simply shown in an oral presentation.

Research design is a technical aspect that should be dealt with in an appendix of a written report or briefly discussed in oral reports. Rather than naming the research design, it is sufficient to simply indicate the ingredients of the design. So, instead of calling it a Before/During Intervention Time-Series Group Design, the practice-researcher might say that forty clients with the same practice goals were measured daily for a two-week period of time on the dependent variable (which is fully described in the report) before intervention and two weeks after the intervention was introduced. In this way, there is clearer communication between the practice-researcher and the consumer. In short, one person's "experiment" is another's "exploratory study"—differences in definition about the naming of designs occurs when researchers and practitioners refer to texts or approaches that have different labels for the same basic designs. On the other hand, if everyone in the agency uses the same labels for designs, communication is facilitated.

Like research design, the details of statistical data analyses should be appended to the report. Observed changes that achieved the criterion of statistically significant change in accordance with a designated statistical test can be noted in written or oral reports. Simple tables and graphs should be shown because they can quickly communicate the essence of the results, along with an interpretation by the practice-researcher. For example, a social worker might report that, since intervention began, the magnitude of verbal abuse of a child by the mother (as registered on a scale of verbal child abuse from "0," no abuse, to "10," extreme abuse) has shown a steady reduction since the introduction of treatment nine weeks ago, as reflected on this graph. Figure 7.2, which depicts this trend, aids the consumer in comprehending the degree of client improvement.

Depending on the purpose of the report, the conclusions that the practitioner is able to make at the time of the report should be outlined. If the practitioner is seeking consultation at this point, it may be helpful to suggest tentative conclusions and then to indicate specific questions or practice decisions to be addressed during the consultation.

Figure 7.3 summarizes the components that should be included in a formal, written report about monitoring intervention implementation and client progress.

Preparing Reports on Practice Effectiveness

To prepare reports on practice effectiveness, the reader must be familiar with all of the concepts presented in this book. Refer especially to chapter 6, in which we discuss designs and present concepts and definitions for evaluating practice effectiveness.

Reports on practice effectiveness build on the informal reports

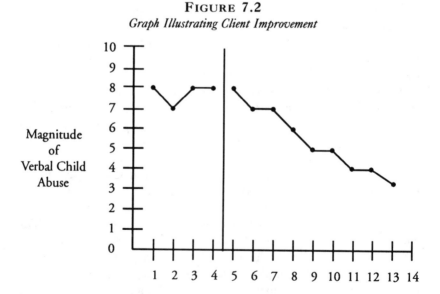

FIGURE 7.2

Graph Illustrating Client Improvement

Magnitude of Verbal Child Abuse

Time at Weekly Intervals

FIGURE 7.3

Ingredients of Reports About Treatment Implementation and Client Progress

Object of intervention
Description of the client(s)
Description of the worker(s)
Intervention goals
Other problems that are not the foci of intervention
Intervention
Client and worker compliance
Progress
Instruments and variables
Research design and data analysis (briefly described)
Simple tables and graphs
Conclusions about intervention implementation and client progress

about treatment implementation and client progress. This is obvious when figure 7.4, which contains the basic ingredients for reports on practice effectiveness, is compared with figure 7.3. The basic additions to a report of practice effectiveness refer to concepts and data regarding causality and generality with respect to practice effectiveness. These reports are generally done after the work with the client(s) has been completed, thereby allowing for time to reflect and analyze the results and the meaning of the interventions for particular clients. Reports of practice effectiveness tend to be more formal, often in the form of a report, a paper for a conference presentation, or a journal article. The primary audiences are administrators, colleagues, professionals, board members, and the community. Naturally, the specific format of the report should be tailored to the primary audience. In a research journal such as *Social Work Research*, the methodology would be thoroughly but succinctly described. In contrast, a report to the agency's board would consist primarily of a brief executive summary of about 5 pages, with detailed methodological considerations such as instrumentation, sampling, and statistical analyses appended to the summary. The point is that the practice-researcher should present the basic ingredients of a report as shown in figure 7.4, but the relative emphasis of particular components or ingredients should vary in relation to the audience.

As with reports of treatment implementation and client progress, the content of the report will differ, depending on whether the target of intervention is a single client system or is comprised of multiple clients. If, for example, one intervention is administered by several

FIGURE 7.4
Ingredients of Reports About Practice Effectiveness

Target of intervention
Description of the client(s)
Description of the worker(s)
Description of the intervention
Evidence of intervention implementation
Intervention goals
Other problems that are not the foci of intervention
Definition of practice effectiveness
Instruments for measurement
   discussion and evidence of reliability and validity
Description of sampling procedures
   discussion and evidence of generality
Description of research design
Discussion and evidence of goal attainment and internal validity
   control
Conclusions about practice effectiveness
Limitations of the study
Recommendations and future directions

workers to several clients in different locations, the practice-re-searcher needs to be sensitive to the problems of variation among workers and clients as well as factors that might influence variation.

Clients should be described according to characteristics that might vary between clients (such as gender, social class, ethnicity, and religion) and workers and which might be employed to indicate the extent to which the client(s) or worker are representative of other agency clients and workers. Features that might influence the way in which the intervention is implemented or be related to differential practice outcomes also should be described. For example, if an intervention relies on a client's ability to read, the client's level of reading ability is crucial; such information could lead to adapting or redesigning the intervention so that it includes oral rather than written instructions. The worker's basic traits and experiences relevant to intervention implementation also should be described.

To the extent possible, the intervention should be specified over the dimensions previously discussed, such as frequency, amount, location, and contents. More importantly, evidence of implementation should be presented in terms of worker and client compliance. If there were problems in implementation, they should be briefly indicated. This provides some context for the reader who should be given a description of the intervention being evaluated and if it was in fact, delivered to the clientele.

Specifying intervention goals and relevant outcome variables is fundamental. As a result of the intervention, what is supposed to change in the client? Are there other problems for which the intervention is not targeted? The reader should have a good idea as to other potential problems or needs that the client has in addition to very specific operational definitions in the form of variables and instruments for obtaining measurements of client goals.

Practice effectiveness should be precisely defined in terms of goal attainment, generality, and correlation or causality. The reader should know what evidence should be necessary to indicate practice effectiveness, and should expect to read or hear about the extent to which such evidence has been provided in the report. For example, the report should address the following questions : What is goal attainment? Is it an agreed upon definition by worker and client? Is it a clinically and statistically significant change or non-statistically significant lack of change? Is it a change, prevention, or maintenance goal?

Instruments should be simply described with the detailed instructions, items, and possible pretesting data provided in the appendix of the report. Of course, if the instrument consists of a simple daily observation, it could be included in the main body of a report. Questionnaires, interview schedules, observational forms, and the like need not be in the report's main body. There should be, however, some discussion about the reliability and validity of the instrument. Previous research on the instruments' reliability and validity can be briefly mentioned and referenced. Any research by the practice-researcher that provides evidence of reliability and validity should be briefly stated, emphasizing conclusions, with the details being attached in the appendix. The contents of the report should include a brief discussion of why the practice-researcher believes the instrument is reliable and valid for assessing change or lack of change in variables related to intervention goals.

The sampling procedures for the research should be described. The practice-researcher should indicate the population to which the findings can be generalized, indicating which sampling procedures were employed. Populations of interest might be workers, clients, or problems, to name the more obvious ones. Sampling procedures might enumerate every element in the population (such as all active clients) or a portion of the designated population. The report should contain what procedure was used and the extent to which it is believed to produce a representative sample. For example, a simple random sample of 50 percent of active cases in one worker's caseload may be drawn. It would be presumed to be representative of the worker's caseload because it is based on probability theory and because a relatively large number of cases were used. Other evidence of generality might be a demonstration of similar distributions on important characteristics in both the sample and the population. For example, it might be reported that the percentage of males, minorities, and teenage clients are identical in the sample and the entire population. In addition, the practice-researcher should present limitations on generality. As an illustration, it might be said that the results on practice effectiveness of an intervention are a reasonable estimate of practice effectiveness for a particular agency, but that the results cannot be generalized to other workers, clients, and agencies.

The procedures of the research design should be presented. Evidence of goal attainment and its relationship to the intervention(s) should be presented, as well as some discussion of the degree to which there is evidence for assessing that the relationship is causal. Reasons for lack of causality (such as lack of control for specific internal validity factors) should be discussed. This is to ensure that the reader does not overgeneralize from the presentation and has perspective on the findings.

The conclusions of the report should discuss the evidence for practice effectiveness. This includes the evidence of an association between the intervention and goal attainment, control of internal validity threats, and the degree of generality. Limitations of the findings would refer primarily to the possible lack of reliability and validity in the data, absence of an association between the intervention and goal attainment, uncontrolled internal validity threats, and nonrepresentative sampling.

Finally, the report should include recommendations about the effectiveness of the intervention. Questions like the following may be answered from the research. Should the intervention be continued or modified? Should all workers consider using the intervention? Should it be combined with other interventions? What additional evidence is needed to be reasonably sure that the interventions employed by the agency are effective?

References

Barlow, D. H., and M. Hersen. 1984. *Single Case Experimental Designs: Strategies for Studying Behavior Change* 2d ed. New York: Pergamon Press.

Billingsley, F., O. R. White, and R. Munson. 1980. Procedural Reliability: A Rationale and an Example. *Behavioral Assessment 2*:229–241.

Bloom, M. and J. Fischer, 1982. *Evaluating Practice: Guidelines for the Accountable Professional*. Englewood Cliffs: Prentice-Hall.

Blythe, B. J. 1990. Applying Practice Research Methods in Intensive Family Preservation Services. In J. K. Whittaker, J. Kinney, E. M. Tracy, and C. Booth, eds., *Reaching High-risk Families: Intensive Family Preservation in Human Services*, 147–164. New York: Aldine de Gruyter.

Blythe, B. J., and D. E. Goodman. 1987. Agency Board Members as Research Staff. *Social Work 32*:544–545.

Blythe, B. J., and S. Briar. 1987. Direct Practice Effectiveness. In the *Encyclopedia of Social Work* 18th ed., 399–407. Silver Spring: National Association of Social Workers.

Blythe, B. J., and S. Briar. 1985. Developing Empirically-based Models of Practice. *Social Work 30*:483–488.

Blythe, B. J., and T. Tripodi. 1989. *Measurement in Direct Practice*. Newbury Park: Sage.

Blythe, B. J., M. J. Jiordano, and S. A. Kelly. 1991. Family Preservation with Substance Abusing Families: Help that Works. *The Child, Youth and Family Services Quarterly 14*/3: 12–13.

Briar, S., and B. J. Blythe. 1985. Agency Support for Evaluating the Outcomes of Social Work Services. *Administration in Social Work 9*/2:25–36.

Campbell, D. T., and J. C. Stanley. 1966. *Experimental and Quasi-experimental Designs for Research*. Skokie: Rand McNally.

Collins, P., Kayser, K., and Tourse, R. C. 1994. Bridging the Gaps: An Interdependent Model for Educating Accountable Practitioners. *Journal of Social Work Education 30*:241–251.

Cook, T. D., and D. T. Campbell. 1979. *Quasi-experimentation: Design and Analysis Issues for Field Settings*. Chicago: Rand McNally.

Council on Social Work Education. 1991. *Handbook of Accreditation Standards and Procedures*. Alexandria: Council on Social Work Education.

Dillman, D. A. 1978. *Mail and Telephone Surveys: The Total Design Method*. New York: Wiley.

Epstein, I., and T. Tripodi. 1977. *Research Techniques for Program Planning, Monitoring, and Evaluation*. New York: Columbia University Press.

Fabry, B., and R. M. Kaminski. 1991. The Pressley Ridge Schools Follow-up Project Report, Summer 1990. Unpublished report, February.

Fischer, J. and Corcoran, K. 1994. *Measures for Clinical Practice: A Sourcebook*. New York: The Free Press.

Fitz, D., and W. W. Tryon. 1989. Attrition and Augmentation Biases in Time-series Analysis: Evaluation of Clinical Programs, *Evaluation and Program Planning 12:*259–270.

Gillespie, D. F. 1987. Ethical Issues in Research. In the *Encyclopedia of Social Work*, 18th ed., 503–512. Silver Spring: National Association of Social Workers.

Gingerich, W., and W. Feyerherm. 1979. The Celeration Line Technique for Assessing Client Change. *Journal of Social Service Research 3:*99–113.

Gochros, H. 1988. Research Interviewing. In R. M. Grinnell, Jr., ed. *Social Work Research and Evaluation*, 3d ed., 267–299. Itasca: F. E. Peacock.

Gottman, J. M., and S. R. Leiblum. 1974. *How to Do Psychotherapy and How to Evaluate It*. New York: Holt, Rinehart, and Winston.

Grasso, A. J., and I. Epstein. 1989. Integrating Management Information, Program Evaluation, and Practice Decision Making: The Boysville Experience. *Computers in Social Work 4:*85–94.

Hinkel, D. E., W. Wiersma, and S. G. Jurs. 1988. *Applied Statistics for the Behavioral Sciences* 2d ed. Boston: Houghton Mifflin Co.

Holland, T. P., and M. K. Petchers. 1987. Organizations: Context for Social Service Delivery. In the *Encyclopedia of Social Work* 18th ed., 204–217. Silver Spring: National Association of Social Workers.

Hudson, W. W. 1982. *The Clinical Measurement Package: A Field Manual*. Homewood: Dorsey Press.

Koroloff, N. M., and S. C. Anderson. 1989. Alcohol-free Living Centers—Hope for Homeless Alcoholics. *Social Work 34:*497–504.

McCubbin, H. S., and A. I. Thompson. 1987. *Family Assessment Inventories for Research and Practice*. Madison: Family Stress Coping and Health Project, University of Wisconsin-Madison.

McKillip, J. 1987. *Need Analysis: Tools for the Human Services and Education*. Newbury Park: Sage.

McMahon, P. M. 1987. Shifts in Intervention Procedures: A Problem in Evaluating Human Service Interventions. *Social Work Research and Abstracts 23/*4:13–16.

McNemar, Q. 1957. *Psychological Statistics*. New York: Wiley.

Meyer, C. 1987. Direct Practice in Social Work: Overview. In the *Encyclopedia of Social Work*, 18th ed., 409–22. Silver Spring: National Association of Social Workers.

Monette, D. R., T. J. Sullivan, and C. R. DeJong. 1990. *Applied Social Research: Tool for the Human Services* 2d ed. Fort Worth: Holt, Rinehart, and Winston.

National Association of Social Workers. 1987. Code of Ethics. In the *Encyclopedia of Social Work* 18th ed., 951–956. Silver Spring: National Association of Social Workers.

National Association of Social Workers. 1987. NASW Standards for the Practice of Clinical Practice. In the *Encyclopedia of Social Work* 18th ed., 965–970. Silver Spring: National Association of Social Workers.

Nurius, P. S., N. Hooyman, and A. E. Nicoll. 1991. Computers in Agencies: A Survey Baseline and Planning Implications. *Journal of Social Service Research* 14:141–155.

Pagano, R. 1981. *Understanding Statistics in the Behavioral Sciences.* St. Paul: West Publishing Co.

Pardeck, J. T., and J. W. Murphy. 1990. *Computers in Human Services: An Overview for Clinical and Welfare Services.* Chur, Switzerland: Harwood Academic.

Parsons, R. J., and E. O. Cox. 1989. Family Mediation in Elder Caregiving Decisions: An Empowerment Intervention. *Social Work* 34:122–126.

Peterson, L., A. L. Homer, and S. A. Wonderlich. 1982. The Integrity of Independent Variables in Behavioral Analysis. *Journal of Applied Behavior Analysis* 15:477–492.

Posavac, E. J., and R. G. Carey. 1985. *Program Evaluation: Methods and Case Studies* 2d ed. Englewood Cliffs: Prentice-Hall.

Reamer, F. G. 1983. Ethical Dilemmas in Social Work Practice. *Social Work* 28:31–35.

Reid, D. H. 1987. *Developing a Research Program in Human Service Agencies.* Springfield: Charles C Thomas.

Reid, W. J. 1987. Evaluating an Intervention in Developmental Research. *Journal of Social Service Research* 11:17–38.

Reid, W. R., and P. Hanrahan, P. 1988. Measuring Implementation of Social Treatment. In K. J. Conrad and C. Roberts-Gray, eds. *Evaluating Program Environments: New Directions for Program Evaluation* 4:93–111.

Reynolds, D. 1982. *Ethics and Social Science research.* Englewood Cliffs: Prentice-Hall.

Rose, S. D. 1981. How Group Attributes Relate to Outcome in Behavior Group Therapy. *Social Work Research and Abstracts* 17:13–23.

Rossi, P., H. E. Freeman, and S. R. Wright. 1979. *Evaluation: A Systematic Approach*, Beverly Hills: Sage.

Scriven, M. 1967. The Methodology of Evaluation. In R. W. Tyler, R. M. Cogne, and M. Scriven, eds. *Perspectives of Curriculum Evaluation*, AERA, Monograph Series on Curriculum Evaluation, No. 1. Chicago: Rand McNally.

Seaburg, J. R. 1988. Utilizing Sampling Procedures. In R. M. Grinnell, Jr., ed. *Social Work Research and Evaluation*, 3d ed., 240–257. Itasca: F. E. Peacock.

Siegel, D. H. 1984. Defining empirically based practice. *Social Work* 29:325–331.

Siegel, S. 1956. *Nonparametric Statistics for the Behavioral Sciences.* New York: McGraw Hill.

Taber, S. M. 1981. Cognitive-behavior Modification Treatment of an Aggressive 11-year-old boy. *Social Work Research and Abstracts 17:*13–23.

Thomas, E. J. 1984. *Designing Interventions for the Helping Professions.* Beverly Hills: Sage.

Thomas, E. J. 1978. Research and Service in Single-case Experimentation: Conflicts and Choices. *Social Work Research and Abstracts 14:*20–31.

Towle, C. 1965. *Common Human Needs,* rev. ed. Washington, DC: National Association of Social Workers.

Tripodi, T. 1983. *Evaluative Research for Social Workers.* Englewood Cliffs: Prentice-Hall.

Tripodi, T. 1987. Program Evaluation. In the *Encyclopedia of Social Work* 18th ed., 366–379. Silver Spring: National Association of Social Workers.

Tripodi, T. 1974. *Uses and Abuses of Social Research in Social Work.* New York: Columbia University Press.

Tripodi, T., and I. Epstein. 1980. *Research Techniques for Clinical Social Workers.* New York: Columbia University Press.

Tryon, W. W. 1982. A Simplified Time-series Analysis for Evaluating Treatment Interventions. *Journal of Applied Behavioral Analysis 15:*423–429.

Vigilante, F. W., and M. D. Mailick. 1988. Needs Resource Evaluation in the Assessment Process. *Social Work, 33:*101–104.

Walker, H., and J. Lev. 1953. *Statistical Inference.* New York: Holt, Rinehart, and Winston.

Weinbach, R. W. 1989. Agency and Professional Contexts of Research. In R. M. Grinnell, Jr., ed., *Social Work Research and Evaluation,* 3d ed., 25–41. Itasca: F. E. Peacock.

Weissman, H. H. 1974. *Overcoming Mismanagement in the Human Services Professions.* San Francisco: Jossey-Bass.

Yeskel, M., and G. Ganter. 1975. Some Principles and Methods of Sampling. In N. A. Polansky, ed. *Social Work Research,* rev. ed. Chicago: University of Chicago Press.

Young, L. C. 1941. On Randomness in Ordered Sequences. *Annals of Mathematical Statistics 12:*293–300.

Zung, W. K. 1965. A Self-rating Depression Scale. *Archives of General Psychiatry 12:*63–70.

Index